DEADLY WEB

Before a computer in her cluttered bedroom, Michigan housewife Sharee Miller uploaded electronic photos that appeared to show a horrific beating by her husband, General Motors autoworker Bruce Miller.

Hundreds of miles away, ex-cop Jerry Cassaday opened the files and was convinced that the unborn children that he and Sharee had conceived in love had been killed.

"Main thing was to hurt the babies," Sharee wrote to Cassaday in a private AOL chat room.

"I promise I will come," Cassaday reassured.

"If this don't work he will hurt me bad," Sharee messaged.

For eighty minutes, the couple planned revenge, point by point.

"Jerry, don't leave fingerprints," she wrote. "[Wear] gloves."

The crime wouldn't be without a personal touch.

"I want him to know who I am," Cassaday wrote. "He will know, but not for long."

"Just say, 'Hi, I'm Jerry' and get out," Miller urged.

The planning complete, Cassaday walked out to his pickup and soon was on a 700-mile journey to murder.

BOOK YOUR PLACE ON OUR WEBSITE AND MAKE THE READING CONNECTION!

We've created a customized website just for our very special readers, where you can get the inside scoop on everything that's going on with Zebra, Pinnacle and Kensington books.

When you come online, you'll have the exciting opportunity to:

- View covers of upcoming books
- Read sample chapters
- Learn about our future publishing schedule (listed by publication month *and author*)
- Find out when your favorite authors will be visiting a city near you
- Search for and order backlist books from our online catalog
- Check out author bios and background information
- Send e-mail to your favorite authors
- Meet the Kensington staff online
- Join us in weekly chats with authors, readers and other guests
- Get writing guidelines
- AND MUCH MORE!

**Visit our website at
http://www.kensingtonbooks.com**

FATAL ERROR

*Mark Morris
and
Paul Janczewski*

PINNACLE BOOKS
Kensington Publishing Corp.
http://www.kensingtonbooks.com

PINNACLE BOOKS are published by

Kensington Publishing Corp.
850 Third Avenue
New York, NY 10022

All Kensington Titles, Imprints, and Distributed Lines are available at special quantity discounts for bulk purchases for sales promotions, premiums, fund-raising, and educational or institutional use. Special book excerpts or customized printings can also be created to fit specific needs. For details, write or phone the office of the Kensington special sales manager: Kensington Publishing Corp., 850 Third Avenue, New York, NY 10022, attn: Special Sales Department, Phone: 1-800-221-2647.

Pinnacle and the P logo Reg. U.S. Pat. & TM Off.

First Printing: February 2003
10 9 8 7 6 5 4 3

Printed in the United States of America

Murder is born of love,
and love attains the greatest intensity in murder.
—Octave Mirbeau (1848–1917), French journalist

Men freely believe what they desire.
—Julius Caesar

ONE

Stench oozed through the big home overlooking the lake near Odessa, Missouri, and Lyn Lewellen couldn't let another minute pass before finding the source. After rising on the morning of February 11, 2000, she returned downstairs, convinced she faced nothing worse than a sewer backup or rotten food.

As she had done when she first noticed the hint of odor the night before, she checked around the downstairs refrigerator and the bathroom.

Again she found nothing.

From the ground-floor apartment where her husband's cousin, Jerry Cassaday, lived alone, a radio tuned to Kansas City's "Q-104 Young Country" played as it had the night before. Cassaday hadn't yet complained of the smell, but he often worked nights and perhaps had returned home too late to catch anybody awake. Spinning discs as a thirty-nine-year-old part-time disc jockey was hardly a career for Cassaday, an ex-cop and Reno, Nevada, blackjack dealer and pit boss. But it allowed him to make a little money and indulge his love of country music.

Lewellen walked into the small apartment and, from behind, saw Cassaday lying still in a reddish brown recliner, his head poking around the right corner. She called his name but got no response.

He appeared to be asleep or passed out. Cassaday was

supposed to be attending Alcoholics Anonymous and getting counseling for his drinking problem. But Lewellen and her husband, Earl, suspected that he had quit attending both. A few weeks before, they had asked Cassaday to find someplace else to live because he was mooching off the family and not paying his bills.

After that, Cassaday had stopped coming upstairs for meals with the family.

Lewellen picked her way through the cluttered apartment. Cassaday had swiveled the recliner to the back of the apartment, away from its customary place before the TV in the corner. The chair faced three windows overlooking the lake. Lewellen could see that Cassaday, whose divorce had come through not long before, had placed framed pictures of his three sons in the window before him. In the window to Cassaday's right was a photo of Sharee Miller, his Michigan girlfriend, or ex-girlfriend, depending on Jerry's mood that day.

Far to Cassaday's left was the other focal point of his life, a desktop computer, connected to the World Wide Web through America Online, the nation's largest Internet service provider.

Jerry spent hours on that thing, day and night, and never tired of it.

The stench grew stronger as Lewellen cut around the front of the chair and she recoiled from the gory distortion of Jerry Cassaday's once-handsome face.

Blood infused every opening and was caked into his beard. It had bubbled out of his left ear and coursed from his mouth. Before drying, the blood had streaked toward his right ear, which tilted toward the floor. A .22-caliber rifle lay at his left knee. A copy of his divorce decree sat on a lamp table to his right.

Horrified, Lewellen found a telephone and called her husband, Earl, who was in Washington, D.C., that morning on business. He told her to call 911.

* * *

Sergeant Brian Gillespie of the Lafayette County Sheriff's Department soon was at the house collecting the evidence of a tragic, but straightforward, suicide. Picking through the cluttered apartment, he found a report showing that Cassaday had recently been treated for depression at a mental-health center in Kansas City, just down Interstate 70 to the west. He also found several prescription bottles, some for medication to treat depression.

He checked the computer and surveyed the living room for a suicide note, but didn't find one. Nothing particularly unusual about that—not all suicides leave notes. But before long, Barbara Cassaday, Jerry's ex-wife, appeared at the Lewellen home with information confirming that Cassaday had recently talked of suicide.

Barbara Cassaday told Gillespie she recently had received an e-mail from Cassaday's girlfriend in Michigan, who said Jerry had contemplated suicide within the last week. That, plus evidence from the apartment, clinched it for Gillespie.

"It appeared that the victim had probably put the gun barrel in his mouth to kill himself," Gillespie concluded.

But pinning down the time, even the day, of death was tricky. Nobody had heard the shot. And a day or so before, Lyn Lewellen's seventeen-year-old daughter had taken a Priority Mail envelope addressed to Cassaday down to his apartment. She dimly saw him lying motionless on the recliner and assumed he was asleep, so she dropped the letter on a sofa and left quietly.

The Lafayette County coroner would rule that Cassaday probably killed himself on February 9, two days before his body was found. Using a small-caliber .22, Cassaday probably took "minutes" to die, the coroner estimated.

Gillespie wrapped up his investigation at the Lewellen

home at 10:30 A.M., about two hours after he arrived. Employees from a funeral home in nearby Wellington, Missouri, came in to handle the body. They lifted a Bible from Cassaday's lap as they carried his body from the recliner.

Before Cassaday pulled the trigger, he had opened the Bible to the fifth chapter of Matthew, which quotes this ancient Hebrew admonition:

"Do not murder, and anyone who murders will be subject to judgment."

About the time Sergeant Gillespie was opening his investigation into Cassaday's suicide, Sharee Miller, a twenty-eight-year-old businesswoman and widow living in Mount Morris, Michigan, sat at her computer to compose a short, chirpy note to Barbara Cassaday.

Miller had met Jerry Cassaday on vacation the summer before while he still worked as a pit boss at Harrah's Casino and Hotel in Reno. They'd hit it off immediately and began corresponding regularly on-line. They had talked some about getting married and having Miller move to Missouri from her home just north of Flint, Michigan. But when Jerry's alcohol-fueled demands for money became too strident, Miller let the romantic relationship cool, but continued to be supportive. Miller had begun corresponding with Cassaday's family in Missouri, where Jerry had returned in the fall to address his substance abuse issues.

Cassaday's musings on suicide earlier in the week had troubled Miller and she wanted to stay in touch.

"Hi Barb . . . I haven't heard from you, let me know if you have talked to Earl," she wrote, and tapped Send.

Barbara Cassaday would not find Miller's note until late that evening, long after reeling from the initial shock of her ex-husband's death and helping her three

children—including Kenny, thirteen, the youngest—
cope with the news.

"By now, I know that you have found out about Jerry,"
Barbara wrote. ". . . Please remember that [Jerry] was the
one that needed help but didn't choose to help himself."

Barbara wrote that Kenneth was the family member
most affected by Jerry's suicide. Now, more than ever,
Kenny needed to draw close to his family and rely on
them for support. The family was ready to help Kenny,
Barbara wrote, and hoped that he could cope with his father's suicide and "move on with his life without guilt or
blame."

Barb also urged Miller to do the same.

But Miller hadn't heard about Jerry's death, replying
to Barb Cassaday on February 12 with grief and shock.

"Oh my God, he was crying for help and I did not listen," Miller wrote.

Miller noted that she recently had spoken with Cassaday and had mailed him $3,000 to help get his life back
together. Soon Miller would express concern that Cassaday may have left behind an ugly message.

"I am afraid Jerry left a letter saying he did this because I didn't love him," wrote Miller, who still was
coping with the death of her husband the year before.

Miller pressed Barb Cassaday for information about
the funeral service, details about Jerry's death and offers
of money to help with the children. She also proffered
friendly advice on dealing with the death of a husband
and father.

Barb Cassaday was uncomfortable with Sharee Miller's
constant e-mails and insistent demands for information.
Still, she felt that Miller, too, was grieving.

"I keep thinking that he should have [could have]
come to any of his friends or family and we would have
done anything for him," Barb Cassaday wrote. "I pray for
his soul and that God will look after him."

* * *

Anybody could tell by looking at his apartment that Jerry Cassaday was a saver. The place was a wreck, the sofa littered with unfolded laundry and the coffee table covered with papers, cups and an open pack of Cassaday's Marlboro Light cigarettes.

The sad task of cleaning out the apartment fell to Mike Cassaday, Jerry's older brother, who lived nearby and had become Jerry's mentor since he had returned to Missouri four months before.

Working through the bedroom, Mike thumped into something while reaching under the bed. It was a briefcase, brown leather, square and blocky.

This was what he meant, Mike thought as he pulled it out, taking care not to damage some paperwork taped to the cover.

The previous November, Jerry Cassaday had told his brother he was going away for a couple of days to clear his head and scout for deer-hunting stands near the family's lake cabin. But in an odd parting, Jerry had said that if he didn't return by 6:00 P.M. two days hence, Mike was to find the briefcase under the bed and follow the instructions. Testifying later in court, Mike Cassaday said he had been troubled by his brother's instructions. But Jerry Cassaday returned to Missouri in plenty of time and soon Mike had forgotten about the briefcase.

The paperwork was three familial letters: the first to Kenny, Jerry's youngest son, the second to Barb, his ex-wife, and the third to Jerry's parents. Also taped to the case was an envelope addressed to a lawyer whose name was well known in the Kansas City area: John P. O'Connor.

"Mike," read a note in his brother's handwriting, "Do not open <u>alone</u>."

Mike Cassaday picked up the briefcase, walked to his car and locked it in the trunk. He needed to find a telephone.

* * *

John P. O'Connor was one of Kansas City's top criminal defense lawyers. He regularly handled high-profile cases, winning more than his share. His secret was down-to-earth storytelling, which jurors always found more appealing than complex legal theorizing.

One wall of his office at his firm was covered with framed press clippings detailing how he helped a jury acquit one big-name client or another, including a high-spirited Kansas City councilwoman who once was charged with assaulting a local police officer. But when the reporters who wrote those articles appeared in his office for an interview, O'Connor was modest, noting that the clips were there only to reassure clients that they really did have a fighting chance.

Even an O'Connor courtroom loss could be impressive, though. A few years before, he had represented one of five defendants charged with an arson that killed six Kansas City firefighters. Though his client was convicted and sentenced to life, O'Connor's defense left more than a lingering suspicion, even among some federal judges, that prosecutors had indicted the wrong suspects.

O'Connor's background as a former assistant Jackson County prosecuting attorney also had earned him steady work defending police officers who found themselves in trouble.

As a former detective and lieutenant on the Cass County, Missouri, Sheriff's Department, Jerry Cassaday had bumped into O'Connor a few times on cases, mostly those where Cassaday was trying to convict O'Connor's client on murder charges. As cop and criminal defense lawyer, Cassaday and O'Connor were natural adversaries. But they had gotten along well, each respecting the other's proper role in the justice system.

In late January, Jerry Cassaday had left O'Connor a

voice mail message, asking him to call. O'Connor had assumed that Cassaday was looking for investigative work. He had returned the message, asking Cassaday to get in touch.

O'Connor was watching television in his South Kansas City home after work on February 11 when the phone rang. At first, he couldn't imagine why Jerry Cassaday's brother would be calling.

"My brother Jerry . . . Something's happened," Mike Cassaday said.

"Wh-what?" O'Connor stammered.

"He shot himself," Cassaday replied.

"Is he okay?" the lawyer asked.

"No . . . he's dead," Cassaday choked out. "We've got a briefcase here and it's got your name on it for us to bring to you. We'd like to get together tomorrow to look at it when my mom and dad and brothers get into town."

Knowing the family had more pressing business, O'Connor persuaded Mike Cassaday to hold off until Wednesday, the day after Jerry's funeral.

Jerry Lee Cassaday was memorialized on Tuesday, February 15. The traditional funeral was held at St. Paul's United Methodist Church in Cass County, which he once had served as a cop.

Before the service opened, mourners heard a medley of Cassaday's favorite country-and-western songs, which Kenneth had prepared on a CD.

But the funeral service just washed over Jerry's mother, Charlene Cassaday, who still couldn't make sense of her son's death. As the mother of four boys and a former office manager for a Kansas City law firm, she'd spent a lifetime sorting order out of chaos, finding straightforward answers to honest questions.

But from the moment four days before when her husband, Jim, had yanked her out of an exercise class near their retirement home in McAllen, Texas, Charlene Cassaday had struggled with why Jerry had taken his life. The funeral offered little comfort and no answers.

A friend from the Sweet Adelines women's barbershop group sang Jerry's favorite hymns, "Peace in the Valley" and "How Great Thou Art." The service ended with a recorded bagpiper playing "Amazing Grace," a traditional conclusion to police officers' funerals. Barbara Cassaday, who sat nearby, had suggested that touch.

I know he would have liked that, she thought as the last mournful notes echoed through the Methodist sanctuary.

Cassaday's body was cremated, with his ashes spread near the family's lake cabin at a spot where he liked to hunt. The family asked for any contributions to go to a psychiatric counseling center at Children's Mercy Hospital near downtown Kansas City. The request highlighted the family's desire that nobody else suffer the mental anguish that tortured their son and brother in his final months. It also reflected Jerry Cassaday's love for children. Before moving to Reno in 1998, he'd spent years coaching youth football programs in the Kansas City area.

After the funeral, Jerry's parents returned to Charlene's sister's home in Kansas City and retired to a quiet bedroom. There they opened Jerry's last letter to them. The one-page single-spaced letter ripped away any comfort Charlene and Jim Cassaday had garnered from the funeral. The letter presented Cassaday's parents with an agonizing decision.

Should they let Jerry and his memory rest in peace?

Or should they expose their son to the world as a troubled, cold-blooded killer?

* * *

O'Connor had reserved a healthy chunk of time for the Cassaday family on February 16. But even before they were in the office, he already was working on their case.

He was troubled about the briefcase. From the family's description, Jerry was profoundly disturbed about something when he died. O'Connor always had gotten along well with Cassaday, but could Jerry have been seeking revenge for some long-forgotten slight? Had he left a bomb in the briefcase?

Using his ties to the Kansas City police, O'Connor arranged for the Cassaday family to hand off the briefcase to the department's bomb-disposal squad. Officers had agreed to examine the briefcase to make certain it was safe to open, and would not read anything they found inside. The Cassadays would wait at O'Connor's office during the examination and the cops would drop off the bag when it was finished.

Before long, members of Cassaday's family appeared in the lobby of O'Connor's law firm, reporting that the handoff had gone off without a hitch. O'Connor made them comfortable in an office, where he learned of the suicide note to Cassaday's parents. In that letter, Cassaday confessed to murdering a man the previous year.

O'Connor excused himself to take a call from the bomb squad. The officers wanted permission to pop open one of the latches to peek inside. O'Connor said yes, and waited in the law firm's lobby. The briefcase soon arrived.

It had not carried a bomb, but its contents were no less explosive. Amid a welter of compact discs, business cards and casino betting chips, there sat a 3½-inch floppy disk, photographs, e-mails and printouts of what appeared to be Internet chat sessions on America Online.

Two of the e-mails appeared to have come from a person named BDJUNK and taunted somebody named Deviousminds about an abortion that someone named

Sharee was planning. The next day, according to a follow-up e-mail, Sharee appeared to have undergone the abortion. The e-mails were crude and written in all capital letters, the Internet's version of shouting.

"I THINK THE ABORTION WENT FINE. SHE SOUNDED LIKE SHE FELT BETTER KNOWING SHE WASN'T HAVING ANYMORE KIDS."

The letter ended:

"THANK YOU FOR MAKING MY RELATIONSHIP WITH MY WIFE BETTER. WE ARE ON THE MENDS AND IT IS THANKS TO YOU. BRUCE."

Though jumbled and hard to follow, the AOL Instant Messenger chat sessions appeared to show a conversation between someone called SHAREE1013 and someone tagged Jlc1006 who were making detailed plans to kill someone. O'Connor pored through the conversation.

For eight pages, the couple discussed how to find "the yard," what signals were to be passed through hang-up calls to a cellular phone and the sound a gun makes in a closed, confined space. And there was talk about babies.

SHAREE1013: Tell me you forgive me. Tell me one day we can have a baby and nothing will happen to it. Tell me I will give birth to it. Tell me you forgive me.
Jlc1006: We will, honey. You and me. I love you. I forgive you. You have nothing to be sorry about.

And, naturally, the couple made a promise to keep the secret.

SHAREE1013: Are you going to be able to live with this the rest of your life? Because I can. You are so good. Are you sure? I can, you know. The rest of my life we never talk about it, never.

Jlc1006: I love you.
SHAREE1013: Answer me.
Jlc1006: I love you. Yes, I can.

Jerry Cassaday's letter to O'Connor, dated November 7, 1999, connected the dots:

"Should you receive this letter, then one of two things has occurred. One, I am dead and need you to see to things for me. Secondly, I would be in jail for something for which I would need your assistance," Jerry had written.

In the letter, Cassaday explained that for some time he had been in love with a woman named Sharee Miller from Mount Morris, Michigan, a northern suburb of Flint. Miller had once carried his child, though she was married to Bruce Miller, an organized-crime figure involved in counterfeiting, money laundering and drugs. Bruce Miller had abused his wife and killed the unborn child by beating her, Cassaday wrote. There were medical records under false names at a Flint hospital that would confirm the abuse, Cassaday wrote.

Subsequently, Sharee Miller became pregnant again, this time with twins, Cassaday wrote. About then, Bruce Miller had begun taunting Cassaday, threatening to kill the babies. Bruce would never let his wife leave because she provided good cover at his business for his criminal enterprises. To keep her in line, Bruce Miller had beaten and raped her and forced her to participate in his drug deals.

Cassaday wrote that recently Bruce Miller had arranged for his wife to be kidnapped by one of his thugs, Jason. After Bruce again beat and raped her, Jason took Sharee at gunpoint to a rural cabin, where the abuse continued. Believing the babies to be dead, Sharee returned home and e-mailed photographs of her injuries to Cassaday, he wrote. Those pictures, and some e-mails they had exchanged, were in the briefcase.

"Your expenses will be covered by Sharee for my defense, if needed," Cassaday wrote. "She will cooperate in any fashion on my behalf."

O'Connor let out a long breath as he sat alone in the lobby. Generally, an uncorroborated confession from a dead man would not be enough to convict anybody of murder. But in the space of a few minutes, O'Connor had held both ends of the case in his hands: a confession and the corroborating evidence.

"Unbelievable," he said to himself, and turned to walk into the conference room.

The Cassadays listened intently as O'Connor checked off the issues. From his work as a prosecutor, he told them that authorities in Michigan probably could file charges in the case. The decision to let Jerry rest or to expose him as a killer belonged to the family. But from the experience reflected on his wall of newspaper clips, he assured them that media attention would be substantial. Family members should be prepared to find reporters and TV crews camped out at their homes if the information ever became public.

Already reeling from Cassaday's suicide note to his parents, the family sat for a moment in stunned silence.

The Cassadays knew about Jerry's relationship with Sharee Miller. Roger, the eldest son, actually had met her during a trip to Reno the previous fall. Mother Charlene had spoken with her on the telephone and had corresponded with her intermittently through e-mail.

But O'Connor was not inclined to push the family for a quick decision about whether or not to notify authorities.

"There's no rush here," he said. O'Connor suggested they wait a day and allow him to make a few phone calls to see if a murder actually had occurred. Just to see if the details in the briefcase matched a murder in Michigan.

The family agreed and returned to Mike Cassaday's home in Lee's Summit, a Kansas City suburb in eastern

Jackson County. There, the discussion continued. What about Bruce Miller's family? Didn't they deserve justice? True, Jerry's e-mails in the briefcase painted him as a monster, but Jerry's judgment already was in question.

With emotions running deep, the family faced the possibility that a woman who could be responsible for the deaths of two men could remain free if they stayed silent.

O'Connor called the following morning and spoke with Mike Cassaday. The dates and details contained in the material from Jerry Cassaday's briefcase and suicide notes matched those from an ongoing murder investigation in Genesee County, Michigan. Mike looked up from the telephone and glanced over at his parents and brothers gathered in his family room. Their discussion was finished.

"This woman needs to be prosecuted," he told O'Connor.

The Cassadays left the details of notifying the authorities to O'Connor, who soon was on the phone to sheriff's deputies in Flint, Michigan.

"Do you still have an open murder case at a junkyard in or around Flint?" O'Connor asked.

Minutes later, Sergeant Ives Potrafka, a Genesee County Sheriff's Department detective, stormed into his captain's office, shirt and tie askew.

"That bitch did it!" he exclaimed. "That bitch did it!"

Unaware that her ex-husband had left the briefcase and the confessions, Barbara Cassaday continued her e-mail correspondence with Sharee Miller.

Just before the funeral, Barb told Miller that Cassaday had left a note behind for her. Cassaday acknowledged he had made an enormous mistake when he pushed for the divorce.

"He said everything he touched turned bad after I

left," Barbara wrote. "It was something I needed to hear and I am glad he did it."

Miller responded in kind.

"Just before my husband died he told me he loved me," Miller wrote. "It is something that will stick with you the rest of your life."

Miller also said she was disappointed with the suggestion that contributions in Cassaday's name go to the children's counseling center, particularly when Barbara and her sons still were in need. Miller proposed taking a trip to Reno to raise money for the family from Jerry Cassaday's coworkers at Harrah's.

Gracefully, Barbara Cassaday tried to deflect Miller's persistent attention.

"If you and the people in Reno truly want to send things to the boys direct then they can send it to me, but please make it clear that we are fine and they certainly do not have to do it," she wrote.

But the trip to Reno wasn't a spur-of-the-moment expression of Sharee Miller's compassion. A month before, she had announced to her new boyfriend, Jeff Foster, that they should go to Reno.

Before leaving, Miller spoke with a friend in Reno, Carol Slaughter, whom she had met through Jerry Cassaday, suggesting contributions to his ex-wife and children, rather than the children's charity.

Slaughter, who had worked with Cassaday at Harrah's, wasn't optimistic. Cassaday had annoyed some people at the casino, and he hadn't worked there very long. But somebody might contribute something, she wrote in a February 15 e-mail.

Slaughter also was struggling with a request from Miller not to say anything about Jerry Cassaday in front of Foster when they got out to Reno. Slaughter warned her that might be tough.

Everybody at the casino knew about Cassaday and his

troubles, and the subject might come up unexpectedly if somebody recognized Miller, Slaughter wrote. And she warned Miller about being too deceptive with her new boyfriend.

"I would say this, be careful about how much you tell AND how much you withhold from your friend," Slaughter wrote. "It can be WAY too stressful trying to remember what you've told and what you haven't."

Miller and Foster flew to Reno for a weeklong vacation on February 16, about the time the Cassaday family was opening the discussion on her future with John O'Connor.

"I gambled, I vacationed, I seen comedy shows, I drank, I smoked and I slept," Miller would say later.

At the end of the long Presidents' Day weekend, Miller and her boyfriend boarded the flight back to Michigan. Bedraggled, drunk and weary from too much partying, the couple landed at Flint's Bishop International Airport about 10:00 P.M., on February 22, 2000, eager to return home.

Captain Mike Compeau of the Genesee County Sheriff's Department waited for them at the end of the Jetway with a squad of officers. Compeau pulled Miller aside and explained they needed to discuss her husband's case. Other officers corralled Foster as he waited for luggage.

On the drive into downtown Flint, Compeau broke the ice with amiable small talk. But Compeau knew he was in for a long evening. A small, pale yellow interview room waited for them at the sheriff's department. And several miles north, Compeau's officers were poised to serve a search warrant at Miller's home.

Compeau's lead investigators had just returned from Kansas City, Missouri, and he very much wanted to speak with the widow Miller about her husband's murder.

TWO

Sharee Paulette Miller didn't turn heads on an average day. She was plain in a promising sort of way; her long face was punctuated by a firm jaw and probing hazel eyes that drifted to gray, depending on her mood. She topped it off with short, naturally blond hair that she'd augment for special occasions with a waist-length hair extension.

Genetically programmed for middle-aged plumpness, Miller stayed trim, though the waist of her five-foot-two-inch frame had thickened during her twenties. Three children by as many fathers since the late 1980s had seen to that. But Miller had her own particular magic.

As a distributor of Mary Kay cosmetics, she knew just the shade of a luminous brown lipstick that would give proper petulance to her small lips. And sometimes she would tuck foam falsies into her bra to give her figure the boost she'd need to get attention.

But Miller also used personality and talent as makeup. With musical tastes running to George Strait and Faith Hill, Miller came to life in the working-class karaoke bars and bowling alleys of Genesee County, Michigan.

Miller's rowdy northern-tier accent vanished when she sang, and Miller could nail the lyrics word for word in a low, sensuous voice. To keep the party going after she'd finished singing, Miller sometimes would wander up to a table of strangers with the microphone and goad each person to admit before God and Flint that they had masturbated.

But the style that Miller had pulled together by her late twenties hung as a thin veneer on a woman who had endured a difficult upbringing and young adulthood.

Born Sharee Paulette Kitley in Flint on October 13, 1971, Miller joined a middle-class family that provided for her basic physical needs of food and shelter. She was named for a French character that her mother, Donna Jean Stokes, once had seen in a movie. When she was old enough to write, her mom encouraged her to sign her name as "Sha-Ree," thinking that more exotic. But the ever-independent daughter soon simplified it to "Sharee."

Her mother divorced Sharee's father not long after she was born and remarried a few years later.

Sharee later would report that she had a "poor" relationship with her natural father and only "sporadic" contact with him throughout her life.

But the new family that Sharee and her older brother joined offered little but disaster, exposing her at age seven to sexual abuse at the hands of a male relative. As with many sexual abuse victims, she learned to keep secrets well. When she reported at age fourteen the continuing abuse to her mother, Sharee immediately entered counseling. Her mother again divorced and moved.

The young Sharee dealt with the turmoil by writing stories and escaping into imaginary worlds of fantasy. She also enjoyed a modeling school in which her mother had enrolled her.

"I could be someone else," she would say. "I always wanted to look like someone else."

Sharee later would point to the abuse she suffered in childhood as defining her relationships with the opposite sex—men weren't to be trusted and could be used for her own amusement.

"One man is never enough for me," she told an acquaintance in the mid-1990s. "I need variety."

Her experience also taught her something about the criminal justice system. Though her mother reported the abuse to authorities, Sharee's assailant never was charged or prosecuted. That laid the groundwork for a personal crusade that would flower when she became a wife and mother.

About the time she reported her sexual abuse, Sharee began to experiment with drugs and alcohol. At age fourteen, she began smoking one marijuana joint a day. That continued after she ran away from home at sixteen.

After coping with children of her own, Sharee would acknowledge that she had been a "rebellious" teenager and said she was a significant discipline problem for her mother.

Sharee also was adrift spiritually. She refused to attend the boisterous Pentecostal church near Flint to which her mother belonged. Later, she would say the faith practiced at the church, which included speaking in tongues, seemed contrived.

"It scared me," she said. "Those people got God the same time, the same place every week."

She quit using marijuana when she turned seventeen. About that time, she married and became pregnant with her first child, Tommy.

After a brief sojourn in Florida, where Sharee worked in a rest home as a nurse's assistant, she and the young family moved back to Michigan in 1990. Sharee and her husband were divorced the following year. Her ex remained active in Tommy's life, even though Sharee retained custody. And Sharee resumed using marijuana, though less frequently than she had before.

Miller had missed graduating with her class in 1988 at Flint's Kearsley High School, but education still was on her mind. While in Florida, she earned a certificate in nursing assistance. She resumed her studies when she returned to Michigan, receiving her diploma from Kearsley High School's adult education program. And reflecting her desire to someday become a nurse, she later took courses at Flint's Mott Community College to study assisting the mentally handicapped.

Her second child, daughter Angela, was born out of wedlock in May 1993. Sharee married for a second time in 1994, giving birth in June 1995 to her third child, Buddy.

Sharee later would say that the marriage was hopelessly broken six months later when her husband assaulted their infant son. The marriage was dissolved the following year.

To clarify custody issues, Sharee submitted in 1996 to an interview with a psychologist. In the session, she accused her third husband of stalking her after they had separated, calling her 117 times in 29 days.

"He has been very persistent in trying to reestablish a relationship to the point where she feels that he is pursuing this in an obsessive fashion," the psychologist wrote after the interview.

To determine her suitability for custody, the psychologist administered a battery of tests. The psychologist found that Miller functioned within the "low average range of intellectual" ability, but suspected the tests understated her true intellectual prowess.

She scored the highest in tasks that measured her ability to associate numbers and symbols, and the testing found she had very good short-term visual memory.

Though she was twenty-four years old, she read at the eighth-grade level, the psychologist found. But more important to the custody issue, the psychologist found that she was a stable mother.

"There is no evidence of psychotic functioning," the psychologist wrote, though Sharee experienced periodic bouts of mild depression. Overall, the psychologist viewed Sharee "as being a responsible adult."

Ultimately, courts would grant Sharee custody of her youngest child. Despite Sharee's allegations that her husband had assaulted their son, the courts awarded him the right to visit Buddy regularly. Sharee told her psychologist that the whole violent episode had begun when her husband found and read her private diary. What he found there "upset" him, Sharee said. The contents of those diaries still remain Sharee's secret.

It would not be the last time that Sharee's secrets would devastate her personal life. But the episode also cemented her desire to take a much more public role in defending the rights of children. Four years later, that devotion would get a full airing before a national TV audience.

In 1994, Sharee had returned to the nursing-home business, starting out as a nurse's assistant in a Flint-area facility. Soon she was appointed manager of the home, a job she later would describe as "responsible." She lost the position, however, in 1996 because of conflicts with her second husband.

"I was forced to quit because my husband threatened my boss," she said at the time.

She soon returned to a $7-per-hour nurse's assistant job at a different facility. On the side, she also cared for Steven Meyers, the brother of a man whom she was dating. Meyers was recovering from a devastating 1996 car accident. Years later, Meyers recalled how she would remain at his side for hours.

"She took me to my doctor and cooked my meals," Meyers said. "She's a kind person. She didn't have to help me, but she did. I've never seen her hurt anybody."

Laura Ewald, Meyers's sister, immediately was drawn to this woman whose care was so important for her brother.

"Sharee was an angel who came out of nowhere," Ewald said.

Ready for something new, Sharee found a job in 1997 doing the books at B&D Auto Salvage, just outside the town of Clio, north of Flint. But B&D hardly was a place where a fresh start got a fair chance.

Sprawled next to a gravel quarry and the Auto City Speedway, B&D was smallish by Genesee County junkyard standards. It was typical in most other respects.

Acres of wrecked and damaged vehicles offered customers valuable parts at bargain prices. Regular shoppers included men—seldom women—looking for carburetors, bumpers or rearview mirrors for home fix-it jobs. And a living was to be made there by auto salvage specialists, rough and shrewd men who knew how to wring the last dollar out of society's forgotten automobiles. They would comb the lot, looking to buy entire wrecks to use for parts on a similar vehicle they were restoring at their own businesses.

The heart of B&D was a squat one-story white building with a single large window in the office. That allowed the employees to see who was approaching the yard down the five-hundred-yard dirt road that turned to deep mud ruts at the slightest rainfall.

The yard itself was the dumping ground for insurance company settlements and the mangled wrecks from drunk-driving accidents. Cars that weren't sharp enough or fast enough went there to die. Sometimes the yard was the last source of cash for a guy with a car and too many bills. But it also wasn't unusual for employees to arrive in the morning and find a serviceable car just abandoned, parked at the gate with the keys in the ignition and the title in the driver's seat.

But if B&D looked like the end of the line for so many dreams, it was heaven for Bruce L. Miller.

Miller, forty-six, soon would retire after working almost thirty years for General Motors, where he once had the final responsibility for testing engines before they rolled off the line. He would work later for GM's Delphi subsidiary, building airflow sensors. Tall and taciturn, Miller had endured years of the kind of layoffs that native Flint filmmaker Michael Moore highlighted in his 1989 movie *Roger & Me*.

Miller saw the salvage yard as his ticket to a steady retirement income that would finance the great love of his life, rebuilding cars.

"Bruce wanted it for his own pleasure," a friend once observed. "It was more a hobby than a living. He just wanted to play out there."

His devotion to cars began at childhood in a family where a rodeo horse, and not a race car, was more highly prized. Born July 26, 1951, to parents of German ancestry, Miller lived in and around Flint all his life, except for a brief stay in California as a child.

Miller learned to drive long before he was old enough for his license, piloting cars around the ten-acre family farm near Flint. He traded a quarter horse for his first car, a 1961 white Ford, when he was sixteen.

Miller's younger brother—Charles "Chuck" Miller—remembered how Bruce would spend hours under the hood of some junker, looking for a mechanical problem, and then fixing it. Sometimes he and Chuck would haul one of Bruce's cars up north to Bay City for the drag races, a dead certain way to make sure your car would need repairs the next morning.

"He loved tearing them apart and putting them back together," Chuck Miller remembered later. "He would fix them up and sell them to make money. Then buy another."

Bruce Miller was an average student at Mount Morris High School in the blue-collar outskirts of Flint. And though he sported a leather jacket and wore his hair slicked back in the 1950s greaser style, Miller already had developed the personality traits that would mark the rest of his life—laid-back, calm and quiet.

Bruce Miller's future, like that of many kids growing up in the industrial heartland of central Michigan, was programmed by the economy. Graduate from high school, join the United Auto Workers (UAW) and go to work in the "shop." That meant any of the many low-rise GM factories that rambled over the gray Flint landscape, making cars, trucks, batteries and spark plugs. With occasional layoffs in hard times, the shop promised a lifetime's work at good wages that could support a man, his family and his hobbies.

A year after graduating from Mount Morris in 1969, Miller married his high-school sweetheart. Two children soon followed—Jeff in March 1971 and Julie in June 1972. The couple divorced not long after Julie was born.

Miller would marry and divorce twice more through the early 1990s, though he would have no more children. His devotion to rebuilding and tinkering with cars and trucks left him little time for a family life satisfying to his wives. And in one instance, Bruce suspected that his wife had been unfaithful to him, Chuck Miller said. But the two remained friendly after the separation and divorce.

"He just likes being married," Chuck Miller said.

One interest that took him away from home and family was his devotion to NASCAR racing. Three or four times a year, he would fly to Nevada, Pennsylvania or Connecticut to watch the races and follow the success of his favorite driver, iconic badass Dale Earnhardt. A throwback to old-style, fender-rubbin' racin', "the Intimidator" was nothing like the pretty-boy drivers, such as Jeff Gordon, that NASCAR promoted when the rest of America discovered Winston Cup racing in the 1990s. Earnhardt appealed to Miller because he won races with hard-nosed, aggressive determination. Miller liked the way Earnhardt controlled the track, giving no quarter to the weak.

Miller particularly enjoyed going to races in Las Vegas. He'd play a little blackjack, though he was too tight with his money to lose much cash. After the race, he'd top off the trip with a visit to the Hoover Dam. That was Bruce Miller's idea of living large.

Bruce Miller towered a full foot over his new five-foot-two-inch bookkeeper, who had been hired by one of his business partners in 1997. At first, Bruce and Sharee didn't see that much of each other. She worked mornings at the yard and then nights at a nursing home. Miller would come to the yard in the afternoons and stay until it was time to go build exhaust systems at his third-shift job at the Delphi East plant in Flint.

Though Sharee knew little about car parts, she changed life at B&D. Soon after arriving, she set up a display for free samples of men's cologne from Mary Kay cosmetics, which she had begun selling in 1997. And amid worn tires, exhaust pipes and toolboxes, customers couldn't help but notice her. Pretty women—any women, really—are rare items at salvage yards. But that was one of Sharee's special qualities. She always found a way to stand in sharp relief wherever she was, either by grabbing a karaoke microphone at a bowling alley or by pushing men's cologne to tow truck drivers from behind the counter of an auto junkyard.

Both Sharee and Bruce had steady personal interests elsewhere during most of 1997 and 1998. Sharee was living with a boyfriend, who'd taken her in after her second marriage collapsed. Bruce had dated three or four women since his third divorce. He was then seeing a school-teacher, whom he'd court on the weekends.

All that came to a halt on October 10, 1998, a year to the day after Bruce's father died. A little blue about the anniversary, Bruce stopped by the nursing home to talk with Sharee. She followed him to his home on West Francis Road.

"We started kissing on the couch and one thing led to another, and we slept together that night," Sharee remembered later. "The relationship moved pretty fast."

But that relationship wasn't only about sex. Bruce brought a gentle humor to her life that had been sadly missing before.

"He made me laugh," Sharee said. "We had a lot in common. We could talk about anything."

On weekends, they'd go to the Bus Stop, a bar in nearby Birch Run, to sing country-western karaoke, though that mostly was her idea.

"We were the center of attention because of our age difference and our height difference," Sharee recalled.

Still, Miller did not mention his promising new relationship to his family. He saved that for Thanksgiving 1998.

Though the family had dressed casually, Sharee again stood out, spiffed up in business attire, well made up and hair coiffed to perfection. Chuck Miller later said he sensed that day that Sharee was working hard to make a good impression.

Standing at the door of Bruce's mother's home, Sharee introduced her three children, Tommy, Angela and Buddy, and noticed that her daughter had taken an im-mediate shine to Judy Miller, Chuck's wife.

"Would you like to go home with Judy?" Sharee said. "She'd like to have a girl."

Out of Angela's earshot, Sharee then described her daughter as a "mistake." Later, she would add that Buddy had been abused by his father. That was news Chuck Miller said later that he found a little odd for dinnertime conversation.

Still, the Miller family matriarch had urged Sharee to speak freely about her life during dinner. Ruth Miller was dead set on figuring out why her son was dating a woman young enough to be his daughter. They already were holding hands and giving each other affectionate little pecks on the cheek.

Sharee said little to calm a mother's concerns.

"I'm a wild child," she told the family. "Bruce is settling me down."

After the couple had left, Judy Miller cornered her husband to ask whether he had discussed the age difference issue with his brother. Yes, Chuck Miller replied, but Bruce didn't seem all that concerned.

"He said, 'I'm forty-seven years old; I'll do what I want to do,'" Chuck Miller said.

That's not good news, Judy thought. *Bruce is more settled. Sharee's not.*

But Judy Miller pushed it out of her mind. Maybe she was just annoyed about that last scene with Sharee as she was leaving with Bruce, when she again began asking her kids, "Want to go home with Judy?"

"She keeps trying to pawn the kids off on me," Judy Miller said to her husband.

Chuck Miller, concerned about the age difference, began hearing stories about the ever-quickening courtship over the next few weeks. But in this case, Sharee seemed to be pursuing Bruce.

"She sent Bruce flowers," Chuck Miller said to his wife one evening.

Others began noticing, too. John Joel Hutchinson, an old friend who made a living salvaging wrecked automobiles, had slept with Sharee a time or two a few years back when he was separated from his wife. After his wife moved back in, Hutchinson made a point of staying away from the office at B&D when Sharee was around.

Hutchinson had seen how she could stir up trouble between multiple boyfriends. Bruce Miller, quiet and laid-back, just wouldn't tolerate that kind of turmoil, Hutchinson later recalled thinking.

I was fucking her, Hutchinson thought as his friend fell further in love. *She was with everyone.*

He took Miller aside and told him to watch out because Sharee was too sly by half. Miller nodded but didn't say much.

"No problem," he replied. "Don't worry, I know what I'm doing."

Once, after Debbie Hutchinson had moved back in with her husband, she had bumped into Sharee, who wasn't shy about saying she still was interested in John Hutchinson, his house and his cars.

"I want your life," Sharee said.

Bruce proposed to Sharee in early 1999, giving her a two-carat diamond ring he'd received from a woman who visited the salvage yard needing a car. Sharee and her tribe moved in with Bruce long before they set a wedding date. She told Bruce that she had sold her home.

As their relationship progressed, and the couple wanted time alone, Judy Miller became Sharee's primary baby-sitter. And she paid well, giving Judy the impression that she had plenty of money on her own.

One evening, Sharee appeared, three kids in tow, asking Judy Miller to watch the children for the evening. That wasn't a problem, but Sharee didn't bring money that Judy could use to buy food for the children.

"Sharee, I've got to have some money," Miller said. "I'll come by the house in a couple of hours (to pick up the money)."

But Sharee resisted, knowing that Bruce wouldn't approve of her paying $50 for a night's baby-sitting.

"He'd get mad if he knew she was doing it," Chuck Miller said.

Still, life was looking up for Sharee. And soon she would receive an irresistible invitation to revisit one of the most painful moments of her recent past.

The New York studio lights flicked on and Sharee was ready. On January 27, 1999, she appeared on *The Montel Williams Show*, in a program entitled "I Never Thought He Would Kill My Baby!"

Her blond hair styled large, and dressed in a striking fire-engine red business suit with a short skirt, she prepared to answer the host's halting questions with a tight, brave smile.

"Please welcome Sharee to the show," Williams announced. "You live this—live with this now for the rest of your life, not with the memory . . ."

"That's how you live," Sharee began.

". . . but with what's left—I should say what's left—but how your child will have to survive for the rest of his life because of your husband, is that right?" Williams asked.

"Right," Sharee answered, and they cut to a commercial.

Sharee's child Buddy hadn't actually been killed by her second husband, as the program's title suggested. Buddy's brain had been damaged when her former husband had thrown him against a wall when he was only six months old.

The husband had received only a 4½-month sentence for the abuse, and Sharee had made it a cause. She started by writing to President Clinton, then began working down to local elected officials. Finally, she wrote the media, and a letter to Montel Williams worked. The show booked her appearance almost four years after the abuse.

After the commercial, Sharee told the story of how her husband had called her at work saying that Buddy had bumped his head. She rushed home to find Buddy's head swollen to the "size of a basketball." Examinations at the hospital showed injuries consistent with child abuse. But when the courts were finished with her husband, he spent most of his short sentence on work release and retained full visitation rights to his injured child. Her anger with a system that let her former husband off so lightly was palpable.

"Our justice system values children down here," she told the studio audience, motioning down around her shins, "instead of up here," finishing the gesture much higher. "They're our future."

The camera cut quickly to women in the audience— eyes narrowing, they shook their heads in disgust.

Nodding to a female criminal defense lawyer seated next to her, Sharee pushed the point further.

"But attorneys like you, and *girls* like you, are the ones that value them down here," Sharee finished.

Her assault on criminal injustice brought the biggest applause line of the show. Audience members bit their lips. Some wept.

But Sharee soon discovered that her appearance on Montel Williams's show amounted literally to only fifteen minutes of fame. Despite her appearances on national television to argue for harsher sentences for child abusers, local officials were still slow to respond to her letters and calls.

Four months after the appearance, she wrote again to Montel Williams, bemoaning that nobody in Michigan was listening to her. She had hoped to become a public speaker and recognized expert on how mothers can respond to abusive fathers. Her campaign had stalled.

She'd written letters about the problem of child abuse to dozens of government officials, but hadn't yet received a substantial response. She suspected that Michigan officials were just ignoring her, hoping that she and the cause she championed would just go away.

Her dream, she said, was to become a public speaker to help those who, like her, had seen abuse firsthand.

"To help one child would make a difference to me," she wrote.

When marriage beckoned, Bruce Miller headed for Las Vegas. He was frightened of needles, and Vegas marriages did not require a blood test.

"He always got married there," Chuck Miller recalled later.

At a wedding chapel on April 23, 1999, the couple posed for pictures, which only accentuated the differences in their ages. In one, Bruce sat behind Sharee, still towering over her, and cradled her left arm in his hand. He looked vaguely uncomfortable in a suit, and his face showed every one of almost thirty years in the shop. Sharee, however, looked fresh in her white gown; her short hair shimmered a sunny blond. Her hands lay just inches from a single red rose the photographer placed to occupy the foreground.

The rose reappeared in another photo the couple also purchased. Sharee Miller held it as she stood before a floor-to-ceiling mirror, catching every inch of her ankle-length dress and white satin pumps. Two rows of empty white pews stretched behind her, and a white grand piano sat to her right.

The picture captured Miller in one of those soft,

contemplative moments that professional photographers are so good at creating. The real Sharee in the foreground had merely lowered her eyes. Her reflection in the mirror—the image she would see if she just looked up—was altogether different, sharper, more focused and more determined.

Sort of the way her new family soon would see her.

When Bruce and Sharee Miller returned from their Nevada wedding, the new Mrs. Miller was on top of the world and in a mood to celebrate. With a prosperous husband ready to take care of her children, Sharee Miller's life was finally on the upswing, she thought.

"Someone was finally taking care of us, instead of hurting us," Sharee later said. "Someone was actually in my children's life trying to do right."

At a night out with the Miller family, Sharee Miller took the microphone at a karaoke bar and serenaded the group. But as the celebration continued into the evening, Chuck and Judy Miller bumped into a woman who had known Sharee from her days at the nursing home. The woman seemed surprised that Sharee had settled down with somebody respectable.

"Sharee's nothing but a slut and a liar," the woman said.

Other things also puzzled Chuck and Judy Miller.

Once, when they were out for an evening, Sharee pointed to a man in a bar and told Chuck Miller that she once had gone out with him, adding, "I can't believe I dated that guy."

In a small town, anybody can bump into an old boyfriend or two. But with Sharee it happened all the time. *She must have dated half of Flint,* Chuck Miller later said he thought.

Fallout from Buddy's injuries continued to affect

Bruce and Sharee Miller. Even before saying their vows, Bruce and Sharee attended counseling to help her children adjust to life after child abuse. The largest step, however, came a month after they married, when Sharee appeared at the office of Flint attorney Peter Doerr and said that Bruce had decided to adopt Buddy and Angela. Tommy's father was still active in his life. But the prospect of Miller's former husband gaining custody was too painful, Sharee said later.

Doerr explained the complex adoption process, particularly the need to conduct an audit so the court could determine if Buddy and Angela's natural fathers had maintained any contact with them and paid child support. The lawyer said such a report could be ready by early December.

The move to adopt chilled Chuck and Judy Miller, whose greatest fear had been that Sharee would convince Bruce to adopt her children, then divorce him and get all his money.

Doerr began the adoption process for the Millers. Later, though, the lawyer would recall that he only had dealt with Sharee Miller. He never met her husband.

His own kids grown and long gone, Bruce Miller had some adjusting to do. With three school-age children and a new young wife, Bruce Miller quickly moved to make some changes to his home on West Francis Road.

He had the aboveground pool adjacent to the house cleaned up so the kids could swim in the summer. And though he was notoriously tight with his money, Miller paid his brother $1,000 to install a deck.

The house itself remained pretty much the same—an older one-story blue home with a dirt driveway and set well off the road. A generous lawn that Bruce Miller would cut with a riding mower surrounded the home.

And neighbors often would see Bruce sharing his seat on the mower with one of Sharee's kids.

The inside was about what you'd expect of a man who owned an automobile salvage yard. In some rooms, the furniture was worn, mismatched and a little haphazard, not that Bruce cared much about interior design. The kitchen, though, was spacious when compared with that of the trailer home Sharee Miller had occupied during her previous marriage. If it all wasn't Martha Stewart pretty, the house was kept up well and certainly an improvement for Miller and her children.

Sharee Miller's child-rearing skills came under more scrutiny after she moved in with Bruce. Judy Miller soon concluded that her sister-in-law's primary form of discipline amounted to negotiating, begging and pleading with her kids.

When the children tired of their new toys, she would just bag them up, throw them out and buy new ones on Bruce's credit card. Chuck Miller noticed that, too.

"How do you buy something for kids who had everything and appreciated nothing?" Chuck Miller said.

Before long, Sharee Miller had run up more than $46,000 in charges on her husband's credit cards.

Some of her children's behavior problems appeared to be organic. Tommy, an excitable and active eight-year-old, was particularly troublesome. But that had emerged years before Sharee Miller got involved with Bruce.

Though adept at both computers and singing, Tommy had gone to counseling in the second grade to deal with his anger, specifically "violence against his sister," his mother wrote in a school questionnaire.

One of Sharee Miller's best friends, Jennifer Ann Dege, said Sharee sometimes would become distraught with Tommy's behavior. "She was having problems with Tommy," Dege said. "He was kinda to the point where they just couldn't handle him anymore."

Bruce also would go "round and round" with Tommy, Dege said, but mostly about "little stuff, like cleaning his room."

Finally, doctors prescribed Ritalin for Tommy, and his behavior seemed to improve. But even if Miller's performance as a mother was under a microscope, her relationship with Bruce was solid in the first weeks of the marriage.

Sharee told friend Laura Ewald that Bruce was a gentle and patient lover who made her forget the mistrust and violence of earlier relationships.

"She always bragged how gentle he was with her and [said] that he's the first man that she could actually make love with and have an orgasm without feeling the past come back and haunt her," Ewald said.

But Sharee never would describe Bruce as Ward Cleaver. The first time Sharee was alone in his home, she remembered later, she pushed Play on Bruce's VCR and saw a pornographic movie pop up. This delighted Sharee, who tried to get Bruce to experiment with new sexual experiences. But Chuck Miller remembered that his brother once complained that he couldn't develop much enthusiasm for viewing videos of three-way sexual encounters between two women and a man.

"Sharee talked pretty open about those sexual things, but my brother was a quiet man," Chuck Miller said. "My brother was a square."

Chuck Miller's wife found it all pretty appalling.

"We're just a little family from a little town," Judy Miller said.

Bruce Miller never spoke with his brother or his sister-in-law about Sharee's life on the Internet. Soon after they were married, she purchased a new computer at OfficeMax and began her own exploration of fantasy on the Internet.

She viewed the World Wide Web strictly through the

prism of sex and pornography, once saying that she believed that up to 90 percent of the Web sites available to browsers were pornographic. With a new computer and a fair amount of time on her hands, she became adept at finding porn sites that offered lots of content for free. Even at sites that required a credit card, Miller knew how to coax the last available free photograph out of the server before the inevitable screen popped up asking for MasterCard or Visa.

She entered the Web through an account on America Online, the behemoth Internet service provider based in Dulles, Virginia. At the time, AOL served more than 26 million paying subscribers. And through free access to its AOL Instant Messaging software, another 70 million users could find individuals throughout the world for private or group chat sessions in real time.

As a subscriber, Miller could obtain e-mail under a number of different addresses that AOL calls screen names. And most of those screen names could be changed as frequently as she wished. Over the life of her account, Miller used thirty screen names. Some were as simple as SHAREE1013, her name with her birthday, October 13, tacked on at the end. Other screen names she used, such as IWANTTOBELAID and Sexykitten4onlyu, spoke for themselves.

When Miller clicked on her AOL Instant Messaging software, a world very different from e-mail opened to her. Communicating with Instant Messaging, or just IM for short, was more like speaking with someone on the telephone, except the speakers would type their remarks into the computer, hit Enter and wait for the reply. The statement then would immediately be transmitted to the other person, who would type in her reply.

Several people could participate in an IM session. But one could invite someone in a larger conversation into a separate chat room for a private talk, away from others.

Miller quickly found the chat rooms that focused on sex and began participating, sometimes from her desktop computer in the bedroom she shared with Bruce, sometimes with the laptop she would carry to the junkyard. What captured Miller's imagination was twofold: the Internet's anonymity and her ability to reinvent herself.

She could log on and portray herself as a wealthy businesswoman or a porn star, depending on her mood. She shared this world with her husband, who never in his life had shown any interest in computers. She was aroused by the frankness of the chat rooms and hoped they would expand her husband's sexual horizons.

"I did all the typing," she said later. "We would read the chats, then go to bed. . . . When you're on-line, you can be anyone you want to be. Bruce and I both made up stories about who I was."

To give her husband, or at least his business, an e-mail presence, Miller created the screen name BDJUNK. Bruce, however, wasn't a heavy user of e-mail. Friends described his typing style as two-finger hunt-and-peck.

Occasionally, Sharee Miller said, she could get her husband interested in ordering car parts on-line, visiting NASCAR auto-racing sites or using the Web to plan one of his Winston Cup trips.

In fact, Bruce Miller had his eye on a July 1999 NASCAR race he wanted to attend. He suggested that Sharee visit Nevada while he was out of town. Always game, Sharee agreed, and invited her best friend and fellow Mary Kay saleswoman, Laura Ewald, along for a trip.

Unable to decide between Reno and Las Vegas, Miller jumped on her computer to do some research in April or May 1999. In an AOL chat room, a helpful soul using the screen name Renodudes popped up offering information about Reno. The two began corresponding, and soon she learned his name was Jerry Cassaday, an ex-cop from Missouri who lived in Reno and worked at Harrah's Hotel and Casino.

Miller decided she and Ewald would go to Reno so she could meet this Jerry Cassaday. She never mentioned him to Ewald, though.

The trip would change all of their lives forever.

THREE

The state of Missouri defines Middle America, tucked near the center of its forty-seven contiguous sisters. Missouri nestles its 4.9 million residents about as far from New York as California. Likewise, travel to its closest international cousins, Mexico to the south and Canada to the north, takes about the same time as the crow flies.

The state earned its most famous nickname in 1899, when Congressman Willard D. Vandiver said: "I come from a country that raises corn and cotton and cockleburs and Democrats, and frothy eloquence neither convinces nor satisfies me. I'm from Missouri. You've got to show me."

As a police officer for much of his professional life, Jerry Lee Cassaday was comfortable with Missouri's reputation for midwestern decency and for skepticism.

Born in Kansas City on October 6, 1960, Jerry Lee Cassaday was the third of four sons raised by middle-class parents, James and Charlene Cassaday. Charlene was a strong-willed woman who was born in California and raised on a farm near Warrensburg, Missouri.

James Cassaday also was a farmer, but he attended William Jewell College in Liberty, Missouri, on a football scholarship. Later, he transferred to Central Missouri State University in Warrensburg to study drafting and physical education.

Charlene Cassaday was pursuing a business major when the two met. They were married in 1953.

James Cassaday went on to manage and own gas stations around Kansas City. At home, he and Charlene raised Jerry and his brothers, Roger, Michael and Steve.

"He was hardheaded, but also loving and happy," Charlene Cassaday remembered of Jerry. And whatever Roger, the oldest son, did, Jerry would follow. Roger was the catcher on the youth baseball team coached by his father, so Jerry had to be a catcher, too, size or ability be damned.

"Jerry didn't give a hoot; he wanted to do it," Charlene Cassaday said.

Despite his yen to play behind the plate, Jerry usually ended up at shortstop.

"He wasn't a barn burner, but he was more than adequate," Charlene Cassaday said.

The youngster gave his parents little trouble as he grew up. "We had more trouble with Roger as the rebellious one," Charlene said. "We had to step on him. But we always felt Jerry watched his brothers push the parameters and learned what he could and could not get away with."

Throughout his public schooling, Jerry got by on average grades. In the sixth grade, he joined the school choir and moved up to the Raytown Sixth Grade All-School Choir, which included kids from all the area schools.

Cassaday continued singing in the choir through high school. His musical tastes favored country and western, with Johnny Cash emerging as his lifelong favorite.

At Raytown High School near Kansas City, Jerry met his first real girlfriend, Tracy, a cute, slender blonde who was a year older than he. She was a member of the National Honor Society, and her diligent schoolwork paid off for Jerry, focusing him on improving his own grades.

Because of Tracy's strict parents, the Cassadays never worried about their son getting caught up in alcohol and drugs through high school.

Outside the classroom, he played a little football, bowled and worked part-time jobs for pocket money, including a stint at a golf course snack bar and out on the course. He also was a bag boy at a local supermarket. Later, he worked at a restaurant.

Cassaday graduated from Raytown High School in 1979. By that time, he had saved enough money to pay for his first two years of college without any financial help from his parents.

Jerry followed Tracy to Central Missouri State University, where he began a string of appearances on the dean's list. It was about this time that Cassaday surprised his parents, announcing that he wanted to major in criminal justice and pursue a career in law enforcement.

His brothers had been in the service, and Cassaday had contemplated that before settling on a career as a cop.

Michael, his older brother, also had wanted to be a police officer. But after Mike married, his wife objected to handguns in the house, so he never followed up.

But James and Charlene wouldn't dash Jerry's dreams. They had urged all their sons to pursue worthy goals and attend college. They did not want to see any Cassaday kid pumping gas or digging ditches.

"If this is what you want to do, fine," Charlene and James Cassaday told him. "Just be the best doggone cop out there."

Cassaday lived in the dorm his first year but found that too distracting for study. After earning a C in a course there, he moved into his own room the second year. He still came home on weekends and enlisted his mother to type his term papers. A professor once noted on one of Cassaday's reports that "you and your mom have done an excellent job."

During his college years, Cassaday surrounded himself with others who shared his love of police work, joining Lambda Alpha Epsilon, a criminal justice fraternity. Cassaday performed well in his major and was also admitted to Alpha Phi Sigma, a criminal justice honor society.

After graduating in 1983 with a 3.8 grade point average, Cassaday entered the Basic Law Enforcement Academy in Jefferson City. There, Missouri Highway Patrol troopers taught Cassaday the basics of police work: how to preserve a crime scene, fill out police reports, handle a drunk driver, disarm an armed man, question suspects, handle a weapon and when to use deadly force. Cassaday excelled at the academy, earning a gold certificate, graduating with honors and finishing second among his peers.

In 1983, Cassaday joined the Marshall, Missouri, Police Department, learning the ropes as a twenty-three-year-old patrol officer. In one mishap, his cruiser was rammed broadside. Doctors treated his back injuries with prescription pain medication, which he would use for the rest of his life.

But someone in Marshall took Cassaday's mind off his injuries, a honey blond dispatcher named Barbara.

Because Cassaday and his high-school sweetheart were having a rough go and the relationship was about to end, he turned to Barbara for friendship. And that evolved into love.

Barb brought two boys to the relationship from a previous marriage, which had not ended well. Cassaday's parents soon heard about Barb, and their reaction was not surprising. At first, they wondered about their son getting into a relationship with a woman with two kids.

"Then we met Barb, and the more we got to know her, the more we liked her," Charlene Cassaday said. "She became the daughter we wanted and never had."

Later, Barb brought her sons to the Cassaday home

for visits. The boys were leery because they had seen other men hurt their mother. Even Jerry had to work hard to gain their trust and love, but when the two boys met James Cassaday, they took to him like a grandfather.

James and Charlene Cassaday put up Christmas stockings for the boys, and were amazed how the boys showered love on them.

Barb and Jerry eventually married, but the boys' biological father would not pay his child support. Neither would he allow Jerry to adopt them. The father finally consented to the adoption when Barb threatened to ask the courts for an order forcing him to pay the arrears.

Cassaday's career also was going well in Marshall, but he longed for bigger towns, more serious crime and greater responsibilities. In 1985, Cassaday joined the sheriff's department in Cass County, just south of Kansas City, a larger operation that covered a much wider area.

Cassaday was impressed with the credentials of Cass County's newly elected sheriff, Homer Foote, a former Kansas City vice cop, and with those of his right-hand man, Undersheriff Thomas Cook.

It wouldn't be the last time his instincts of whom he could trust would fail him.

Cassaday threw himself into the work in his new department, and in less than six months, he was promoted to detective lieutenant, overseeing the department's Criminal Investigation Division.

Cassaday also screened other department applicants, devised staff schedules and evaluated other employees and their performance.

"I spoke on behalf of the department in areas of narcotics, drug abuse, Neighborhood Watch and crime prevention," Cassaday said later.

And Cassaday worked hard to become a better cop, participating in training programs sponsored by the FBI and the Northwestern University Traffic Institute. He took FBI training to one day become a firearms instructor. And he took a class on advanced criminal investigation techniques from the Missouri Deputy Sheriff's Association.

Cassaday began to think a lot of his policing skills. In a conversation years later, he bragged about how he used to catch crooks and bad guys.

"When I was a detective, I thrived on that," he said. "I loved for people to answer my questions. I loved to talk because I would ask questions I knew the answer to. I wanted them to lie to me because then I knew I had them.

"If they would lie about little things, I knew the big ones were lies, too. People always offer more information than they should. Always. People like to talk. It's in their nature."

Cassaday learned that a corroborated confession was the cleanest way to lock away criminals. He would brag to friends that he solved a higher percentage of his cases than any other officer in the Kansas City area. He also was proud of his nickname, "the Chameleon," which reflected his ability to blend in well with suspects and coax confessions smoothly.

Cassaday joined the Metro Squad, an elite task force that investigated murders and other major crimes that were too big for small police departments to handle alone.

And he earned a reputation—even among criminal defense lawyers—as the honest cop working in a department that too often cut corners and bent the rules to suit the whims of its chief, Sheriff Homer Foote.

"Jerry was one of the good ones," said John Lozano, a Harrisonville, Missouri, lawyer who regularly had to defend clients that Cassaday had arrested.

As Cassaday grew as a cop, Cass County also changed. The boyhood home of President Harry S. Truman,

Cass County once was a sleepy rural enclave largely over-looked by bustling Kansas City to the north. But with more industry and residential growth sprawling into the area, the department's tired, good-old-boy way of doing business no longer could withstand scrutiny.

Cassaday's initial problems with the department were irritations. Foote had promised to send his young lieu-tenant to the FBI police training academy in Quantico, Virginia. That never happened, and Cassaday was left disillusioned.

Cassaday also had counted on Foote to put a good word in for him at the U.S. Marshals Service, which he had hoped to join. Cassaday had applied when the fed-eral agency was about to relax a hiring freeze and fill several openings in the Kansas City area. Cassaday be-lieved he had all the necessary qualifications and thought he was a shoo-in.

But later, Cassaday found that Foote had never fol-lowed up with the promised recommendation. Indeed, Cassaday discovered that his employment in the Cass County Sheriff's Department, and his supposed close-ness with Foote, had actually worked against him, blackballing him from any position with the Marshals Service.

When interviews were scheduled, Cassaday never was contacted.

Cassaday also was upset with the way the department treated his wife.

When the two left Marshall, Barb also had been hired by the sheriff's department to work in the office. But when she became pregnant, Cook, the undersheriff, told her she ought to quit. While Cook had suggested that she leave in the interest of her health, Barb Cassaday believed that it was because Cook did not want a pregnant woman working in the department. She quit, nevertheless.

Later, a county attorney told Cook that he could not

simply fire a female employee just because she was pregnant. Barb then was offered her job back, but she decided against it, fearing repercussions for her husband and his chances for promotion.

Cassaday's real trouble started in 1992, when he could no longer abide the department's shabby practices. He saw prisoners being illegally detained and strip-searched in the county jail, which caused a surge of civil lawsuits against the county. Senior officers were rigging bids in purchasing police cars.

When a set of the sheriff's department's emergency flasher lights went missing, they turned up on a truck belonging to one of Cook's relatives.

And Cassaday saw cops being asked to violate laws, rules and regulations to obtain convictions. In May 1992, Cassaday and another deputy heard from an officer that Cook had asked him to doctor a police report. Cook had ordered the officer to show that a driver had been intoxicated, when, in fact, he wasn't.

Unable to sit quietly as the department crumbled around him, Cassaday decided to speak out, and he picked an eleven-year-old murder investigation as his battleground.

The case involved the kidnapping and slaying of Cheryl Morris, a Belton, Missouri, restaurant worker. Officers were certain they knew who the culprit was—they just didn't have enough evidence to charge him. But in 1992, police dispatch logs turned up that appeared to match the license plate number and description of a car belonging to the suspect at about the same time of Morris's abduction and murder. Cassaday and others thought the new evidence was fishy, because some of the information appeared to have been added to the reports much later in the investigation.

One day, Cassaday happened into Cook's office and saw him studying the old case file.

"There's a lot of discussion in the office about who might have made those entries," Cassaday said as he peered over Cook's desk at the documents.

Fixing his eyes straight at Cook, Cassaday threw out an accusation that would forever change his career in law enforcement: "Tom, it kind of looks like your handwriting."

Cook's face burned red and he glared at Cassaday.

Cassaday took his suspicions to Cass County prosecuting attorney Dennis Laster.

Laster, who later would become a university professor of criminal justice, had his own suspicions about the veracity of Cass County Sheriff's Department dispatch logs.

And with Cassaday's observation, Cook emerged as the likely culprit, since he had furnished police logs that appeared to have been altered.

County officials took some information to Foote and asked him to fire Cook. But Foote refused. Cassaday earlier had believed that Foote had overlooked Cook's conduct to give him the benefit of the doubt. Cassaday now had to consider that Foote was as tainted as Cook.

Laster also was troubled. He knew that as a prosecutor, he had to work closely with Foote and Cook to prosecute legitimate cases the sheriff's department presented. And that conflict of interest had the potential to ruin even good cases brought by a less than honest department. Still, Laster also knew something had to be done.

Laster recused his office from any probe and asked for a special counsel to investigate the Cass County Sheriff's Department.

But even with a new special prosecutor in place, the investigation took some time. Finally, more than a year later, on July 21, 1993, the special prosecutor began the public process to remove Foote from office.

This came months after Cassaday had testified before a grand jury. And Cassaday's whistle-blowing did not sit well with his superiors in the sheriff's department.

On the same day the special prosecutor filed a civil lawsuit to remove Foote from office, the sheriff ordered deputies to hand-deliver a termination notice to Cassaday at his Raymore home.

Fighting for his job a week later before the county's Personnel Appeals Board, Cassaday testified that he had no choice but cooperate with the special prosecutor.

"A barrage of complaints have been lodged against our department," Cassaday said. "We have cooperated fully with the investigating agencies. . . . I know beyond a shadow of a doubt I was terminated because of my co-operation with the grand jury."

The board backed Cassaday and quickly reinstated him and another deputy who also had testified. Foote relented but added that he would only rehire Cassaday "under protest."

Cassaday returned to the department but found himself demoted to patrol. And again, the review board rescinded Foote's illegal action.

Foote countered by ordering other employees within the department to have only limited contact with the rebellious deputy, saying Cassaday had lost credibility and Foote no longer had confidence in him.

And for those employees who stood with Cassaday, Foote added a forbidding message: communication with Cassaday could jeopardize their careers. Foote even hired a rookie as detective and began assigning all the cases to him to further limit Cassaday's duties.

For the next several months, Jerry and Barbara Cassaday endured near-constant harassment. He would receive telephone calls at home, in the middle of the night, threatening Barb or the kids.

The callers would say, "Watch your back" or "You've got a pretty wife."

The calls were so upsetting that Barb began carrying a handgun. Once, deputies were ordered to retrieve Cassaday's patrol cruiser from his driveway in the middle of the night, sending Cassaday into a scramble to retrieve a suit and wallet he had left in the car.

Cassaday's suspicions grew deeper. Though he thought he was the only deputy with a key to the evidence room, he learned that Cook also had a key and was making regular visits to it when Cassaday was not around. He imagined that his superiors were going to make evidence disappear, then blame him for it.

In the midst of this turmoil, Cassaday slipped off a curb, injuring his leg severely. His six-month disability leave after two surgeries at least got him out of the office and gave him time to consider his future. While he could stick it out during the department's investigation, Cassaday also knew that, win or lose, his days in the Cass County Sheriff's Department were about over.

Cassaday was vindicated on June 21, 1994, when a U.S. Secret Service documents expert testified that indeed the murder evidence had been fabricated. The expert said inks used in the dispatch logs were not commercially available when the logs were filled out.

"The questioned entries are fraudulent," said Susan Fortunato.

Foote and several of his cronies soon were booted from office. But for Cassaday, the damage had been done. Like a veteran marine returning home from Vietnam, Cassaday was no hero. His chances for promotion blown, he became an outcast in the department, upsetting the good-old-boy network by becoming the Serpico of Cass County.

Cassaday gave some thought to running for sheriff after Foote's ouster but set it aside. Too many people would argue that Cassaday had helped engineer Foote's departure to smooth his own way to the top. He knew that wouldn't be right.

Rather than fight the inevitable, Cassaday resigned in

the summer of 1994 and looked for new ways to support his wife, Barbara, their new young son, Kenneth, and the two boys from her previous marriage.

"It destroyed him," said Charlene Cassaday, Jerry's mother. "We encouraged him to get back into police work, but his heart wasn't in it."

He found new opportunity in an unlikely place.

Riverboat gambling in Missouri surged in the mid-1990s, and a giant of the industry, Harrah's, was building a hotel and casino in North Kansas City. A new casino needs qualified security officers, and ex-cops fit the bill.

Cassaday had interviewed with the casino during the trial but was reluctant to tell Harrah's personnel people about his role in the investigation. However, one Harrah's official, a former FBI agent, made some discreet inquiries and learned that Cassaday was being hounded out of the department after exposing its corruption. The former agent recommended Cassaday's hiring almost immediately.

Cassaday joined Harrah's as a security supervisor on July 18, 1994. His photo ID, taken by the Missouri Gaming Commission in September, betrayed none of the turmoil that had marked his professional life to that point. It depicted a fresh-faced thirty-three-year-old Cassaday, sporting a mustache that did little to hide the baby face that his older brothers had teased him about for years.

As a security supervisor for Harrah's North Kansas City Hotel and Casino, Cassaday was responsible for the safety of the facility, its employees and patrons.

"I conducted all internal and external investigations and worked as the liaison officer to area law enforcement agencies and prosecuting attorneys," Cassaday wrote in a later résumé.

Family members would recall later that Cassaday was immediately struck by the contrasts with his old job. Instead of the darkness and suspicion of the sheriff's department, the casino was, by design, a happy place to work. Employees mingled freely with customers and encouraged a carefree party atmosphere.

But as Cassaday shifted gears from investigating murders to rousting drunks and catching card cheats, the lingering scars from his experience in Cass County became manifest. Charlene Cassaday said that the bitter fight with Cook had altered the loving man she once knew.

"His personality changed," she said later. "That's when he started this problem with severe depression. It's kind of sneaky. He could put on a good front and everyone thought he was fine, but it was eating him up."

He began to drink more, mostly beer, but he combined it with the painkillers he used for his leg and back injuries. And into that soup, he ingested a new medication, Prozac. About this time, Cassaday was diagnosed with clinical depression, but the Prozac did little to heal his mind and he rejected any form of counseling.

"We thought once he got completely out of [the sheriff's department], he could put it behind him, but he couldn't," Charlene Cassaday said. "It cost him the career he loved. He began to get very bitter."

In 1996, Cassaday started a new job, dual-rate table games supervisor—or pit boss, in casino parlance. Here, Cassaday learned how to become a dealer. After his training, he was able to work the craps, or dice, table, as well as deal blackjack, Let It Ride, Caribbean stud and double-down poker. The job also gave him his first taste of computers, of which he had little experience before.

By 1998, with his addictions firmly rooted, Cassaday's relationship with Barb began to fray. Family members said that Cassaday, once a social drinker, now was spending more time in Kansas City bars with the guys after work. And since he worked nights, while his wife worked days, he saw less and less of Barb. Coupled to this the pain medication and antidepressants and Cassaday began to live in his own world.

"Before he had always been up and optimistic," Charlene Cassaday recalled. "He loved people and made allowances for people's problems and gave them the benefit of the doubt."

But now he became paranoid and wanted out of Kansas City. He leaped at the opportunity in 1998 to transfer to Harrah's bigger casino in Reno, Nevada. While he also considered a transfer to New Orleans, he and Barb believed Reno offered a better place to raise the boys.

By now, Barb was working in a Kansas City law office with her mother-in-law and was being groomed to become office manager when Charlene Cassaday retired. But Jerry saw the Reno transfer as a way to advance his new career and learn more about the gaming industry.

Jerry transferred to Reno in June 1998, while his wife stayed behind for some surgery. In July, Cassaday returned to Kansas City to pick up his wife and move their life and belongings to Reno.

The marriage cracked on a summer night in August, just a month after Barb had left a good-paying job in Kansas City to pack her three sons to Nevada. Cassaday announced that he was going out for a walk but didn't want company.

"I want to walk by myself," he said.

After returning, he presented Barb with a letter, ordering her out of their home.

"He suddenly walked in, handed his wife a letter that he had written on the computer and told her he wanted her to go back to Kansas City," Charlene Cassaday later recalled. "He didn't know what he wanted, but he didn't want her."

Cassaday put an entirely different spin on the breakup

to his parents. In September 1998, he called home and discussed the spilt.

"We got this whole song and dance about how un-happy he was and how he felt so controlled," Charlene Cassaday later said.

James Cassaday, her husband, was less than sympathetic to the problems that, he believed, Jerry had created for himself.

"He needs to have his head examined," he told Char-lene Cassaday.

They tried to convince Jerry to opt for a trial separation rather than file for divorce, but Cassaday already had made up his mind. They also urged Cassaday to get coun-seling for his marital problems, his depression, his pain medication addiction and his alcoholism. He refused.

But what to do about Kenneth? He already had started school in Reno and desperately wanted to stay with his father. Barb relented, but only after exacting a promise from her husband.

"As long as [Cassaday] kept his act together, she would not fight him on this, because this is what Kenny wanted," Charlene Cassaday said.

Schools in Reno operated on a three-months-on, one-month-off system. So Barb and Jerry decided that Kenneth would go to school in Reno and spend the one-month vacations in Missouri.

But if Barb had *any* indication that Cassaday was not being a good father, the deal would be called off.

After Barb moved out, another woman moved in with Cassaday to help with the rent. But when that didn't work, Cassaday and Kenny moved to a smaller apartment in nearby Sparks, Nevada. Barb returned to Missouri, devastated and unable to understand what had hap-pened to her marriage.

She soon filed for an amicable divorce.

On the surface, Cassaday was flourishing in his new job,

despite the breakup and his addictions. By all accounts, he appeared to be an exemplary casino employee.

On January 25, 1999, a Milwaukee man on his first trip to Reno took time from his adventure to drop kudos on the Harrah's staff. On a customer service card, he praised Cassaday and other casino employees for top-notch service.

"I've never been so knocked out by such a wonderful, helpful and courteous staff," the man wrote.

Cassaday immediately got a pat on the back from a casino vice president in a perk that the casino called WOW Bucks.

"Thanks for demonstrating the attitude that really makes a difference," wrote Vince Donlevie.

In January 1999, Cassaday led a class on new casino procedures, which pleased his superiors.

"Thank you for your time and hard work Jerry," the bosses told him in a memo.

And as Cassaday reinvented his professional life, he also tinkered with his appearance, growing a full, though neatly trimmed, beard. But like the mustache, the beard did little to hide his youthful appearance. Cassaday still looked like a high-school drama student playing an older man in the class play.

Even if some customers and his bosses thought this young man was nothing short of superb, Cassaday's parents saw someone who could be as different as night and day, depending on which day or night they spoke.

Charlene Cassaday heard it in his voice during occasional telephone conversations.

"He was up one day and down the next," she said. "Not mean, though. Just moody."

By July 1999, Cassaday was working night shift on the Harrah's gaming floor, watching the people who crowded in at all hours looking for the jackpot that could make them instant millionaires.

Although Cassaday defined himself as an ex-cop and displayed the mannerisms that he had picked up from those lost days, he also had no trouble fitting in with the camaraderie of the graveyard shift at Harrah's.

The team included Gloria Taylor, who worked a roulette wheel, and Carol Slaughter, a blackjack dealer. And Cassaday fit in for the most part, becoming a member of the crew, exchanging profanities, risqué humor and observations on their betting clientele.

During his off hours, Cassaday learned how to use the computer that he shared with Kenny, using America On-line to surf the Internet while looking for adult companionship in the X-rated world of sex chat rooms.

Cassaday had a plethora of screen names and used them to communicate with a number of people, mainly women. His primary screen name was Jlc1006, but Cassaday could get creative. Depending on his mood or his chatting partner, Cassaday could be Deviousminds, Twowayman9905212, GovagentJ, Jack100660, Jerrynreno, WrmfireOpnhrt, Martha961022980, Werelookin4u, Downandoutinkc, Myster8552, or Renoman711.

While surfing the Net in April or May 1999, Cassaday met an intriguing woman from Flint, Michigan, named Sharee. The chance meeting would bring a new screen name, one that Cassaday would cling to and use thousands of times in the months to come: Sharesfool.

Cassaday soon told Slaughter and Taylor about this Michigan woman he'd met on-line.

"He started talking about this gal he met on the computer," Taylor said.

He told his friends that he and Miller had exchanged many e-mails. Most remarkably, Cassaday said he was falling in love with Miller, even though he never had met her. Knowing that on-line relationships were often built on faceless lies, Slaughter and Taylor warned Cassaday to be skeptical when swimming in the Internet's dark waters.

"Jerry was at a point in his life where he was like a little kid in a candy store," Slaughter said.

The two women thought it odd that Cassaday, an ex-cop, could be so easily sucked into such a tenuous relationship and wondered why his police radar wasn't seeing through the lies that often went into that kind of correspondence. Cassaday told Taylor that his on-line forays were just part of his search to see if he still appealed to women, since he recently had broken up with his wife.

Even Cassaday's parents tried to warn him after they heard of his new Michigan angel. His divorce with Barb was not yet final, and they felt he was jumping into something he wasn't emotionally prepared for.

"Before you start something permanent with someone new, you'd better get your old life taken care of," Charlene Cassaday told her son.

But Cassaday would not heed anyone's advice. His communication with Miller only intensified.

"They had been e-mailing for quite some time, and that soon led to telephone conversations between them," Slaughter said. "Jerry said they started talking on the phone because he wanted to hear her voice."

Taylor remembered it similarly.

"He told me his telephone bills were astronomical," Taylor said.

But Cassaday was under a spell, smitten with a faceless woman.

He told Taylor that Sharee Miller was "wonderful" and that they had "so much in common."

Still, while Slaughter and Taylor listened to Cassaday's tales of Sharee, they thought the on-line romance was a joke.

But the joke became all too real when Cassaday told them that Miller was flying out to Reno to meet him.

"They finally decided they wanted to meet," Taylor said.

"Everybody here knew she was coming," Slaughter said. "Jerry was so excited. He kept telling us how gorgeous she was, how sweet she was."

The trip was set for mid-July, and just before leaving, Miller sent Cassaday a page-long single-spaced letter, composed at work on a typewriter without benefit of spell checker.

"Boy, I think I am spoiled by the computer," Miller groused. "I would not know what to do if this was not electric."

Soon Miller cast a spell to capture Cassaday with coyness and promises of unknown pleasures and mystery. Miller sent along a song, saying she loved it because it reminded her of Cassaday.

Miller had tried to call Cassaday the previous night, but she got no answer because he was out on a date with another woman. She teased Cassaday about that date, saying she could get jealous, not knowing whom he was seeing. Had they spoken, Miller said, she would have sung Cassaday a love song. She also wished she could have joined him for a late drink.

Tempting him with her own jealousy, she even asked if his friend was pretty.

Cassaday had begged Miller to stay with him on her trip to Reno. She declined, but cautiously.

It probably wasn't a good idea to stay at his house on her first visit, she replied. Wouldn't it be better if they met first, to see how they got along before they made more intimate plans? But again, she teased Cassaday, offering hope that their relationship might work out and that she could spend time at his house, and in his bed.

Who knows, she said, they might hit it off so well they could test the hot tub in her room?

With Cassaday's interest piqued, Miller told him that she might not immediately identify herself when she arrived at the hotel. That would force Cassaday to scrutinize every short blonde who sat at his blackjack table.

But she assured Cassaday she would announce her arrival without making him guess.

Miller then hooked Cassaday, the hopeless romantic, with a preview of her perfect romance. She wanted a *Pretty Woman*–type romance, one where he would hold her gently, kiss her deeply and then lead her to bed.

Miller ended the letter on a note of sweet promise. She peppered Cassaday with questions that hinted she was ready for domestic, as well as physical, intimacy. She asked about the kinds of things that couples notice about each other from living together.

Did Cassaday like to cuddle, or did he need room to sleep? Did Jerry snore, or was he a sound sleeper? She said she could learn a lot about him by just watching him sleep.

"See you sooooooooonnnnnnn," she concluded. "Your woman in Michigan."

Sharee Miller was on Jerry Cassaday's mind almost every waking moment. Before her visit, he mentioned something to Taylor.

He said Sharee Miller was young and vivacious, and she hadn't had sex in years.

From Cassaday's point of view, he had hit the jackpot.

FOUR

The video arrived in the summer and added a sensual sizzle to Jerry Cassaday's growing passion for his Michigan angel, Sharee Miller.

She titled the ten-minute clip *For Jerry's Eyes Only,* and it became a staple in the Cassaday VCR, keeping him company and occupying his thoughts and desires while Miller was hundreds of miles away. The video would further cement their sexual bond.

The lights are low, and the music—a country duet—is warm and romantic.

A small VHS-c camera catches a digital clock in the lower left-hand corner. It's 11:55 P.M.; her kids are in bed, and her husband at work. The stage is set for simple, sensual pleasures.

Miller is wearing a beige night slip, decorated with flowers. Her full blond hair is pulled back from her face and curls cascade down her neck.

As Miller begins to lip-synch the song, her camera whirrs away, capturing her reflection in the mirrored headboard of her gently rolling water bed.

Flickering candles bathe Miller in a soft glow, subtly darkening her hair and adding warmth to the room. Miller settles into the rolling water bed and impishly pulls her night slip up and over her knees, exposing a blond tuft of hair.

Slowly, Miller begins to knead her ample breasts, pinching,

*pulling and rubbing her nipples until they stand out erect
against the darkness of the room.*

*Writhing in the bed, Miller sits up and gently continues her
breast massage with both hands as a sleepy, dreamy look covers
her face.*

*Sharee lifts her breasts to her lips to kiss the nipples and bring
them fully erect. She moistens her fingers at her lips and they disappear between her legs.*

*Miller now lies back and spreads her legs apart, inviting the
viewer to bring her to climax.*

*She inches her hand down, down, down. Then the fingers of
her right hand are performing a masturbation ritual.*

*Slowly at first, and then with growing urgency and antici-
pation, her fingers explore the area, settling on a spot that is
sensitive.*

*Her hands begin to flutter, lightly at first, then faster and
faster.*

*As the music reaches its pinnacle, Miller pitches her head back
in satisfaction and parts her lips in a soft exhale. She straight-
ens her back, squeezes her thighs together and shudders with
the deep relief of orgasm.*

There's more. Miller has noticed that it was too dark
in the room for the video to record her properly.

*The second act soon begins, now lit adequately for Cassaday
to gulp it all in without a moment of mystery.*

*Miller pulls the night slip down, gathering it at her waist as
she rubs, licks and flits at her breasts, once again bringing the
nipples to full erection as Sarah McLachlan's "Angel" plays
softly in the room.*

*Lying on her side, Miller gazes into the headboard mirror,
back at the camera, playing with her left breast. She rolls over
and again massages both breasts, arching her back upward so
the nipple can be seen peeking over her legs.*

*She spreads her legs and again begins to massage, licking her
right index finger as she touches her breast, and then between
her legs, then back to her breast.*

In a sudden move, the finger disappears inside her.
And then it is over. Miller smiles coyly, draws her clothes around her and shuts off the machine that has recorded her secret pleasures.

Sharee Miller produced her home video weeks after she met Jerry Cassaday in person and became intimate with him in Reno in mid-July 1999. Before that meeting, and long before she produced and mailed the video to Nevada, her only knowledge of Cassaday had come from talking with him in phone calls and in on-line chat rooms.

The July trip had come at Bruce Miller's suggestion, and Sharee and friend Laura Ewald decided to spend a week in Reno. Ewald later said she knew nothing of Cassaday; Miller had never mentioned him.

Miller and Ewald stayed at Harrah's Casino and Hotel, an enormous, glitzy edifice that dominated an entire block in downtown Reno. The pair crammed as much fun into a day as possible, shopping and sunning during the day and attending shows at night. They rested maybe five hours a night, opting to party and leave the sleep for when they returned to Michigan.

On July 17, 1999, following a quick breakfast, the women hopped into their rental car and headed for Lake Tahoe. "It was a beautiful drive up into the mountains," Ewald remembered later.

After detours to roadside shops, the two ate lunch at a little picnic spot, enjoying the lovely lakes and sights of the area. Back in Reno, they stopped at a store across the street from Harrah's and bought some expensive-looking costume jewelry. The trinkets, which cost $14 each, looked as if they could be worth much more

The faux diamond rings were the finishing touches for Miller's outfit for the evening. Before heading out to a music and magic show at the casino, she dressed in a black evening gown and added a blond hair extension that showed off tresses down to her waist. She topped off the outfit with a white suit jacket.

After the show, Miller and Ewald headed to the Harrah's gaming floor.

Ewald was a slots person, but Miller enjoyed the camaraderie and conversation at the blackjack tables. Finding an open spot, she played a few hands and began using her looks and chatty nature to pass the time. Occasionally, she'd slip a Mary Kay business card, each bearing her Michigan phone number and e-mail address, to one of the ramblers who invaded the casino's night scene.

For weeks, Jerry Cassaday had been waiting for this woman to sit at his table. His beard groomed neatly to perfection, he watched Miller and did his job, handling the computers and dishing out the complementary service cards for regular players. Still, the couple took care to hide their friendship, pretending to be strangers. They appeared to be nothing more than casino pit boss chatting up a new customer. Miller would recall later that he seemed very friendly.

"He was really focused on the fourteen-dollar rings instead of my wedding band," Miller said.

Cassaday also took one of her business cards announcing for anyone listening at the table that he knew someone who used Mary Kay products and might be looking for a vendor.

Before long, Miller left the table and went looking for Ewald. She found her in a forest of slot machines. Sharee had a story ready for Ewald if she had seen Miller talking with Cassaday at the blackjack table.

"She said there was a person at the blackjack table giving her a hard time," Ewald said. "He kept wanting her to go out for a drink, even though she told him she was married."

Miller said she had a solution.

"I told him that the only way I would go out for a drink is if you went with me," Miller said.

Soon Miller had returned to Cassaday's table. But with her marriage to Bruce Miller only three months old, she was guarded with Cassaday. She told him she recently had married a man named "Jeff," who had been injured working on the roof of their new dream home. Now Jeff lay comatose, with little hope of recovery, in a Flint, Michigan, nursing home.

She also filled Cassaday's ears with stories about businesses she owned—a salvage yard and some nursing homes—and of lawsuits with lucrative pending settlements.

"I told him a lot of stories that day," Miller recalled.

But even with talk of her marriage, the stories only heightened Cassaday's interest. And after he clocked out that night, he and Miller met. Unnoticed by Ewald, they slipped up to Miller's room, as they had planned for weeks.

The culmination of that evening rested fondly in Cassaday's memory for months. He would recall it later in a long e-mail to Miller.

Cassaday wrote that he vividly remembered that special evening because it had brought purpose and desire to a life that had seemed to be going nowhere. July 17, 1999, Cassaday said, was the day his life began anew with none of the emptiness that had marked his first thirty-eight years.

"That one special night, an angel came to me," Cassaday wrote. "She opened my eyes, she opened my heart, and she taught me what it is to truly love from deep within."

The next day, Cassaday would sit with Miller and Ewald as they had dinner at a casino restaurant. The meeting was brief, Ewald recalled. Cassaday only wanted to know how they were doing with their bets and if they would be in the casino later. The women were noncommittal and Ewald never gave the pit boss a second thought.

Miller and Ewald returned to Michigan on July 20, 1999, flying Northwest Airlines from Reno. Her friend never noticed it, but something inside Miller had changed profoundly. And it had everything to do with Jerry Cassaday.

Miller's friend Jennifer Dege soon learned more about the trip. Miller had dated Dege's uncle years earlier, but the two fought all the time and the couple split. But Dege, Ewald's nineteen-year-old niece, remained friendly with Miller and the two lived together briefly in Millington, a small city near Flint.

A few days after returning from Reno, Miller told Dege that she had begun an affair with a well-built guy named Jerry, whom she had met on-line. He was a private investigator, Miller said, and had a son.

Still, Miller acknowledged that she felt bad about cheating on Bruce—but not so bad as to cut Cassaday out of her life.

To capture the buildup to their first sexual encounter, Miller sent him a photograph. The picture depicted Miller standing in the entryway of her home, dressed in the same outfit she had worn the night they met—a long black dress, accentuated with a white coat.

On the back, Miller wrote: "July 17, 1999. The first time we made love. Sharee!"

The July trip to Reno had aroused excitement and wonderment in Miller, who began a torrid exchange of e-mails that burned with sexually charged themes and anticipation of more physical encounters with Cassaday. But e-mails, phone calls and the nightly Instant Messenger chats weren't enough for Miller.

She decided she had to get back to see Cassaday and

began making plans to visit him again in August. His e-mails were passionate and devoted, she remembered.

"His e-mails were so intense—it was like a fairy tale," she said. "I was addicted to it. I wanted to see if this was the same person who was writing me."

To go without arousing her husband's suspicions, she concocted a lie for Bruce Miller, saying she had a Mary Kay sales meeting in Reno. She again booked a room at Harrah's.

Cassaday met her at the airport, but the couple spent little time in Miller's room. Company rules prevented Cassaday, a supervisory employee, from staying in hotel suites with a guest. Instead, the two passed the days in Cassaday's two-bedroom apartment in Sparks.

Miller reconnected with Cassaday and found that he was just as gentle, devoted and romantic as his e-mails had promised. And Cassaday was in heaven! Sex with a beautiful Michigan blonde and her proclamations of wealth all intoxicated Cassaday.

His friends Gloria Taylor and Carol Slaughter met Miller and sized her up as decent-looking enough to be seen in public with any man.

"She seemed like a real nice gal," Slaughter said. "And when they were together, Jerry was over the moon. His eyes lit up. He looked like he was completely infatuated. He had this mushy feeling. And she was very affectionate."

Cassaday's friends also learned that Miller was ten years younger than Jerry, but she was willing to swing from the vines with her older lover. Cassaday could not wait until his shift was over so he could parade about the casino with his new gal, showing off his trophy to his casino friends who also worked the graveyard shift.

They touched; they held hands; they giggled like high-school kids in love for the first time, friends said.

"They just had their hands on each other all the time,"

Slaughter said. "Sharee would stay up all night playing and gambling.

"Every time [Cassaday] went on a break, she would take a break from gambling and . . . they would go for a walk outside. And whenever he was outside of the pit, not performing his job, they were either holding hands, arms around each other. They were extremely affectionate."

Taylor remembered watching from her roulette wheel as Miller and Cassaday sashayed in at about 3:00 A.M.

"They were happy and looked like they were having a wonderful time," she said. "He was showing off the woman he adored. He showed her off all over the place," Taylor said.

"This is the love of my life," Cassaday would tell people.

Taylor said Miller was just as responsive, just as much in love.

With her arms and lips all over Cassaday, she told Taylor, "I'm trying to get him upstairs into the hotel."

Miller also told Cassaday's friends about a suffering husband back in Michigan, Jeff, who was injured in the construction accident. Such news would have surprised her real husband, Bruce Miller, who was far from brain dead, running his own junkyard and working for General Motors.

She also told Taylor and Slaughter about Bruce, Jeff's brother, who had moved in to help her care for Jeff, and now lived in an apartment that was attached to their home. Miller said Bruce would help with Jeff when he came home to visit on weekends.

She also told them that Jeff's health was very fragile, and he did not have long to live. So it came as no surprise that Miller and Cassaday began making plans for their life together after Jeff had left the scene.

And knowing that Sharee owned a junkyard and nursing homes and had pending lawsuit settlements just made Miller more attractive to Cassaday.

"Jerry thought he hit the lottery," Slaughter said.

Taylor also knew that Cassaday was vulnerable after his breakup with Barb and that he used the on-line chats with Miller and other women to validate that he was still attractive to women.

Miller filled all his needs, Taylor said—young, attractive, sexually active, with the promise of money.

"It was like he was looking for the genie in the bottle to appear and he rubbed the bottle and, *poof,* out comes Sharee," Taylor said later.

And Miller seemed to need Cassaday also, explaining to Slaughter and Taylor that she visited Reno periodically just to get away from the daily stress of caring for Jeff and to have a little fun.

One afternoon during the August trip, Miller and Cassaday took off to find their own future dream home. Cassaday knew Jude Crane, a casino employee who moonlighted as a real estate agent for Keystone Realty.

Crane also had seen Miller and Cassaday hanging all over each other at Harrah's, gambling and drinking and having a good time, and later recalled a conversation with the two lovebirds. Cassaday ambled over with Miller and said he would "like to look at some homes," Crane said.

He noticed that Miller was also interested.

"Yeah, I'd like to get a house," she said, saying she was in the process of selling property back East.

The couple made plans to meet Crane the following Saturday, so he blocked out five or six hours and he met Cassaday, his son and Miller. The four drove to a high-end neighborhood, where houses started about $300,000 and went up to $750,000.

As a $49,000-a-year casino pit boss, Cassaday could hardly afford such homes, but Miller assured Crane she could manage it.

"It would be in my name," she told Crane.

After looking at about eight high-priced houses, the couple settled on one that would have earned Crane a handsome commission and began picking out rooms for their children—Cassaday's son and Miller's three kids.

But the couple never returned to close the sale.

"They fell off the face of the earth," he remembered later.

During the trip, the couple went to an annual event called "Hot August Nights," which featured scores of classic cars. They walked around together and looked at the expensive antiques, occasionally talking to the owners, but generally just enjoying each other's company.

But Miller's plans also confused Cassaday's friends.

Although she spoke of having cash, Miller asked Slaughter to recommend her for a future job as a casino cocktail waitress after she moved in with Cassaday. Slaughter thought this odd. Why would an independently wealthy woman want to work as a cocktail waitress and put up with all the crap and come-ons of drunken gamblers?

The August trip came to a crashing halt when Miller received bad news from Michigan. She passed it along to Cassaday in a four-page note, written on a Harrah's notepad.

Something awful had happened, Miller began, wondering if she should even tell Cassaday the entire story. Guilt permeated the missive. While she and Cassaday were making love at his apartment, Miller had received a message at her hotel room. Jeff, her injured husband, had just been moved into intensive care and was in grave condition.

"In my heart I am believing this is payment for loving you," Miller wrote. "I've never cheated, Jerry, and I just did and look what has happened."

Jerry Cassaday sent Sharee Miller back to Michigan;

he believed her anguish was genuine but knew that his own opportunity was at hand.

Back again from Reno, Sharee pulled into the long driveway of Chuck and Judy Miller's modest clapboard home, just north of Flint. Stopping to chat for a moment, she peeled off $500 to pay her sister-in-law for watching the kids.

The baby-sitting had become more regular for Judy Miller that summer, and she didn't mind.

"Sharee paid me well, but it was all coming out of Bruce's pocket," she later recalled.

The money was almost too good—$50 for overnight stays and $150 each week to watch the kids while Bruce and Sharee were at work. The $500-a-weekend rate began earlier that spring when Sharee and Bruce had gone to Las Vegas.

From his own experience and from talking to others who had known Miller over the years, Chuck Miller knew that his sister-in-law was a spendthrift.

"That Sharee," Chuck Miller later said, "she can't keep a penny in her pocket or her pants on."

A few days after Sharee returned from Reno, Judy Miller's suspicions were seriously aroused. While visiting Bruce's home, Judy Miller saw Sharee accept a dozen roses that were delivered to her door.

It wasn't Valentine's Day, Sharee's birthday, or her and Bruce's anniversary.

Roses are not just a spur-of-the-moment gift, Judy reasoned, and are certainly not given just for the hell of it. Roses are supposed to *mean* something.

"I thought it was odd, and her reaction was even odder," Judy Miller later recalled. "She didn't want me to know who they were from. She was crying when she read the note, and then told me they were from her brother. But the way she acted, I didn't think they came from her brother.

"She just told us a lot of stories that didn't make sense."

Cassaday also was into storytelling about this time.

He called his parents, Charlene and James Cassaday, with an update on his new true love. His parents knew of his drug and alcohol problems.

"Mom, I've got some things to tell ya," Cassaday opened one telephone conversation.

"He just told us that she was great and wonderful and she had come in to visit him and they had spent some time together and she was everything he'd ever dreamed of," Charlene Cassaday remembered.

"He was just head over heels."

Despite the doubts that his friends had about this new relationship, Cassaday clung to Miller with a love that some would call blind.

But Cassaday's eyes worked fine, particularly when he watched his favorite video, which arrived in August. His e-mails revealed his infatuation with the images of the masturbating Miller. In an August 29 message, Cassaday rhapsodized over the video, intensely re-creating each detail and imagining that he was there with her.

"I know in your mind it was me that was there with you," Cassaday wrote. "They weren't your hands rubbing your body, they were mine."

Cassaday's e-mails betrayed more than a passing familiarity with pornography, or at least letters to *Penthouse Forum*. He described gently massaging Miller's clitoris and bringing his drenched fingers to her lips for a taste.

Cassaday reveled in an account of how he would perform oral sex on Miller and then passionately kiss her so she could again taste herself from his lips and beard.

The video lived in his imagination and Cassaday could picture himself participating. He remembered the moment at which Miller arched her back, and he believed, completely, that she was having an orgasm.

By late August, Miller was considering a September trip to Reno, so Cassaday signed off with a promise to abstain from masturbation until she arrived. He would just dream of his Sharee and watch her videotape each day.

Responding with sensuous e-mails of her own, Miller said she also was aroused and recounted how she had masturbated after receiving his letter. She assured Cassaday that her videotaped orgasm was real. And though she was touched by his promise, Miller gave him permission to masturbate.

"Just wait a couple of days before I get there," Miller wrote. "You wait all these days and you will blow my brains out when you have one in me."

With his finances deteriorating and his issues with prescription drugs and alcohol growing more urgent, Cassaday had more problems in his life than he could manage. However, he could chase them all away by simply flicking on his VCR. Sharee Miller and *For Jerry's Eyes Only* always beckoned.

He couldn't imagine how she could become one of his problems.

FIVE

After Miller returned to Michigan in August, she sent Cassaday the inevitable bad news of her husband's death. Jeff Miller, she said, never came out of his coma, his body eventually following his lifeless brain into death. But as word trickled back to Reno about Miller's loss—the "love of her life" who was mortally injured building their "dream home"—Jerry quickly saw his opportunity to win Sharee Miller begin to slip away.

In her grief, and out of a sense of obligation to Jeff's family, Miller claimed she had quickly remarried, this time to Bruce Miller, Jeff's brother. Before Jeff's death, Bruce had moved into an apartment attached to the dream home and had helped Sharee manage his brother, who was much taller than Sharee and too heavy for her to move alone.

Miller said that during Jeff's long period in the nursing home, she and Bruce would bring him home on weekends and lay him gently on the living-room floor. That would allow the children to roll over him and play with their stepfather. Miller said that Bruce had been such help during those difficult months.

The lightning romance between Miller and her brother-in-law was hazy, but later she would give this explanation to Slaughter, one of Cassaday's closest friends.

"[Bruce] finally confessed that he had always loved her," Slaughter said. "She told me that Bruce was the one that introduced Jeff to her. He didn't think that it would ever work out. But when it did work out between Sharee and Jeff, he was happy to step back, knowing that his younger brother was happily in a relationship."

Miller said Bruce had shown a romantic side she had never seen, Slaughter recalled.

"Now that Jeff was gone, [Bruce Miller] felt like he needed to come clean and tell her exactly how he felt," Slaughter remembered. "She said that he then stood up, gave her a long kiss on the lips, which he had apparently never done, and [said] just think about it. Just sleep on it. Just think about the possibility of us being together."

Miller, however, told Slaughter that she had some misgivings.

"She told me that she was extremely concerned because of the age difference, that she had never looked at Bruce in a romantic way. [She] couldn't imagine it and didn't want to lose him as a friend."

The news was difficult for Cassaday, but it soon became worse, if that were possible. Sharee told Cassaday that Bruce Miller was a man whose life as a union autoworker and small business owner covered his criminal involvement in counterfeiting, money laundering and drugs. Almost immediately after the sudden marriage, Bruce Miller had begun to leech money out of his wife and her businesses. Bruce didn't yet know about his wife's lawsuits and the pending settlements, but that was only a matter of time, Sharee Miller said.

As an ex-cop, Cassaday was shocked at news of Bruce Miller's criminal ties but understood why Sharee had told him. Through it all, her devotion to their love remained strong. She just wanted him to know exactly what he was getting into. And more than anything, Miller needed the support that Cassaday could offer.

"You are, as usual, on my mind and in my heart," he

wrote in an e-mail from late August. "I love you and truly hope all works out."

He usually signed his letters: "Your fool for life, Jerry."

Cassaday never spoke with Miller's husband on the telephone, but Sharee told Cassaday that Bruce had somehow figured out that his wife was having an affair. She said Bruce considered the affair just a bit of unresolved emotional baggage from Sharee's marriage to Jeff, but Cassaday's calls to Miller's home and salvage yard were too frequent and, at times, too insistent, not to raise suspicion.

Sharee Miller once told Slaughter that Cassaday had called her at work, asking to speak with her. When Cassaday was told she wasn't there, he blew up saying, "Get her on the phone; I need to talk to her."

That incident drew a strong rebuke from Miller. In an angry e-mail, she ordered Cassaday to stop calling the junkyard after noon, when her husband would likely pick up the phone. She scolded Cassaday, telling him that if he could not reach her at home, she had errands to run.

"I do have a life beyond working and talking to you on-line," she harped. "Continuing to intentionally piss Bruce off is not making me want to come there quicker."

But even with a new and sometimes frightening husband, Miller consented to a third trip to Reno, this time in September, knowing Bruce would accept the explanation that she had customers for her cosmetics in Nevada. Miller wrote that she had broached the topic of divorce with Bruce. Perhaps the marriage had been too hasty and poorly thought out.

Cassaday took over planning for the September trip, making Miller's airline reservations and booking a complementary room for her at the casino hotel. He also urged her to come to Kansas City immediately afterward to meet his family at the wedding of his oldest son, Jeremy. Miller wouldn't commit to the Kansas City trip, but said she was ready for Reno and thinking about Cassaday and a life they would share, if only for a few days.

"I love you with all my heart," she wrote. "I can't wait to be in your arms again."

With a little tinkering, Cassaday cobbled together twelve days off through mid-September while burning only five precious vacation days. A week of that would go for the trip to Kansas City, but the rest would be spent on his most ambitious project in years. Beginning with her arrival in Reno on September 9, Cassaday planned to sweep Sharee Miller completely off her feet, to the point she would decide right then to leave Bruce Miller, move her children to Nevada and begin a fairy-tale life in the High Sierras.

"I can't wait to go dancing with you, to sing to you, to hear my angel sing to me, to kiss your face and hold you close," he wrote.

To build anticipation, Cassaday included in almost every e-mail a countdown to the minute she'd arrive.

"Guess what?" he chirped on August 28. "Only 278 hours to go, 16,680 minutes or 11.58 days or 1.655 weeks until I'm holding you tight in my arms."

His promises also were frank and physical.

"My balls are so heavy and full, but I won't do anything about it," Cassaday wrote in a follow-up e-mail. "I want to save it all for you."

For Miller, Cassaday's letters and phone calls were a portal to adventure.

After getting off work the morning of August 28, Cassaday found Miller on-line and soon they were in a private chat room. For several minutes, Miller indulged Cassaday in a provocative lesbian fantasy.

Miller: I could feel her hair on my inner thighs. I just imagined it was your beard.

Cassaday: mmmm

Miller: I felt her hands running up and down my legs and I just thought about your hands on my body.

Cassaday: I love your body.

Miller: . . . I took out my toy and she lay next to me. She was playing with my breasts, licking them, sucking them and then she moved to my neck. I started playing her with the vibrator.

Cassaday: Did she like that?

Miller: She was so excited. I knew she wanted more, but I just didn't want to. She started moving her hips and moaning.

Throughout, Miller kept Cassaday at the center of the fantasy.

Miller: Do you realize how many orgasms women can have?

Cassaday: I know how many you have with me.

Miller: I know I had a lot of orgasms with you, but Jerry I didn't think I could have so many with a woman. But I think that is because I saw your face, not hers.

Some of their sexual correspondence was more playful than erotic. Early on, Miller nicknamed Cassaday's penis "George," after a country-western artist they both admired. She then incorporated the nickname in a screen name she occasionally would use when chatting on-line with Cassaday: Isgeorgestrait.

Such exchanges were a welcome break from Miller's deadening routine of work at the salvage yard and her family responsibilities, such as shuttling her grandmother to her mom's home and taking the kids to school.

But Sharee knew that Jerry also hungered for some of

those calming daily routines. So earlier that summer, she had given him a taste of what life would be like with her and the kids by sending another video to Reno. Unlike the intimate moments she shared in *For Jerry's Eyes Only*, the second tape was all wholesome domesticity, minus the dark overtones of her disturbing marriage to Bruce.

Entitled *My Family 1999*, the video opens with her six-year-old daughter, Angela, lip-synching, karaoke style, to Martina McBride's "I'm Little But I'm Loud."

Her brushed auburn hair catching the light of a radiant summer afternoon, Angela fidgets and gamely takes her mother's direction. Sharee softly sings along behind the camera, her sweet soprano betraying none of the hard Michigan twang of her speaking voice.

After Angela is finished, Sharee asks, "Do you think she's drop-dead gorgeous?"

"I'm drop-dead gorgeous!" Angela giggles.

The scene shifts quickly to the enormous grassy yard of the Miller home, full of rambunctious kids. Children cartwheel through the frame, climb over picnic tables, banter with Mom and generally ignore her good-natured bossing.

"Can you handle all this energy?" she asks Jerry on the soundtrack. "You sure you can handle this?"

Less idyllic is her tour of the salvage yard, where she points out cars cracked up in drunk-driving accidents.

"This is work," Sharee tells Jerry dismissively. "Not as attractive as your work."

She points the camera to a sad-looking green family sedan, one of dozens of cars she owns with her husband.

"There's my antifreeze-sucking bitch of a car." She sighs.

But there's some lightness at work, salvage yard–style humor. Miller swings the camera through her office and settles it for a moment on a sign over the counter: IF YOU BOUGHT THE WRONG PART, YOU'VE GOT A SPARE!

The tour of her home reveals a knickknack decorating scheme punctuated by eruptions of toys and children's videos. The camera frames an antique-doll collection.

"How'd you like that in your room?" she teases.

The tape concludes with excerpts of Miller's triumphant appearance on Montel Williams's show, a troubling reminder that she, too, is still searching for a more settled life.

Miller's hopes for a future with Cassaday were so intense that she began to dream about him and how he would fit into her family. Dreams were particularly vivid for Sharee late that summer. She seldom got much sleep because of her late-night Internet explorations and chats with Cassaday, so she often awoke the next morning in the middle of a dream.

In late August, Miller dreamed of going to Cassaday's apartment in Reno and finding her mother sitting on his couch. Her mother had arrived, bearing a particularly domestic gift, a new stove. Cassaday's range was old, so her mother had replaced it with a model that Miller preferred. At dinner, Cassaday raised a topic that was on Miller's mind at that point, a new family.

"Honey, when do you plan on telling [your mother] she is going to be a grandma again?" Cassaday asked in the dream. Miller's mother didn't react with surprise to news of a pregnancy. Cassaday must have told her already, Miller surmised. And her mother seemed to like Cassaday.

The dream faded out with Cassaday leaving for work at the casino and the couple going out to gamble later on. But the dream's tantalizing promise of family and home only heightened Miller's anticipation of the upcoming trip.

In an e-mail describing the dream, she signed off by encouraging Jerry to watch the AOL chat rooms that night for a friend, Jennifer, who would be on later. They might like to talk, she said.

Cassaday enjoyed his connection with Jennifer. She was close to Miller and could keep him apprised of how she was doing and of what he could do to reassure her of his love.

Cassaday often seemed to meet Jennifer on-line when she was at the Miller house for baby-sitting or something else. In fact, Jennifer often seemed to log in under Sharee's AOL screen name.

Several years younger than Miller, Jennifer Ann Dege also was a heavy Internet user who enjoyed flirting in the AOL chat rooms. She talked daily with Sharee, either on-line with IM or by telephone, and remembered that Sharee had once co-opted her on-line identity for a sex chat with a complete stranger.

But that was typical Sharee. Anonymous fun was all part of the harmless adventure of the Internet. Jennifer also knew Cassaday and had participated in a three-way chat with him and Sharee. Months later, she could recall very little about it.

"It was an everyday conversation," she said. "Just joking around."

But she was a little surprised when Miller revealed that her on-line romance with the Nevada pit boss had blossomed into a full-blown affair. Her marriage to Bruce Miller—whom she considered "well-mannered, laid-back and quiet"—seemed way too solid for that.

"It was very good and loving," she said. "They got along great."

But Miller was concerned about Jennifer and whether Cassaday enjoyed her company a little too much. Miller once had become annoyed when she found that Jerry's phone number had popped up on Jennifer's caller ID.

"Well, the way I feel is if you are getting so involved with Jennifer, you should just take her phone number and start talking with her," she scolded Cassaday that summer. "I am not going to play this game with either one of you."

Late the night of August 29, Cassaday opened an e-mail that purported to be from Jennifer but was written under Miller's e-mail address. In it, the writer let slip something big: Sharee was considering a vacation with Bruce to mend fences in their young, troubled marriage.

"[Bruce] told her that he would give her the divorce if she went on one last trip with him," the e-mail stated. "Do you trust her and this shit you think is love?"

The news wounded Jerry: just when he was preparing to prove his commitment to Sharee, Bruce got in the way—and Sharee appeared to be going along with it!

Within minutes, he was on the phone to Sharee, demanding to know how she could consider traveling with Bruce when she had pledged her eternal love to him. Sharee's e-mail response was reassuring, but diamond hard.

"I would rather not have you telling me how scared you are [that] I am going to fuck someone else," she wrote. "Yes, Bruce asked me to go with him, nothing unusual, but it was something I was going to talk to you about."

The invitation from Bruce Miller was not at all casual, she explained. She confirmed the terms that the earlier e-mail had revealed. If she went on the trip and then decided she didn't want to stay with her husband, Bruce would give her a fast divorce. But if she didn't go, the separation would be long, painful and possibly tie up her life, children and money for years.

Sharee Miller wrote that she had wanted to discuss it with Cassaday, but only after she had figured out how she would deal with Bruce. Miller firmly told Cassaday that she couldn't stand this much conflict in both her marriage with Bruce and in her relationship in Reno. She craved an easy, calm life without turbulence.

Still, Miller assured Cassaday that her feelings had not

changed. Her love for him was boundless, she wrote soothingly.

Word of turmoil in Miller's household reached others in Reno. Slaughter recalled a conversation with Miller in which she said her husband was urging her to choose between him and Cassaday.

Here's how Slaughter recalled what Sharee Miller told her: "Bruce sat Sharee down and said: 'Sharee, look at your life. Look at what Jerry's done. He's turned your life upside down.'"

To bolster Cassaday's sagging spirits, Miller exploded with a cheery patter of upbeat e-mails over the next couple of days. She described buying racy underwear from Frederick's of Hollywood.

"Do you want me? I bet you do," Miller wrote. "Are you going to love me when I am there? I bet you will."

But Cassaday—always tuned to quiet messages—didn't respond. Bruce Miller, his fiercest competitor, had adopted Cassaday's strategy for winning Sharee's heart: romance her away from the familiar environs of home.

Sharee became uneasy with Cassaday's silence. So she tried heating up her e-mails with the simple decisions of what to pack for her trip to Reno. She described a new pair of tight jeans she had purchased.

"You didn't seem to have a problem with me in jeans the night we went to the bar," she wrote. "In fact you were hard all night."

Miller's assurances worked, for the time being, anyway. Cassaday soon was back on-line, doggedly pursuing the woman he loved. Through a travel agent friend, he'd upgraded her flight to Reno to first class.

"First one on the plane, first one off and in my arms," Cassaday bubbled. "Your man in the mountains and your fool for life. Jerry."

* * *

Plagued by a lack of sleep and burgeoning pressure in her personal life, Sharee was certain of one thing the morning of September 3, 1999:

She was uncertain.

Bruce wanted her to stay in Michigan. Cassaday wanted her to move to Reno. Because of his criminal activity, life with Bruce wasn't working out, but at least they had a long-standing relationship to depend on. Bruce also had asked her to go on a vacation with him to patch things up.

Cassaday offered the promise of romantic ecstasy, but Jerry and Sharee could also argue, mostly about her feelings for Bruce. But because Cassaday was so focused on the wealth Sharee had described, they also quarreled about money. And Sharee was more and more convinced that Jerry's contentious nature was tied to his drinking, mostly beer but sometimes boosted with whiskey and pills.

Early that morning, she took a stab at expressing some of her conflicts and resolving at least one of them. In an e-mail to Cassaday, she started by telling him that she wouldn't go to the wedding with his family in Kansas City. With her trip to Reno already dead certain, a side excursion to the Kansas City wedding would mean that her children—Angela, Tommy and Buddy—would have to spend too much time with Chuck and Judy Miller, Bruce's brother and sister-in-law. She also wouldn't be comfortable meeting Cassaday's family while questions of the divorce still hung in the air, particularly since Barb would be there with their children.

It wasn't fair to make her compete with his ex-wife that weekend. In fact, she said, the scheme would backfire, angering Cassaday's relatives and staining their relationship.

She remained uncertain about how to respond to Bruce's request that she vacation with him.

Bruce was upset, she wrote, because she had not given

him an equal shot at her love. And she had kept him at arm's length. Again she told Cassaday that she had not yet made the difficult decision between two men.

Choosing between a man she liked, but often feared, and the man she loved, but often argued with, was tearing at Miller. But she pleaded with Cassaday to win the contest.

"Make me see that nothing is worth losing this love," she wrote. "Make me see that I need to run as fast as I can to be there with you in a perfect love."

But perfect love came at a price, Miller wrote. Cassaday had to begin working on his alcohol problems and his abuse of prescription pills before she would consider moving to Reno and living with him. Cassaday's solution—just having her move to Reno—would not be enough to change him, she said. That change needed to come deep from within Jerry Cassaday, she wrote. She said she could not have her children live with a weak man whose crutch was stronger than he was.

In unmistakable terms, Miller had set down markers for Cassaday: make me love you more than I like Bruce, and deal with your drinking or I won't live with you.

But ultimatums were just goals for Cassaday. His confidence in his ability to win Miller's love and lifelong affection never wavered.

"You, Sharee, are my angel," he replied. "My love for you will never die."

The days before her September visit to Reno were a blur of activity for Sharee. She took her children to a fair near Flint to see the truck pulls and a rodeo. Tommy got into some poison ivy on September 6 and had to go to the doctor for the rash.

But after mowing the grass, doing the dishes and closing up the big aboveground pool and taking the kids to the Dairy Queen, Miller wrote to Cassaday:

"I can't wait to kiss . . . suck . . . [and] make love to you all over . . . to dance all night with you . . . to spend my time with you making long passionate love."

She also e-mailed Cassaday nude photos and some provocative pictures of her wearing a tank top and panties. An old boyfriend had taken the pictures when she was nineteen. Cassaday responded with rhapsodic predictions of how well he and his son, Kenny, would get along with Sharee.

Bursting with parental pride, Cassaday described how well Kenny would fit into the blended family that he and Miller already were planning.

"He's anxious to finally meet you," Cassaday wrote. "He knows how much we love each other and what we mean to each other."

Miller's life was consumed with nailing down details before the Reno trip in September, so she never responded.

But near the eve of Miller's departure, Cassaday wrote a preface to the adventure worthy of *Star Trek*.

"We are about to embark on a journey no one has ever known," Cassaday wrote. ". . . We have both chosen to leave the life we know behind and venture into this endeavor together."

By any measure, Miller's visit to Reno was a success.

After packing the kids off to her sister-in-law's home the evening before, Miller caught a 4:45 A.M. flight for Reno on September 9.

Cassaday met her at the Reno airport that morning. The next three days went almost exactly as they had planned. Cassaday and Miller focused on love.

In a letter describing the weekend, Miller remembered that, at first, their lovemaking was rushed and wild. Later, their closeness became sensual and relaxed. She told Cassaday that he had healed her, made her forget her troubles and worries and brought peace to her mind, heart and head.

"Do you understand that it is so much more than sex to me?" she asked. "It is a coming together of our souls."

Cassaday's take on the weekend was just as positive.

"You prayed that when you left me this time, you would only want to come back," Cassaday soon wrote. ". . . I think we accomplished that."

Even Miller's time with Kenny went well. In a letter after he returned to Reno, Cassaday described how Kenny stood up to sing at the wedding in Kansas City. He praised Sharee for showing Kenny how to turn fear into courage.

"You gave him the confidence to do that," Cassaday wrote. "It took courage and you are responsible for it."

Cassaday also took a moment to quiet any fears Miller may have had about Barbara, his former wife, who was at the wedding with their sons. Though Cassaday said he still was concerned for Barb's welfare, his love for her was gone. In Cassaday's heart, there was only room for Sharee, he wrote.

But the centerpiece of the September weekend in Reno wasn't so much love, devotion or sex. It was letting Cassaday's friends and family in on a secret he and Sharee had been holding: Miller was carrying Jerry's baby, conceived in Reno earlier that summer.

Gloria Taylor was the first to hear. Before Miller arrived, a distraught Cassaday told her that Miller had become pregnant after they had made love on her first visit in July.

Taylor was suspicious, wondering how Miller knew she was pregnant after only a few weeks. Though she was friendly with Miller, Taylor had heard enough of incapacitated husbands and sudden pregnancies. She urged Cassaday to be more skeptical and curb his infatuation.

"You don't know her well enough to believe her," Taylor said.

"No, no, no," Cassaday replied. "This is the one. I'm not in it for the money."

Cassaday then embraced the idea that this woman, the love of his life, was pregnant with his child. Taylor remembered Cassaday going out to "tie one on," celebrating her pregnancy.

The prospect of a new child became even more real when Miller sent Cassaday an elegant card of a pretty pink baby asleep on a mountain of fluffy towels.

After Miller arrived, Slaughter recalled the couple talking about her pregnancy.

"Jerry was over the moon," she said. "He was thrilled."

But in a private moment, Miller confided to Slaughter that she could have problems with this pregnancy.

"She said her doctor said she probably couldn't carry it to term," Slaughter recalled.

News of Miller's pregnancy frankly dismayed Cassaday's parents. Given that Cassaday's own divorce wasn't yet settled and that Jerry had other personal and financial issues to face, was a new child really a good idea?

"This doesn't ring true," Charlene Cassaday said.

"This is ridiculous," her husband echoed.

Returning to Michigan, Sharee Miller stopped by her brother-in-law's home to pick up the kids, peeling off the usual string of $100 bills for baby-sitting. Her explanations that the frequent visits to Reno were Mary Kay sales meetings were wearing thin for Chuck Miller. And he was certain that was the same with his brother, though Bruce Miller never spoke about deeply personal concerns with anyone. Chuck thought of his brother as "the quiet man."

As Chuck Miller watched Sharee pull away with the children, he let his imagination roam.

She's going out there being a whore, Chuck Miller later remembered thinking. *She's always coming back sick, sore and tired.*

* * *

Cassaday displayed no inkling that Miller might have trouble with this pregnancy, but he knew she was completely devoted to him after her September trip to Reno. When he returned from the wedding in Kansas City, Cassaday opened his e-mail.

After a cheery "You've Got Mail!" he read a note from Miller that again rekindled their warm romance. The weather in Michigan had turned chilly and the night was perfect for a crackling fireplace and cuddling.

"Winter is only good for one thing," Miller wrote. "That is getting snowed in and loving all day."

Cassaday's plan had worked out better than he had hoped. Miller was carrying his baby, and she was in love with him. But Bruce Miller always had a way of crowding into the picture, even at the peak moments.

After waking up on September 23, 1999, Jerry got some very bad news from Miller. Earlier, Jerry and Sharee had been talking about money. Cassaday, always in need of a dollar, had urged Sharee to just pick up and bring everything out to Nevada. Sharee said Bruce, as usual, was resisting. Bruce couldn't accept the idea of living under a different roof from Sharee.

Sharee tried to be reassuring, but things had suddenly gone very badly at home with Bruce. In a message thick with confused and conflicting emotions, Miller told Cassaday that Bruce had accepted that she could never fall out of love with Jerry and then fall in love with him. Nevertheless, she said, things had become complicated at home. So much so, that Cassaday should think about getting on with his life, without Miller.

"I love you and you deserve so much more," Miller wrote. "Maybe that is why I think you should let go, because I love you and right now I can't give you what you deserve."

Miller's message to Cassaday was clear: get on with your life because something has gone terribly wrong with mine.

Jerry Cassaday logged on to America Online the night of September 23 and waited for Sharee. Before midnight, she appeared and Jerry tugged her into a private IM chat session.

There Sharee told him that her life in Michigan was far worse than he ever could have imagined.

SIX

Any cop who's answered a domestic violence call knows the symptoms of battered woman syndrome.

The condition was defined and codified in the late 1970s and its characteristics now are familiar to everyone in law enforcement and the general public through a host of domestic-violence education programs, books and TV movies.

In the syndrome's earliest stages, a battered woman often is in complete denial, refusing to admit a problem in her marriage and blaming her injuries on "accidents." Later on, she realizes there is a problem but rationalizes that she deserves the beatings and the other abuse.

And with her judgment clouded by financial insecurity, the battered spouse usually sees little way out of the abusive relationship.

For three months, Miller had sent Cassaday subtle hints that there was a much darker side to her life than a love-less marriage to a petty criminal. She was attracted to Cassaday but clung to Bruce and always blamed herself.

"I am going to lose a friendship or a love. . . . I know this," she wrote in a moment of indecision. "And I deserve to lose one because, Jerry, I made this mess of my life."

Before she married Bruce, Miller had sent Cassaday suggestions that something was amiss. Sharee told Cassaday that when Jeff was rushed to intensive care while she was in Reno in August, she blamed herself, believing it was God's punishment.

Even small annoyances, such as being without telephone service for a couple of days when workers accidentally cut the line, triggered sweeping self-pity that suggested far deeper issues.

"Why do bad things always happen to me?" she wrote. ". . . I just wish just once, something would go smooth for me and these children."

But if Cassaday had any doubts that Miller was an abused spouse, she erased them entirely in a long IM session on September 23.

Alone in her home, not far from the salvage yard, Miller opened a bottle of wine and logged on. Cassaday soon joined her. Slowly, under his persistent coaxing, Miller peeled back the layers of her marriage to Bruce.

It began with financial blackmail.

Cassaday always had assumed that with her money and businesses Miller had the means to just pull up stakes and move to Nevada. He learned from Sharee that night that Bruce's control of her finances were now so complete that she was reduced to pilfering relatively small sums from him.

Bruce had stolen $5,000 from Sharee. She tried to get it back by cashing some of Bruce's checks, but Bruce had discovered it and threatened to go to the authorities.

The agonizing details zipped in real time across the Internet from Michigan to Nevada.

Miller: When I signed his name on the checks, he said he was going to the police if I didn't deposit the money. Let me handle this, Jerry.
Cassaday: How, by giving in every time? By doing what he wants?
Miller: I can't, or won't, have you here in the middle of this. I am working on things. Trust that . . .

Cassaday: Tell me what you are doing. . . . I don't want you doing anything stupid. . . . You have kids.
Miller: Everything I do is stupid.
Cassaday: They need you. I need you.
Miller: I am not doing anything that stupid. I don't like jail.
Cassaday: Then, tell me what you are doing. . . .
Miller: Jerry, I am trying. This is hard enough, tonight, telling you, letting you know how stupid I am. That I am not the woman you thought . . .
Cassaday: The only thing I think is stupid is you're not getting the help you need to deal with the problem.
Miller: I am trying.

The evidence of abuse coalesced quickly for Jerry Cassaday, the ex-cop. He pressed Sharee to begin talking about physical abuse.

Cassaday: How often does it happen?
Miller: It is not something I want anyone to know right now. Just when he thinks I have had contact with you.
Cassaday: Don't make me go through all this, again. Just answer my questions.
Miller: Jerry, please, this is not easy. . . . I don't want to think about it. Why are you making me?
Cassaday: When was the last time? Last night?
Miller: . . . Last night. I need you to let go. Just let go. . . . I am not worth all this. It is my fault.

Miller tried to evade Cassaday's policelike questioning. She still had secrets to hide, but he kept pushing.

Cassaday: Do you love me?
Miller: Yes, but something tells me you can't handle the next question. . . .

Cassaday: I don't know I can handle any of this. So just tell me. It can't be any worse.

Miller: Are you letting go? Are you ready to run? Are you letting go yet?

Cassaday: NO.

Miller: Why?

Cassaday: Because I love you.

Miller: Why are you taking all this? Can't you see where this is my fault?

Cassaday: Absolutely not.

Miller: You want to know how many . . . times? I don't . . . know. I lost count. Every time he hears your name lately; Every time he thinks the smile on my face has to do with you; Every time I get a phone call from you; Every time he sees your number on the Caller ID, HE MAKES HIS FUCK-ING MARK, because he knows I love you. But he knows you won't love me if you know he is fucking me.

Cassaday: Leave him.

Miller: I CAN'T.

Cassaday: Take the kids and get out.

Miller: You wanted to know. So now you are going to hear.

Sharee took a few minutes to gather her wits. Cassaday probably wasn't prepared to hear the rest of what she had to tell. "Do you understand what he did to me the other night?" she asked. "I don't think you know. I don't think you understand."

Cassaday fumed.

Cassaday: What a piece of shit he is. Why do you protect him from me? . . . Is that the kind of man you want around your kids? . . . How can they not see what is going on?

Knowing they were speaking on the Internet, Sharee cautioned Jerry never to show any of the conversation to anyone. "If you do," she said, "I will go to jail and never see you. And my kids won't have a mom. Promise."

"I swear it," Jerry promised. "Now talk."

Miller: This next part will be hard.
Cassaday: Talk to me. . . .
Miller: When he gets like this, it is not only physical. It is something else, and I don't want him near me since [I met] you. . . . I can't handle it. He needs to be in hell.

Sharee's momentum collapsed in fear and confusion. Cassaday was pushing her too fast. "You have to know what I am doing is right? Wrong? I . . . don't know," she wrote. "But I can't take it anymore. It hurts and I can't deal with it. This is why I think you should back away [and] leave me alone."

Then the news just tumbled out:

Miller: I lost my baby, Jerry.
Cassaday: No.
Miller: I went to the hospital because I was hurt, not the baby, but I lost the baby. Now he will pay. It will just take me time. Give me the time.
Cassaday: WHAT HAPPENED?

Sharee fumbled about, trying to tell Jerry about a visit to a hospital in Detroit, about an hour's drive from her home near Flint. Jerry went silent, waiting for her to come to the point. Finally, she did.

Miller: I never thought I would ever tell you that he hits. I got in trouble because I was with you. . . . I fell.

Cassaday: Bullshit. What happened? What did he do?

Miller: . . . Jerry, I fell outside on the deck and the lining was already thin and the baby couldn't make it. I was cleaning the pool and I fell.

Cassaday: You're lying.

Miller: Now, please let it go.

Cassaday: Not till I know the truth.

Miller: Now, do you hate me?

Cassaday: Sharee, you can tell me now, or in person when I beat it out of him. . . . Tell me or I'm coming.

Miller: DON'T THREATEN ME. THIS IS NOT THE PLACE FOR US.

Cassaday: Stop yelling and talk to me.

Miller: DON'T THREATEN ME. . . . I GET ENOUGH OF THAT. . . . It was my fault. I started the fight . . . When he started, I told him I made love to you all night. Wrong thing to say. He hit, I hit. And everything was fine for a few days. Then it wasn't.

Cassaday: Where did he hit you? . . .

Miller: I told the hospital I was cleaning the pool and fell. . . . Do you know what it did to me losing it? . . . It made me start having bad thoughts of killing him.

Cassaday: Where did he hit you? . . .

Miller: Goddamn it, Jerry. I can't tell you.

Cassaday: Sharee, please.

Miller: He didn't hit me, Jerry. He raped me. There, are you . . . happy? Leave me alone. I am done. . . . Why did you make me tell you? Why are you doing this? Why don't you just leave things alone? I am upset. I don't want you to know these things.

Cassaday: Sharee, I understand that. But that was my baby. I have the right to know. I love you. . . .

Miller: He fucked me on the deck of the pool. I lost the baby because of the force. Now, do you still love me? He consummated the . . . marriage. Leave it alone.

Cassaday: Yes, I still love you.
Miller: Let me handle this one. . . . It was my fault.
Cassaday: Bullshit.
Miller: I provoked it. . . .
Cassaday: So that gives him the right to rape you and kill my baby?
Miller: Jerry, don't worry. He will pay for the baby.
Cassaday: How?
Miller: He will. . . . Just know that. I wanted her.

The couple signed off quickly. Cassaday fiddled with the software for a moment, sending a transcript of the chat session to his printer for a permanent record. Miller sensed Cassaday was profoundly shaken by the conversation. In an e-mail later that night, she told him that she still wanted to leave Bruce to live in Nevada, but she had opened a door that was, perhaps, best left closed.

She lashed out at Cassaday for pushing her to describe the assault. Miller assured Cassaday that she was stashing money away and planned to leave Bruce someday, but only on her own terms, and only when she was ready.

And Miller acknowledged having dark thoughts about her husband that she could not share with Cassaday because they could send her to jail.

"Understand that I do not really want him to die," Miller wrote. "Yes, it would make things less complicated, but that is not what I want."

Jerry's protective instincts immediately emerged. Sharee's suffering was his fault, not hers. He also was buoyed by her willingness to endure harsh physical suffering for their forbidden love. All of her suffering was for him, he thought. How could he ever return such love?

Any plans that Jerry or Sharee had discussed the night before to free her from the bondage of her marriage had been shadowy and ill formed. But now, Cassaday was determined to do something, anything, to end her marriage to Bruce Miller.

The morning after the IM session, Cassaday wrote that he had been devastated by Miller's account of the rape and miscarriage. His first instinct had been to fly to Michigan and confront Bruce Miller to redeem the name and honor of a very miserable woman.

"No one, I mean no one, is going to get away with the things he has done to you, I assure you of that," Cassaday wrote. "I assure you Jerry will take care of that."

Sharee Miller pulled herself out of bed the morning of September 24, her head pounding from a wicked hangover and too little sleep. The chat session with Cassaday had gone late into the night.

After rustling up breakfast for the children and scooting them off to school, she logged on to AOL and found Cassaday's letter. "Jerry will take care of that," she read.

Cassaday's forceful response again pushed Miller to try and end her long-distance affair. Everything was too complicated right now. Miller had told Cassaday that she'd hoped Bruce would give her a divorce after learning about Cassaday, but he hadn't. Her plan had been to anger Cassaday so he would quit calling and let things in Michigan settle down for a while. Then she could think about leaving her husband and moving to Reno. She pulled up her e-mail program to plead with Cassaday to let her handle her husband. She again blamed herself and urged Cassaday to find someone else.

"Just move on with your life and find a strong good woman," she wrote. "Let me go because I see no hope."

However intense, the emotional fires from the IM session and the follow-up e-mails the morning of September 24, 1999, could not be sustained.

By that night, Sharee and Jerry were chatting on-line,

and this time Cassaday, at least, was more clear-headed. He used his experience as a homicide investigator to show her that any plot she might hatch to take Bruce's life likely would fail.

Killers usually trip themselves up, Jerry noted.

Cassaday: Mostly, they talk too much by either making people suspicious or telling them or involving them. When I was a detective I thrived on that.

Miller: Then I should not have told you. So I [messed] up already.

Cassaday: You don't have to worry about me. I loved for people to answer my questions. I loved to talk because I would ask questions I knew the answer to. I wanted them to lie to me. Because then I knew I had them. If they would lie about little things, I knew the big ones were lies too. People always offer more information than they should. Always. People like to talk. It's in their nature.

Miller wondered how she ever would be considered a suspect if her husband died suspiciously. The Millers, after all, were considered "an ideal couple," she said.

"But Jerry," she wrote, "if we were in a bar together in a town where everyone thinks we are a perfect couple . . . why would they even doubt me?"

It would get around, Cassaday assured her.

"I'm just telling you: Loose lips sink ships," he wrote.

"Fine, then I will wait here until he . . . dies," Miller replied.

But Sharee seemed distracted by Jerry's reminiscences about his investigative prowess. She wanted to know how she could stymie a police interrogation.

Cassaday: I don't want to brag, but when I did that . . . for a living, I had the highest clearance rate in

the metropolitan area for cases solved. And of those, I had the highest confession rate. I was good at what I did. I had a nickname. . . . Are you there?
Miller: So if I am asked a question, I just continue to say, "I don't know. I loved him so much. Who would do something like this?" and cry and cry. Are you saying I am too honest for this? I would tell, is that it?

Miller had broken Cassaday's spell, so he just played along.

Cassaday: I love you very, very much.
Miller: Jerry, the only other option is waiting until he kills himself.
Cassaday: Or helping him to.
Miller: I don't know how. I buy him cartons of cigarettes all the time.
Cassaday: Weak heart.
Miller: I feed him grease.
Cassaday: Cancer.
Miller: I feed him a ton of shit.
Cassaday: What speeds up cancer?
Miller: You said it yourself . . . people like him live forever. . . . Just forget it, I can't do it. . . . I don't know if I could live with myself. I don't know if they wouldn't break me if I did it.
Cassaday: Then just save your money and get out.
Miller: But I bet they couldn't [break me]. . . . Want to bet money on it? Do you think I would make it? Or do you think the cold would shine through in my eyes?
Cassaday: I don't know. A lot depends on the detectives and their resources and experience.
Miller: OK, you scared me out of it. Next subject.

Which was exactly what Cassaday wanted. As an ex-cop, he knew that Miller automatically would become a suspect

if her husband was killed. Miller was lost in the under-
brush of a bad marriage, unable, for now, to see a way out.
Murder, Cassaday reasoned, was too extreme a solution,
particularly when she hadn't yet tried to leave Bruce.

Cassaday's message to Miller was simple: depend on
me to help you out of this. He advised her to begin keeping a diary so she could document the dates and times
of her husband's abuse for future investigators. But
Miller remembered the time her second husband had
found and read her diary. He'd damn near killed their
son. She resisted the prospect of keeping a diary of
Bruce's abuse.

"If he found it I would never talk to you again," Miller
wrote. "I wouldn't be able to."

Miller was paying for staying up so late the night before. She was tired and wanted to sign off, but Cassaday
kept her on the computer. For a long time, they touched
on some topics with which she was all too familiar:
money and future travel plans. But in each instance, she
found ways to remind Cassaday that her husband remained an obstacle and even a threat.

Cassaday asked her if he could buy a Chevy Camaro
sitting at B&D. That way, he could sell the Ford pickup
whose payments were eating a hole in his wallet. Too difficult, Miller responded. Bruce would have to see the
paperwork, and that wouldn't be good, she noted.

"If he was not living, [it] would be easier," she wrote.

Cassaday also was considering a trip to Flint and
wanted Miller to find time to be with him. Cassaday suggested that Miller tell her husband she had to go to
Chicago to discuss the lawsuits and the pending settlements. Miller resisted again, saying Bruce probably
would want to accompany her on such a trip. He didn't
yet know about that particular lawsuit, and she didn't
want him to find out about it, Miller wrote.

"I might die when I get [the settlement]," Miller

wrote. "That is a lot of money. People act weird. . . . I am not ready to die."

After hearing the whole story of Bruce Miller's violence two nights before, Cassaday was more and more convinced that he was destined to rescue Sharee. He would be a coward to leave after seeing the courage with which she faced an abusive husband and suffered torture for their love. More than ever, he was committed to Sharee, his "angel."

God had put them together so they could help each other.

On September 25, Cassaday wrote Miller that he needed her to stand by him and give him support and inspiration. And Miller, Cassaday wrote, needed him to care for her and give her the love she had never known.

"Baby, I am that man. . . . We will be together, forever," Cassaday wrote. "It will happen, and it will happen soon."

Miller's money and businesses were firmly under her husband's control, Cassaday concluded, so they would have to pool their resources to make her escape possible. With Miller's fiscal sense, Cassaday could get his own financial house in order, perhaps by cutting back on his expenses, he wrote on September 26. With a settlement pending on one of her lawsuits, Miller would have the money for a new house and a fresh start, Cassaday assured her.

But hopeful words wouldn't get Miller out of a bad marriage. Cassaday offered Miller a strategy well short of murder. If she just left Bruce, he probably would die of humiliation.

Cassaday pressed Miller to imagine Bruce living alone in their "big house," tortured each day by the memories of his failed marriage, drinking and smoking himself to an agonizing and solitary death.

Cassaday also reminded Miller of her husband's violence and what it already had cost them. Bruce had stolen her life, her freedom, her money and her happiness. And never forget how "that worthless piece of shit" had killed the baby that Cassaday and Miller had conceived in love, Jerry wrote.

And after the rape and physical abuse, Bruce had forced his wife to take the blame, when she had the spirit to resist his attacks. Bruce Miller was less than human, Cassaday wrote.

Cassaday concluded by borrowing from Sharee's brutal vocabulary when she spoke of her husband. But he was careful to show Sharee how satisfying a nonviolent and psychological confrontation with Bruce could be.

"Baby we can do this, we will get him right where we want him, and then BAMMMM!" Cassaday wrote. "We will cause him to self-destruct from the inside."

SEVEN

Miller responded with stark news to Cassaday's proposal to humiliate her husband. In a heart-to-heart talk with her, Bruce had continued to press for a vacation to patch things up, with separate bedrooms if she wanted. But it was the destination that chilled Cassaday's blood: Reno.

On September 26, Miller wrote that her husband had explained that he only wanted what was best for her and tried to explain his reasons for wanting to go to Reno. Bruce had told her that if she hadn't done anything wrong, traveling to Reno should not be a problem.

Miller wrote to Cassaday that she had worked hard to dissuade her husband from Reno, arguing she was bored with the city and would much prefer a second honeymoon in Las Vegas, where they had been married. Bruce Miller rebuffed his wife's protests; he hadn't been to Reno in ten years and wanted to see how it had changed.

Miller bravely had asked her husband whether his plans for Reno had anything to do with her on-line friend, Jerry Cassaday. Bruce responded that he had no interest in bumping into Cassaday or picking a fight with him.

The e-mail quickly devolved into a panicked scramble. Miller was petrified at the notion of Jerry and Bruce meeting in Nevada. Then she wrote the words that pierced Cassaday's heart. If she had to go on vacation with Bruce to mollify him, she would do it.

"I want you to know that this is getting worse," Miller wrote. "I think maybe you should just turn around and walk away."

In a later phone call, Miller told Cassaday that Bruce had assured her that he would not hurt her again and that he would get professional attention for his anger. From his police work, Cassaday knew that such assurances were usually worthless. His e-mail response was a howl of pain and rage.

"That asshole killed our baby!" he screamed. "That lying piece of shit tells you he won't do it again and everything is okay—until he beats you again, which he will, until he hurts your kids, which he will."

The money issue also had become a thorn in the relationship. The Camaro at B&D, which Cassaday had hoped to buy cheap, would be no better for Jerry than the Ford pickup he'd been driving, Miller reasoned.

"Jerry, in my eyes, I see a man who likes to live well beyond his means," Miller lectured. "There are other options, other cars."

But the only option Cassaday wanted Miller to consider was his plan to humiliate her husband. Now she was turning this into a thing about money, he thought. Cassaday just wanted Miller to enjoy her kids and her life. He'd told her dozens of times that he didn't want her money.

"That's something that piece of shit has never told you," Cassaday wrote. "In fact, he just turned around and . . . stole it, and beats and rapes you when you bring it up or ask about it."

Cassaday again rejected Miller's pleas to forget about her, but he did consider her request to put off a trip to Michigan to spend a few hours with her. Days passed with little news written between them. Cassaday's plan to extract Miller from a violent and abusive relationship had failed miserably; it had collapsed into acrimony over money and commitment.

Miller maintained that she still wanted to leave her husband, but she said the timing wasn't right. Cassaday, stung over her refusal to help him with his mounting money problems, couldn't seem to convince her they could work out all those issues after she left Bruce.

Still, Jerry Cassaday always could find a way to add even more turmoil to his life.

The morning of Friday, October 8, 1999, Cassaday left work dressed in the smart uniform of a Harrah's pit boss—black shoes and pants topped with a white shirt and neatly finished with a black bow tie, purple vest and black apron. Before heading home to the apartment and checking on Kenny, Cassaday drifted to the nearby Cal Neva casino for drinks and a few hands of blackjack.

Taking a rest room break a few hours later, Cassaday left his chips and money on the blackjack table, assuming the dealer would watch it for him. When he returned, they were missing. Knowing that the Cal Neva, like all Nevada casinos, was heavily invested in video surveillance equipment, Cassaday called over the pit boss and suggested he run their security videotape back twenty minutes to see who took the money and chips. When the pit boss hesitated, Cassaday became quarrelsome. As security officers gathered and tried to calm Cassaday, he ratcheted up the confrontation with profanity.

Officers asked him to leave and Cassaday refused. Finally, a security guard began reciting a Nevada law that would require Cassaday to leave or become subject to arrest for trespassing.

Cassaday still refused, prompting a call to Reno police. Now surrounded by casino security guards, Cassaday was led down an escalator to the doors on the street. Walking through a set of double doors, Cassaday slammed one behind him, striking the arm of a trailing security guard. Reno police arrived and arrested Cassaday on charges of misdemeanor battery and trespassing. He was jailed immediately.

It wasn't Cassaday's only recent scrape with the law. A few weeks before, he had earned a driving-while-intoxicated citation after passing out behind the wheel of his truck at a stoplight. He awoke in the cab to a policeman's flashlight shining in his eyes. They hauled him downtown and he had to walk miles back to his truck after making bond.

This time, however, he couldn't even make bail, which totaled $755 on the two counts. With his money stolen while he was in the rest room, he had only forty cents in his pocket when he was arrested.

Back at his apartment in Sparks, thirteen-year-old Kenny wondered why his dad was so late getting home from work.

Several hours later, Carol Slaughter was logged on to AOL when Sharee Miller appeared, her software inviting Slaughter for a private chat.

"Kenny's home alone," Miller wrote, explaining that she had just heard from Cassaday's son, who said Dad was hours late from work and hadn't called. Kenny sounded frantic, Miller said. She suggested that Slaughter check if Cassaday had been arrested.

"Let me get off the computer and make a few phone calls," Slaughter replied. "I'll come back and let you know what I find out."

A call from Slaughter to the Washoe County Jail confirmed what Miller already had suspected. Cassaday was in jail. Miller soon was on the phone to Jerry's mom in Texas, trying to figure out what to do with Kenny.

Charlene Cassaday, whose concern for her son's mental

health had only grown since his separation from Barb, was decisive: Figure out a way to get Jerry out of Reno and back to Missouri, where he could begin drug and alcohol counseling. In the meantime, get Kenneth on a plane back to Kansas City immediately so he could live with his mother, Barbara.

Charlene Cassaday promised to call Jerry's brothers for help. She also said that whoever was taking care of Kenny also needed to clear the firearms out of Jerry's apartment. Cassaday would be depressed enough after spending the day in jail—no need for anything drastic to happen.

While Carol Slaughter took care of Kenny, the guns and the flight arrangements, Sharee Miller composed a note to Cassaday's son. Recently, they had spoken and chatted on-line about his dad, birthdays and a new Web site Kenny had just constructed. The notes were teasing and a little wistful.

"Kenny, I want you to know that if it never works out for your dad and I, I will never forget you," Miller had written just four days before. ". . . I think you are a wonderful man and deserve the best."

Miller's e-mail of October 8 offered love, hope and comfort to a son frightened about what his father had become. Softly, Miller urged Kenny to go back to his mother in Missouri and promised to find help for Jerry. Alcoholism, she explained, was a disease that could be treated.

"I have to have faith that he will get better," Miller wrote. "Tell him, Kenny, tell him how his drinking makes you feel."

Kenny was waiting for his flight when his father was released from jail on bond at 11:54 P.M. As Jerry Cassaday walked out, a county employee slapped a release form into his hands. Three notes had been attached to the form: "Call your wife"; "Call Sharee"; "Call Parents." Cassaday phoned his mom, but he didn't really sound like he was ready to accept responsibility for his alcohol-fueled anger at the casino.

"Mom, I did not hit the man," Cassaday said. "I jerked the door and slammed it back and it turns out . . . the door hit the security guard."

The vanguard of Jerry Cassaday's intervention arrived the next day. While Cassaday recovered at home on October 9, Slaughter was at Reno's airport picking up Roger Cassaday, Jerry's older brother who lived in Texas.

The night before, Roger had met Sharee on AOL IM and together agreed that the first order of business after Kenny got back to his mother was to convince Cassaday to return to Missouri. Charlene Cassaday was arranging with cousins for Jerry to live in Odessa, a small town about forty-five minutes outside Kansas City. Jerry could live with James Earl Lewellen, a minister.

With support in more wholesome surroundings, Cassaday would stand a better chance of recovery, his family reasoned. And with convictions for battery and trespassing, Cassaday could lose his license to work in a Nevada casino. Returning to Missouri was a natural choice.

The following day, Roger Cassaday took his turn standing in the Reno airport, awaiting another volunteer in the campaign to clean up his brother's life. Since he'd never met Sharee Miller, Cassaday held up a sign reading YANKEE BABE, one of his brother's pet names for Sharee. She'd told Cassaday family members it would take her a couple of days to clean up some business before she could make it out.

Roger Cassaday came away with a good impression of Sharee Miller. From the way she spoke, she clearly loved his brother and was concerned for his welfare. Back at the apartment, Roger could see that the love was mutual.

"They were a very affectionate couple, almost like newlyweds," he would remember later. "Lots of hand holding, kissing, whispering, that sort of thing."

Over dinner, they got to know each other. Roger Cassaday learned that Miller was a businesswoman, who owned a rest home, a junkyard and a nursing home that she had inherited from her grandmother. She was planning to sell the nursing home so she could focus more attention on the salvage yard, Roger Cassaday remembered.

He also quickly concluded that both Sharee and Jerry were committed to spending the rest of their lives together.

Sharee said they had looked at homes, which she planned to purchase, and even had considered buying a dude ranch in Colorado, which both she and Jerry could work when he was feeling better.

Until Cassaday recovered, the Colorado plans clearly were a fantasy, but Cassaday admitted to being a dreamer and that the idea strengthened him at his lowest point. He once told Miller how exciting he found the prospect of creating lifetime memories for children, their own and others, who would visit their dude ranch.

"So much about it is so attractive, being with you and the kids all the time," he said. "They could help run the place, [and] we could live such a beautiful, clean, healthy [and] safe life."

Cassaday once had mentioned to his mother that he and Sharee were considering a life in the mountains. She laughed.

"That girl really is your dream, isn't she?" she said.

Roger Cassaday stayed at Harrah's that night in a complimentary room booked under Miller's name. He offered to stay at the hotel because he wanted to give the couple some privacy. And they clearly wanted it, he remembered.

Monday, October 11, was hardly the stuff of dreams. A visit to the casino's human relations department secured Cassaday a medical leave, which would hold his job until he recovered. Afterward, he would return to Reno or perhaps transfer back to the Harrah's casino in North Kansas City, where he had started with the company.

The visit to the lawyers was even less pleasant. The charges he faced were misdemeanors and not particularly serious in the criminal scheme of things. Still, it would take money to deal with them, money that Cassaday did not have. Even a $375 attorney's bill to stay out of jail was a load for a man who was falling further and further behind on his truck payments.

Miller said she was prepared to step up.

"I'll take care of the lawyers; money is no object," she said, easing at least one immediate worry.

Still, when time came to rent the U-Haul truck necessary to take Cassaday's life back to Missouri, Miller could not help with the deposit. She had left her credit cards in Michigan. Roger already had left, so Cassaday called his mother and asked to put it on her Visa card. Charlene Cassaday agreed but said she would need to be repaid before the credit card bill came due. Miller agreed.

What couldn't get packed in the truck got stashed in a commercial storage locker—a barbecue smoker, a lawn mower, a TV and about thirty boxes of other items.

Another brother, Mike, arrived soon to help Cassaday drive the truck back to Missouri. Mike Cassaday lived in Lee's Summit, Missouri, not far from Odessa, and had been charged by the family with looking after Jerry and making certain he was doing well.

But before getting on the road, Jerry and Sharee stopped at Carol Slaughter's home for a final evening with her. Slaughter had agreed to tidy up some of Jerry's business in Reno, checking his mail and making bank deposits when necessary.

The evening was jarring for Slaughter. When Cassaday was out of the room, Miller told her she really wanted to break her ties with Cassaday. Given what Slaughter had seen over the last week, she didn't blame her. When Cassaday reappeared, though, Slaughter was amazed to see how easily Miller seemed to fall back in love with Jerry.

Why these mixed signals?

Gloria Taylor, another of Cassaday's friends at Harrah's, got the same feeling from Miller.

"Her stories keep flip-flopping," Gloria said.

Later, when Miller had returned home, she complained to Slaughter that Cassaday was calling and e-mailing way too much. Slaughter dismissed her concern. Dealing with a persistent former boyfriend hundreds of miles away was simple.

"Change your phone number," Carol said. "There are things you can do if he lives so far away."

Returning to Flint, Miller picked up the kids at her brother-in-law's house. Judy Miller remembered the scene before Miller left for Reno a few days before. She had come crying to the house, saying Bruce didn't want her to go, but Sharee had argued that she had Mary Kay cosmetics to sell. If she didn't sell it, someone else would.

"Bruce was a penny-pincher, but he'd always say, okay, go ahead," Chuck said.

Bruce Miller, his brother said, was not pleased with his wife's frequent trips to Reno and was unhappy he couldn't go with her. But Bruce had owned the yard for only a short time and still had work to do.

After a while, Bruce began quietly grousing to his brother about all the money Sharee was spending. Bruce Miller was a difficult man to read, Chuck Miller said later. He'd never talk about marital problems. He'd just get quiet.

"And he was getting real quiet," Chuck Miller would say later. "She was running him ragged, so he started taking nights off work. Sharee would not be there."

For a time, he even changed shifts at work, working days instead of nights. Sharee disliked that even more, Chuck Miller said, because now Bruce was home at night to check up on her.

Sharee Miller's friend Laura Ewald learned of the October trip when Sharee told her she had to go to Reno to help a sick friend, somebody named Carol.

Jerry Cassaday was comfortable pouring his life into a computer, and not just for Sharee Miller. Just after he returned to Missouri, he took a moment to reflect soberly upon his life and its misdirection.

On October 19, he dropped an e-mail to a Kansas City friend and put his life in candid, but typically upbeat, perspective. He shared both good news and bad.

"The good news is I finally met the woman of my dreams, an absolutely wonderful woman," Cassaday wrote. "She has been very good for me and I can only see it getting better."

Then came the laundry list of problems. The alcohol and drugs finally had caught up with him. And he had been too slow to get help. The arrests had brought his whole life tumbling down.

Cassaday knew that his return to Missouri was his last chance, his final opportunity to pull his life back together. He had vowed to get into a counseling program and stick with it. Otherwise, he'd lose his job, his son and his new girlfriend, too.

He asked that his friend not tell others that he was back in Missouri. More temptation was the last thing he needed.

When Cassaday wrote to Miller the next day, his optimism took on an almost frantic edge, as if he were trying to convince her that he still was the man she had grown to love.

"It's gonna work!!!" he wrote on October 20. "I will make it!!!"

Miller fed that optimism, offering Cassaday a pretty picture of their lives together someday. Cassaday needed to hear comfort, not lectures about his finances, and certainly not the private doubts she had shared with friends about whether their relationship really was working out. Her promises were explicit.

She promised Cassaday that she would wrap up her life in Michigan and join him in Odessa. She'd be at his side for his counseling appointments. Miller said she was growing impatient with waiting and had dreamed of making love to him after they had spent a lazy evening talking and watching television together.

Cassaday would have had no reason to doubt her affection or her devotion to his well-being.

"I love you Mr. Jerry Cassaday," she wrote. "One day soon it will work."

But Miller's biggest news was just hours away.

EIGHT

Just after Bruce Miller went to work the night of October 20, his wife held the wand from a home pregnancy test up to an electronic camera and clicked away. Soon the images zipped through cyberspace, from Michigan to Missouri to Jerry Cassaday's computer.

The first set of eight pictures showed Miller holding the wand, and they may have bewildered Cassaday. But the last photo showed the home pregnancy test box and bore a caption from Miller written in bold letters: **"ONE LINE NOT PREGNANT. TWO LINES PREGNANT."**

A follow-up e-mail confirmed the message:

"NOW YOU TELL ME, DO YOU THINK I JUST GOT PREGNANT?" Miller crowed.

Unbelievably fertile, Miller claimed to have conceived earlier in the month during her short visit to help Cassaday pack in Reno.

Minutes later, Cassaday found another stack of pictures from Miller. In one, Miller smiled contentedly and rested her face softly on her left hand. Another photo depicted her torso with her hands cradling the breasts that would nurture the child growing inside her. The next day, Cassaday responded to the news and the photos with elation.

"I love you," Cassaday wrote. "We will be together, we will live a wonderful, happy life together."

With Cassaday's assurances of love still on her mind,

Miller spent the day nesting, furiously cleaning her home and waiting impatiently for Cassaday to call with more reaction.

Sitting alone in his basement apartment, Cassaday logged on to America Online about midafternoon under one of his lesser-used screen names, Deviousminds. There he found Bruce Miller, beckoning him into an IM chat session under the screen name BDJUNK, his business e-mail address.

Confronted at last by the man who had forced the miscarriage of his child, Cassaday dodged Bruce Miller's questions, hiding the news of Sharee's latest pregnancy to prevent another savage explosion of domestic violence. BDJUNK signed off soon, however, and Cassaday waited on-line, knowing that Miller would have to go to work. Cassaday watched the clock for nearly half an hour before an e-mail arrived.

Cocky and taunting, BDJUNK noted that he only had been off-line for about twenty minutes, but already he had learned everything he needed to know. With the leverage of Sharee's new pregnancy, getting her to talk now was easy, he wrote.

Slowly, BDJUNK began to pick at Cassaday's insecurities. He bellowed how Sharee loved him, and Jerry had better leave them alone and get used to it.

BDJUNK blasted Cassaday for calling his business and his home and then hanging up if he answered. Cassaday was violating the sanctity of their marriage vows. When Jerry called, Sharee paid the price, BDJUNK noted. She always suffered "consequences" for reminders of her infidelity.

Did it make Jerry feel good to realize that she was suffering for their love? No matter, BDJUNK said. If Sharee really loved Jerry, she would be with him, not in Michigan.

BDJUNK also warned Cassaday against encouraging Sharee to assault him. He revealed that she already had come after him with a kitchen knife, and he would file attempted murder charges against her if it happened again.

So, again, Sharee Miller had to defend herself against her husband's anger. She hadn't mentioned that to Cassaday in her e-mails. Bruce Miller was exactly what Cassaday had come to expect from Sharee's descriptions, mean and brutish.

And, of course, BDJUNK couldn't resist digging at Cassaday's jealousy, reminding him of a plan to take a second honeymoon at Harrah's in Reno.

Cassaday wilted. Sharee had lied to her husband about where Jerry now lived. She probably had done it to protect Cassaday, but at what cost if Bruce Miller discovered the lie?

BDJUNK wrapped up with twin promises: He would leave Cassaday alone if Jerry would just butt out of his marriage. Otherwise, he would file charges against Sharee for the knife assault.

"Because she loves me, she is still here with me in our happy home," BDJUNK wrote. "I guess you are not smart enough to see . . . she will never leave me."

Cassaday could not have imagined what Sharee Miller had endured in the preceding twenty minutes. Bruce Miller had learned of the pregnancy and then boasted of how he had coerced the news out of his wife. After Bruce Miller left for work, Sharee quickly e-mailed two photographs of her husband to Cassaday.

One showed him sitting in a chair, looking menacingly over his right shoulder toward the camera. The second showed Bruce, wearing his black NASCAR jacket, standing next to a woman.

"This woman is as tall as I am," Miller wrote in a caption.

Neither Cassaday nor Sharee Miller would get much sleep that night.

Early the next morning, October 22, was little better. Cassaday began by offering weak encouragement.

"Baby, love you," he wrote. "I just don't know what else to say anymore. This all hurts so much."

Later, he resorted to the optimism that had occasionally pulled them through. His love, he wrote, would never fade and he always would love her.

He begged Miller to believe that his love for her was real and told her to call him anytime she needed comfort. And he told her to never forget that someday soon she would become "Sharee Cassaday."

But communications were fragmented, broken by plans they could not reconcile. Cassaday wanted Miller to gather up the children and leave Bruce and come to Nevada at first, then Missouri. Sharee had been hesitant, making darker suggestions that Cassaday always had rejected.

In an e-mail the morning of October 22, Sharee Miller bemoaned that she and Jerry couldn't talk much anymore. She again began to push Cassaday away, begging him to concentrate on his own problems and raising his son. She was causing him more trouble than she was worth, she wrote.

"Somehow I feel every time I receive a bruise, a broken bone, a broken spirit, I deserve it for what I let happen to my children," Miller wrote. "I am the asshole. . . . Can't you see that?"

Miller's letter confirmed the worst for Cassaday. She was pulling away and giving in to her husband's brutal abuse. Cassaday's reply was desperate and written in large, bold letters: **"I WOULD NEVER HAVE GOTTEN THIS FAR WITHOUT YOU, WITHOUT THE PROMISES YOU MADE [AND] THE HOPE YOU GAVE ME. WAS IT ALL LIES?"**

Miller responded by throwing in Cassaday's face the countless e-mails, phone conversations and IMs in which he had urged her to just leave Bruce. Cassaday often had followed such pleadings by accusing her of staying with Bruce just because she couldn't leave with all her money.

No, she assured Cassaday, it wasn't all about money. Her love for him was real and undying. But Sharee wrote that she, too, was being torn apart about the effect that Bruce's blind jealously was having on Cassaday.

She wrote how the torment was consuming her. She couldn't sleep or eat. Just getting through each day was a struggle, and she fully expected to be hospitalized soon for her mental anguish.

And all Cassaday could talk about was the money! Sharee lashed to the bitter core of the letter. She promised to leave her husband, but it would cost her soul and her pride.

She would leave Bruce, but he never would suffer for the emotional and physical damage he had inflicted on her.

"I will sit in [Kansas City] worrying about going to the grocery store and having a bullet put in my head," Miller wrote. "I will sit in [Kansas City] and become a rotten bitch, knowing he is still breathing here."

Though she finally had committed to leaving her husband, the letter aggravated Cassaday. If her fears weren't driven by money, then what was she afraid of? Sharee responded mysteriously but offered new insights into her troubled marriage.

She opened by begging Cassaday to quit asking so many questions about her fears and about why she was so afraid to leave her husband.

"For the sake of my life and my children's lives, please, please do not make me tell you right now," she wrote. "Trust me on this one, honey, it could kill me."

Still, she noted that when she was ready to escape from Bruce she wouldn't need a moving van.

The e-mail photographs of Bruce from the night before were critical to Cassaday's understanding of her life, Miller said. Cassaday needed to see Bruce Miller's eyes and know the fear they instilled in her, she wrote. But she couldn't have Cassaday just come up to Michigan to confront her husband. If Jerry could be goaded into a fight, then Bruce already would have won, Sharee said.

She then urged Cassaday to think about her lifestyle and what that said about her husband. How could a small business owner and GM shop rat afford to buy his wife a $100,000 ring? And how could he afford to give her a jewelry stash—valued at over $300,000—that she never could wear around Flint?

Listen to the fear in my voice, Miller pleaded. Can't you tell that something bigger is in play here? Take, for example, the last trip to Reno, she said. She left without Bruce's knowledge, but he learned of her whereabouts even before she got off the plane. And he knew virtually everything about where she was and who she was with every moment she was there.

Miller wrote that she was afraid of her husband for solid reasons that she could not yet articulate. The fear had made her life agonizing. And to see it ruin Cassaday's life was unbearable, she wrote.

By the morning of October 23, Cassaday was beginning to see the picture of Miller's reluctance to leave, but he was still annoyed with her evasiveness. With a $300,000 jewelry stash, Miller could easily leave without a moving van, as she had written.

The jewelry, obviously, represented the laundered proceeds of Bruce Miller's career in crime, he reasoned. And surveillance of Sharee's last trip to Reno clearly suggested mob ties.

Big deal, Cassaday thought. As a cop, he had handled hardcase criminals before and Sharee knew that. So was she really willing to move? Cassaday turned on his computer and wrote a letter to seize the opportunity.

Cassaday emphasized the positive, assuring Miller that news of her decision to leave, however difficult, had given him the happiest day of his life. All of his pleading and cajoling finally had convinced her that he could take care of her and the children. But to get her out would require careful planning, Cassaday wrote. Already he had begun to plan a false forwarding address to cover Miller's tracks as she escaped from Flint.

He pleaded with Sharee to tell him more about what she would be bringing with her when she left Bruce: Money from stocks? One car, two cars? Did she want to rent a home when she arrived, or did she want to buy right away? Was she planning to work after she arrived, or did she want to just stay home with the kids?

The subject was delicate because Miller always had been sensitive about Cassaday's infatuation with her wealth. But if Miller was coming to Missouri soon, Cassaday reasoned, he had to know what he would be dealing with.

And though Cassaday suspected that Miller might have been telling him only what he wanted to hear, he attributed her vagueness to Bruce Miller's oppressive presence.

"I don't know what that . . . piece of shit did to you since we talked, but obviously he did something," Cassaday wrote. "Every time he does, you do this to me."

In her living room, Miller scanned the letter in which Cassaday still insisted that she leave her husband, but said nothing about her fears. She never had been crystal clear with Cassaday about her plans for Bruce Miller. She hoped that Cassaday would take the initiative but knew he would resist any suggestion of a violent resolution.

After deleting Cassaday's e-mail, she began composing her own.

What emerged was a two-page "fairy tale," as she described it, which detailed the plight of a lonely married woman in love with another man.

* * *

The story centered on a woman named "Stacy," who was compelled through poverty to marry a man twice her age. The husband, Miller wrote, had been married several times and had children with his previous wives. The ex-wives had not been happy since their separations. One of the women lost everything in a nasty divorce. And though she lived nearby, she was watched constantly. Another of his ex-wives had begun cheating on him and left him. Alas, no one ever saw her again.

So the man married again, this time to a woman named "Debbie," who also was unfaithful, even though they had two children together. He followed her and began tape-recording her when she began cheating.

Debbie remarried, but her second husband was always getting in trouble and landing in jail, for reasons he never could understand. Bad things always seemed to be happening to these women. Terrible accidents befell them. And none of them ever understood why.

The man soon married Stacy, his fourth wife, though they had no children. But Stacy quickly fell in love with another man. More than anything, Stacy wanted to leave her husband to be with her new love.

Stacy's husband knew of his wife's lover. But to protect him, Stacy told her husband she didn't have much affection for her lover. Eventually, her husband came to believe that his wife's lover had grown tired of waiting for her and had moved on with his life.

But how, Stacy wondered, would she resolve this mess? She prayed for her husband to die of natural causes. Even if he died a violent death, few would question whether he deserved it. And if anyone asked if Stacy was involved, she would respond with hysterics. Soon everybody would forget about Stacy's husband and she finally would have her life back.

Yes, Stacy decided, death was her answer.

And none of it was about her husband's money,

earned through a life of crime. Even if a heart attack took his life, she stood no chance of holding on to his money. His criminal friends already had made that clear to Stacy. A life without fear would be reward enough, Stacy reasoned.

In the fairy tale, Sharee Miller also said the other ex-wives, who had paid a lifetime of consequences for once being married to this man, would have their lives back. Stacy ached to tell her lover the complete truth about her husband, to make him see what she had been living with. But very bad things already had happened to the other women in her husband's life when they had shown any sign of independence.

Stacy knew what would happen to her if she tried to leave. Her husband simply would find her, and nothing would change. Stacy lived in agony, Miller wrote, knowing she had a solution to her problem but never having the "tool" to carry it out.

Stacy considered setting her lover free and living alone in quiet anguish. But their love was too real and intense. He continued to wait for her, even though fear had locked Stacy in its cage.

Miller concluded the story, begging Cassaday to read between the lines and find the moral of the tale. Stacy was trapped. Though she knew what she wanted, she didn't know how to get it. Stacy, she said, was crying for help.

"See if you can come up with a beautiful ending to this nightmare, since I know you would not agree to her ending," Miller wrote.

October 23 ended with two more e-mails from Miller. Her soft suggestion that her husband needed to die caused another argument. Cassaday was too focused on his own plans to even listen to Miller discuss her fears.

"We can't make a plan screaming at each other," Miller wrote. "We can't make a plan if my concerns are not important to you."

Less than fifty minutes later, Miller again pleaded for Cassaday's support while she tried to get out of her marriage.

"I thought that the love we felt would get me through this," Miller wrote. ". . . I can't lean on someone who is always pushing me away."

Miller never wrote explicitly in her e-mails how she preferred to get out of her marriage, though her suggestions of "death" hardly were subtle.

The fairy-tale e-mail spoke of getting rid of a person— death was Stacy's only answer, and she needed only the tool to do it. Rough justice was part of Sharee's thinking.

Less than a week before, Miller had written Cassaday, urging him to watch a movie on CBS that night.

It was the 1996 film *Eye for an Eye,* where Sally Field played a suburban mother whose daughter was raped and murdered by a psychopath. The killer was freed when police bungled the DNA evidence, so Field took the law into her own hands. She joined a vigilante group set on making its own rules.

"Very enlightening movie," Miller wrote.

NINE

To revive Miller's flagging spirits, Cassaday tried reminding her that a life with love and babies awaited her in Missouri. But all too often, those discussions dissolved into acrimony as Cassaday dismissed her trepidation out of hand. Miller was afraid, and she told Cassaday that he wasn't listening.

"How come you won't let me explain my fears?" she wrote.

Changing tactics that Sunday morning, Cassaday tried being relentlessly upbeat, suggesting that the contrast between the hope in his life and the despair in hers would push her toward a decision.

Breathlessly, Cassaday wrote to Sharee that he was going to church, confessing that he had not been in the Lord's house for a long, long time. But it excited him now.

"I want to get close to God again," Cassaday wrote.

Cassaday said he yearned for the peace that his faith had given him years ago and hoped that it could be rekindled. He promised to pray for Sharee Miller, her children and the baby she now carried in her womb. For himself, he would pray for forgiveness, healing, guidance and the Lord's protection. Cassaday wrote that he could feel his life turning around.

"I have you to thank for that," he wrote.

Somehow, that struck a chord for Miller, who never

had been particularly religious. A year before, she had told school counselors that her eight-year-old son, Tommy, had no religious faith. But in a wistful response, she painted a picket-fence scene, imagining that she was part of Cassaday's immediate present. She imagined she was in Missouri, in her own house, waiting for Cassaday to pick her up for church.

But Cassaday's enthusiasm forced Miller to reexamine her own life, which only brought sadness.

"Now, I am stuck in a world I cannot get out of while you are turning your life around," she wrote.

With Cassaday at church and spending the day on a fishing trip with Kenny, Miller spent that Sunday morning composing a melancholy series of e-mails, some answering questions from the latest argument, others pleading with Cassaday to remain a pillar of hope for her.

One of the problems the night before had been Cassaday's insistence that she and the children move to Odessa and immediately set up housekeeping with him. Miller warned Cassaday to be ready for baby steps, not giant leaps. Miller wrote that she never had said they would live together immediately. She said they needed time to grow and learn about each other before they moved in together. In short, they needed to date.

"Real dates where I can send you home at night," she wrote. "I would send you home at night, and let you come back over and over."

The issue that might hold her in Michigan, however, was Tommy's new desire to move back in with his natural father because he no longer could stand living with Bruce. Miller took that as a profound rejection of her. Losing Tommy was a substantial blow and she blamed her husband for the loss of two children—Tommy and the first child she had conceived with Cassaday the summer before. Bruce had aborted that pregnancy with his rape of her on the pool deck, she'd written.

"How many more have to leave before I can find the strength to run?" Miller wrote. "How many have to die in my soul before he dies in my sight?"

But Miller no longer vacillated between choosing between Jerry and Bruce. Her hatred for Bruce Miller now was clear.

"I wish Bruce would not wake up from his nap," Miller wrote. "I wish his heart would stop beating so mine could beat again. I want to live again, and living is what I will do when he dies."

Abandoning the romantic connotations of the angel metaphor that had marked her relationship with Cassaday from the beginning, Miller portrayed Jerry as a biblical guardian angel—the protector and bringer of light, warmth and justice.

"Every time I turn around, when I am lost and when I am found, like an angel standing guard, there you are," she wrote. ". . . My desire is to stand by the fire that burns in you."

She begged Cassaday not to let arguments cool their love. Their separation was killing her, making her unable to sleep or eat.

In dreamy, surrealistic prose, Miller saw herself clinging to Cassaday's hands. Idly, she would trace his name like a schoolgirl. And she asked Cassaday to be there when she needed to run from Bruce Miller.

". . . This woman needs a safe place to land, the strength in your hand," she wrote.

Cassaday's fishing trip ended a little early when the battery on the boat's trolling motor gave out. He had lost the family fishing derby. Kenny hauled in two fish to his father's one. Cassaday spent the early evening at his brother's house in Lee's Summit, then headed home. He checked his e-mail and found Miller was watching out for him.

"I hope and pray you are being good tonight, Jerry,"

she wrote. "I just get nervous when it gets so far past the time we are supposed to be talking."

Cassaday also found a note from his old Kansas City friend whom he had written after getting back to Missouri.

The e-mail was full of sympathy for Cassaday's rehabilitation issues. Usually, Cassaday wasn't inclined to share his weaknesses, but this friend was touched that he had. He also gave Cassaday encouragement about the new woman in his life.

"So, you hit my curiosity button—tell me more about this new wonderful woman that's got you goo-goo," his friend wrote. ". . . You definitely deserve to have some happiness, and somebody to share it with is a bonus."

She's certainly special, Cassaday must have thought. When he finally reached Miller through e-mail, she discouraged him from phoning.

"Jerry, I have to watch the phone calls on here. . . . Too many collect [calls] will draw attention," she wrote. "For the things going on it is better if not much shows up on the phone bill."

Cassaday did not respond immediately to the heap of morose e-mail that had accumulated in his in-box that Sunday. When he did, he again offered encouragement that their love would prevail.

Discouragement in the face of despair was too easy, he wrote. But they had to grow stronger every day and never give up.

"We have to know that we are soon to be free, to love, to make love, to share love," Cassaday wrote. "Honey, I . . . am and always will be your fool."

With a new work and school week starting on October 25, Miller felt a fresh burst of domestic energy, throwing herself into cooking, cleaning and child care. In breaks between chores, she teased Cassaday about not being around the telephone when he'd gone out for a pack of cigarettes. And she e-mailed him a fresh stack of photographs of her distended belly.

Cassaday reacted with giddy enthusiasm and announced he wanted to travel to Flint to see her now that she was pregnant again.

"Hey, my little baby factory, how ya doing?" he asked. "How can I spoil you rotten if we are this far apart?"

Miller rewarded Cassaday's encouragement by baking a batch of chocolate chip muffins and shipping them to Missouri so they would be there by the end of the week.

"You have to put them in the microwave for ten to fifteen seconds before eating," she advised, sounding motherly. "It melts the chocolate chips inside and makes it wonderful."

Cassaday detected the up tick in her mood, and he supported it by assuring her that her birthday present to him, a ring, would remain with him always.

He also sought to dispel any notion that he was considering reconciling with Barb, whom he saw regularly because of his outings with Kenny.

"My heart has only room for you, no one else," he wrote. "I only love you, my baby, my sweetie, my lover and the mother of my babies."

But the psychological lift Sharee Miller received from the domestic activity usually wore off toward the end of the day. On October 27, after whipping up cupcakes for Angela's Halloween party, Miller announced to Cassaday that she was exhausted with depression, her spirits dropping lower and her hopes fading each day.

Miller blamed some of her restlessness on the hormones from her pregnancy. She needed to be with her baby's father, she wrote.

And again, Miller nudged Cassaday to at least consider a swift resolution of her situation, on her terms.

"It is driving me insane, trying to find something or someone to help me end this . . ." she wrote. "I am to the

point of going to Detroit, picking up a bum on the streets
and paying him a small fortune to do what I want."

Later that night, she drove home her lonely point by
sending along photographs of her at home alone, her
hands cradling her breasts.

Since Miller revealed her brutal miscarriage in late
September, glum longing had replaced much of the
frisky passion that had marked their early correspondence. But Miller could still light the fires, particularly if
she felt Cassaday's mood was beginning to match her
own. Before taking off work in late October to work on
Angela's ladybug costume for Halloween, she took a
minute to make certain Cassaday woke up with a smile.

She asked Cassaday to imagine what it would be like
for him to wake up with an erection and find her lying
next to him. In lush, steamy terms, Miller imagined Cassaday approaching her from behind as she still slept.
Slowly, he began to rub his swollen member against her,
but she remained asleep. He entered her, finding her
still wet from an encounter the night before. She awoke
and the pace quickened. Cassaday pressed ever deeper,
until he finally reached his climax.

Dreamily, Miller reveled in the thought of going to
sleep with Cassaday deeply seated inside her, and awak-
ing the next morning to find him coming back for more.

"Wouldn't that be nice to have every morning and
night?" she asked. "An answer to your morning, noon
and evening hard-on."

In another message, she restaged in an e-mail a scene
she depicted on video in *For Jerry's Eyes Only.*

"I put my nipple in my mouth and started sucking
hard," she wrote. "I could see your lips on my breasts
while I was sucking."

Miller also told Cassaday they should consider continuing their cyber relationship, even if they were living in the same house someday. The house, she said, would have several telephone lines for computer links. Jerry and Sharee would sit in separate rooms and message each other on AOL.

"This is how we met," Miller wrote. "Some things are easier to tell on this computer."

For days, Miller had suspected this pregnancy was un- usual and was prepared to give Cassaday a complete account of her October 29 prenatal-care visit. As she de- scribed it to Cassaday later that evening, the appointment began with an ultrasound examination by a nurse.

After smearing cold sticky goop over Miller's belly, the nurse moved the probe around, looking for the fetus. Miller watched a computer monitor while the nurse searched. With the probe low on Miller's belly, the nurse found the fetus's heartbeat. Miller recalled that the sound was like "hearing a sunrise."

"Wait a minute, here," the nurse said, and pointed to another tiny heart beating on the monitor. "Mrs. Miller, I do believe you are having twins!"

Miller cried happy tears as the doctor hustled in to confirm that Jerry and Sharee soon would be the par- ents of twins.

And, given the nature of her relationship with her husband, she gave Cassaday the opportunity to confirm his parentage. She offered, without hesitation, to take blood tests to confirm that Jerry was the father, though she assured him that the babies were his.

Cassaday's response was rapturous, declaring his de- sire to be with her for all future appointments and skipping completely over the issue of whether he was the father.

"I would have loved being there with you when you

found out for sure we are having twins," Cassaday wrote. "I would have kissed you so deeply and passionately the minute we heard!"

Cassaday later exuberantly demanded that Miller e-mail the pictures from the ultrasound examination, the kind that became the standard first picture in late-twentieth-century baby albums.

"Where is that picture of my babies at?" he asked excitedly. ". . . Give me live shots of my babies in your belly!"

On Sunday morning, October 31, Miller still had not sent the ultrasounds and begged Cassaday for patience. She promised to scan the pictures that night, after Bruce had left.

"It is hard to do right now when someone is watching my every move," she wrote.

Miller sent four murky ultrasound photos to Cassaday via e-mail, confirming in his mind that she indeed was pregnant with his children. After digesting them, Cassaday saved them to his hard drive. He never noticed the date stamps on the pictures, which put them in different years in the early 1990s.

Halloween was a blur for Miller, taking the kids trick-or-treating, dressing Angela as a ladybug and taking her to the party. But by early evening, she had a moment to send Cassaday a photo of a beautiful mountain lake at sunset, perhaps a view they would someday share at their Colorado dude ranch.

"Please let this end," Miller wrote in the caption. "I hate being away from you."

Later, she would add: "All my days are filled with tears right now. Please take them away."

Miller had hoped that news of the twins would cheer up Cassaday, but it had begun to weigh on him, snuffing out his exuberance for the future. Too many miles and too much emotional distance separated them. Cassaday dreamed of a life with Sharee and the children, but he could not find a way to free her from the chains of her marriage. She couldn't find her own way out of Michigan and she had rejected his plan.

With time to kill before a November 1 counseling appointment, Cassaday shared his growing despair with Miller. Yes, he wrote, he was beginning to lick his substance abuse problems. However, that was a hollow victory without Miller by his side. He missed Miller terribly and needed her in his arms and in his life. He wanted Kenny back; he wanted to be with Sharee and her children; he wanted to be with his babies.

"Honey, I wish I [had] the answers for you, for me, for us," he wrote. "[But] nothing I pray for happens."

The counseling appointment didn't help much. Afterward, he wrote: "So many things are so screwed up right now. I know you are hurting, but I also know you love me."

Sensing his morose outlook, Miller urged him to take encouragement. She had her own plans to end her marriage with Bruce that Cassaday could not be a part of. She was making plans she never had imagined, Sharee wrote mysteriously.

She had grown leery about disclosing too much to Cassaday, but she assured him that she was working every day to resolve her mess.

"I am talking to people I never dreamed I would . . ." she wrote. "But this is a dangerous situation and one person is controlling it."

She concluded by saying that she would not speak of this to Cassaday again. Everything she was planning, however, was for Cassaday.

In a telephone conversation, Cassaday pressed Miller to talk about her plans and learned she had a pistol. He always had believed that murder wasn't a solution, even for a life of brutality and rape. When they returned to the Internet, Miller assured Cassaday that she had cleaned the pistol inside and out and heaved it into a local Dumpster.

The gun no longer played a role in her plans, she wrote, warning Cassaday that he might not hear from her for a while. Bruce Miller never would understand that his abuse of her was a crime. And none of the abuse would stop until Sharee took care of the problem. Otherwise, she would be haunted forever.

Miller said she was envious of Cassaday's work to recover from alcoholism and drug abuse, but she doubted she could straighten out her own life. She was shamed by her own weakness.

"You are strong enough to do it, and I am not," she wrote. "I am not shit in this world."

Cassaday awoke with a sense of urgency on Tuesday, November 2. He and Miller had fought on the telephone the day before. She had said Cassaday still didn't understand why her situation was "uncontrollable." Afterward, he had gone over to his brother's house for the evening, leaving Miller to stew.

"You didn't deserve all this, Jerry," she wrote while Cassaday was out. "You never asked for it and you didn't deserve it."

For all his hopelessness, Cassaday did not want Miller pushing him away again. His solution was another trip to Michigan.

The next morning, Cassaday sent an e-mail that contained Internet links to flight schedules and ticket prices.

"I'm coming to see you baby, real soon," Cassaday announced. ". . . Can't find anyone to trade cars with for a few days, but I have to come."

Miller resisted mildly, admonishing him to follow his doctor's advice and continue to attend his Alcoholics

Anonymous meeting. She concluded, though, on a resigned, almost disinterested note.

"I don't even know what to say to you today or what to
write," Miller wrote. "I guess I am going to get ready for
work and end this."

Still, she sent Cassaday directions to the salvage yard.
She could see him there when Bruce wasn't around in
the morning. Maybe they could get together later.

Soon Cassaday was behind the wheel of a rental car for
the thirteen-hour drive to Flint. Already months behind
on his truck payments, Cassaday didn't want to take his
Ford F-150 on the road.

In a week, he would show no such hesitation.

Early on November 3, Miller reserved a room for Cassaday at the Holiday Inn Express in nearby Birch Run,
paying for the room with her own Visa debit card. Cassaday appeared at the salvage yard and she took off work
and followed him to the motel.

Later, she and her kids—Tommy, Angela and Buddy—
met Cassaday at the Chuck E. Cheese's near the Genesee
Valley Mall, the largest shopping center in the county. To
a disinterested observer, they would have appeared as
two friends who had unexpectedly bumped into each
other and stopped for a casual chat as the kids played
the arcade games. They spoke as old, dear friends.

After spending the night with Sharee at a local motel,
Cassaday began his return to Missouri on November 5.

Though she later would say she viewed his trip to Flint
with extreme trepidation, an e-mail she sent to Cassaday
the day he left recounted her mood. She thanked Jerry
for visiting and apologized for not being able to spend
as much time together as she wanted. But she would
never forget the visit, she wrote.

"Did you know that every time we make love I have the
most wonderful orgasm?" she asked. "Then every time I
feel you having one, it makes me have another."

But one of her fondest recollections of the rushed visit was listening to Cassaday as he talked in his sleep.

"It was in that moment I realized how much you really do love me," she wrote.

Upon arriving in Odessa, Cassaday called Miller's home number, let it ring once and then hung up. It was their signal that he had arrived home safely. To leave the telephone line open if she decided to call, he worked off-line on an e-mail he had been composing in his head all the way back to Missouri. Cassaday noted that Sharee had finally agreed to leave Bruce Miller soon.

"The only thing that kept me going, honey, is knowing that you love me and in just a matter of days I will be coming back for the last time," Cassaday wrote.

He gushed about her pregnancy and her smart and wonderful children. And he thanked her for sneaking around Bruce to see him.

"I know the chances you took just to be with me, just to let me see my babies," he wrote.

Cassaday logged on and sent the e-mail automatically. He checked his Instant Messaging software looking for Miller, but she wasn't on-line. So he composed a quick e-mail to nudge her along the next time she checked.

"You're late!" Cassaday wrote. "I'm here, where are you, baby?"

To pass the time waiting for Miller, Cassaday checked his e-mail, though he wasn't expecting much. Sharee was his most regular correspondent—almost 150 e-mails between them in the last two weeks alone. Mail from her wasn't likely, though. He had just seen her, and when he left her late afternoon the day before, she seemed tired and ready to go to bed early. She may not have even awoken yet.

Still, he checked his e-mail.

Sitting on top was a message from BDJUNK, the AOL screen name Miller had assigned to her husband and his business. Miller, however, would occasionally use the address by mistake.

"YOU SHOULD READ THIS" was the subject line.

Cassaday clicked it open to find a message that realized all of his worst fears. It was written in all capital letters, the Internet's crude version of "shouting."

The letter was cruel, cold and obscene.

"SHAREE IS GROWING FAT WITH TWO BASTARDS IN HER," BDJUNK screamed. Sharee no longer wanted the excess weight and had decided to have an abortion. Tauntingly, the writer said Sharee had decided she would rather "SCREW EVERYTHING IN SIGHT" than have Cassaday's children.

Cassaday instantly knew the message was from Bruce, a very dangerous man. BDJUNK said that Sharee had made a smart decision to have the abortion. It also was a good decision for Jerry, the writer needled. That way, Cassaday wouldn't have to pay child support for the kids. No need to worry about "TWO BASTARDS FLOATING AROUND WITH YOUR LAST NAME."

BDJUNK blasted Sharee for screwing Cassaday without using condoms, and having risked turning herself into a "HERPES INFECTED BITCH WITH TWO BASTARDS IN HER."

Bludgeoning Cassaday at every turn, BDJUNK said that Sharee had been sleeping with everyone in town, but she still had decided to stick with her husband. "SO YOU SEE. ALL WILL BE DOING GOOD. YOU WITH YOUR WIFE. ME WITH MINE AND THE THINGS IN HER STOMACH GONE."

For nearly three pages, the taunting continued. Cassaday again learned how Sharee had threatened to kill Bruce, but still "THE LITTLE BITCH" had changed her mind and decided to return to him.

BDJUNK also said that Sharee's daughter had told him of meeting a strange man with her mother the day before. Now, Cassaday concluded, Bruce knew almost everything.

BDJUNK also pressed Cassaday for advice, asking whether Sharee needed professional help after a dual abortion.

"I HAVE HEARD THAT THE LOSS OF A BABY COULD MAKE YOU CRAZY. WITH HER KILLING TWO, DO YOU THINK SHE MIGHT NEED HELP AFTERWARDS?"

Still, Sharee seemed intent on "KILLING THESE BAS-TARDS. SHE DOESN'T WANT THEM INSIDE HER IS WHAT I HEAR HER SAY."

Cassaday reeled from the blunt-force trauma of the e-mail. It tore at his most tender places: his inability to convince Sharee to leave her husband, his agony over her helplessness and his own money troubles with that crack about not being able to "support the bastards."

The bitterly calculated description of the babies as "bastards" ripped at Cassaday. The characterization of Sharee—Jerry's "angel"—as a whore and slut tore at his love. And guilt welled inside Cassaday as he imagined his angel dealing with a bastard like that, and he remembered the times he had argued with Sharee that killing Bruce wasn't the right solution.

Frantically, Cassaday worked the telephone to find Miller, but with no luck. She wasn't registered at any Flint-area hospital under her own name. Nobody was picking up at her house, and she wasn't answering her cell phone. Quickly, he sent an e-mail, knowing that Miller would look for him on-line.

"I'm worried!!!" he wrote. "Where are you, honey?"

Hours passed as Cassaday debated whether to stay on-line or leave his only available phone line open for calls. Finally, he gave her a trail to follow if she could just find a telephone.

"If you come on here, call my house, even if you don't

talk I will know it's you," he wrote. "Then I will meet you on here."

Just after noon, another message from BDJUNK appeared. The note was still and dark.

"Jerry, This is Sharee. I am going away for a few days. I will contact you next week sometime."

Two hours later, a pile of Web links, sent again by BDJUNK, appeared in Cassaday's e-mail in box.

All of them offered emotional-support material for women who had lost their pregnancies.

As time passed, Cassaday's rage began to quiet. Cassaday welcomed the grip of cold resolve and waited by his computer.

"Still checking for you honey," he wrote. "Love you."

TEN

Jerry Cassaday always had imagined himself Sharee Miller's champion and protector, but a lot of good *that* had done. Cassaday had offered her little but safe advice from half a country away. In the meantime, she had endured her husband's brutality, carried their babies and pleaded with Cassaday for help. And as an ex-cop, he always had been reluctant to even talk of getting rid of Bruce.

But that moment grew closer as Cassaday waited by his computer.

BDJUNK returned to the Internet the next day, November 7.

Again in swaggering capital letters, BDJUNK announced that Sharee would be home soon, the abortion complete. In fact, Sharee seemed to be feeling much better, knowing that she wouldn't be having more children.

BDJUNK ridiculed Cassaday's silence, suggesting he was a coward for not confronting him directly. BDJUNK also stated he was finished delivering messages from Sharee. She would be speaking directly with Cassaday soon.

The news wouldn't be good, the e-mail said. Sharee Miller was finished running around on her husband and had promised she no longer would be Cassaday's "whore."

To drive the point home, BDJUNK described how Sharee had performed oral sex on him just the day before, yelling his name, Bruce, and telling him of her love. Leave Sharee alone, BDJUNK growled. His wife was happy in his bed and in his home, he wrote. Indeed, Sharee had begged to stay in his house and promised that she never again would try to kill him, the e-mail stated.

The e-mail dismissed the abortion as insignificant, with BDJUNK feigning indifference and saying he didn't know where she went for the procedure. He gave the knife a twist by again noting that Cassaday should be happy because he wouldn't be responsible for any "little bastards."

BDJUNK wrapped up with an acid conclusion, certain to drive Cassaday over the brink.

"THANK YOU FOR MAKING MY RELATIONSHIP WITH MY WIFE BETTER. WE ARE ON THE MENDS AND IT IS THANKS TO YOU. BRUCE."

Several hours later, Cassaday and Miller connected by telephone and spoke about what had happened. Miller told Cassaday that Bruce again had gone wild, beating and raping her with such a force that she now feared her unborn children were dead.

But Bruce Miller liked to make each violent episode just a little special, and a little worse.

He had ordered two of his junkyard thugs to take Sharee to a remote cabin and rape and beat her again to make sure she understood the consequences of her relationship with Jerry Cassaday.

But Sharee Miller needed rest, so she and Cassaday made plans to meet on IM later that night. Miller promised more details of the torture and even proof in the form of e-mail photos showing her bruises.

With hours to kill, Cassaday began his own plans. He called his brother Mike and told him he was going to the Cassaday family cabin at Lake Pomme de Terre to scout deer stands for the upcoming hunting season. He also needed a couple of days just to get his head straight from all his drug and alcohol problems.

But the Sunday telephone conversation raised more questions than answers for Mike Cassaday, who heard a lot that didn't make sense.

"Hey, look, Mike," Jerry said. "If anything ever happens to me, there's a briefcase under the bed at home. Get hold of the briefcase and you'll know what to do with it."

Mike Cassaday pressed his brother to cancel this trip and just tell him what the hell was going on.

Jerry then rattled off a deadline, a hard deadline.

"Look, Mike, if I'm not home by six o'clock, Tuesday evening, get hold of this briefcase," Jerry said.

Jerry hung up, and Mike thought for a moment. Mike knew that his brother had just lied to him. Jerry didn't even have a key to the lake cabin.

If this goes south, I'm going to need a plan and a lawyer, Jerry Cassaday must have thought.

Cassaday flipped on his word processor and wrote to John P. O'Connor, a Kansas City criminal defense lawyer. Although O'Connor had never represented Cassaday, the two met years before when Cassaday was a Cass County deputy working near Kansas City. O'Connor also had a terrific reputation for defending cops who'd run afoul of the law.

"Should you receive this letter, then one of two things has occurred," Cassaday's letter began. "One, I am dead and need you to see to things for me. Secondly, I would be in jail for something for which I would need your assistance."

If he was dead, Cassaday told O'Connor to settle his estate, giving his things to his sons and his brothers.

But if he was still alive and in jail, Cassaday told O'Connor that he would retain him "at any cost" and that Sharee Miller would help with the bills.

In short, succinct sentences, Cassaday told O'Connor

that Miller lost their child because of Bruce Miller, who was involved in organized crime, counterfeiting, money laundering and drugs.

Cassaday wrapped up the letter quickly and dug out his old briefcase. In it, he placed the letter and copies of some e-mails with Miller.

That evening, Cassaday logged on to AOL. Sharee joined him on Instant Messenger two minutes later.

In the cluttered bedroom of her home, Miller uploaded electronic photos of her bruises from the beatings, taken from a tiny Web camera atop her computer monitor.

Cassaday knew what to expect. He'd written loads of domestic-violence reports, but he was anxious to see proof. It would steel his resolve.

Still, the pictures were slow in coming, so Cassaday pressed Miller to describe her injuries.

Cassaday: What about your back and legs and face?
Miller: Jerry, you said you were not going to look at them. You promised. . . . My face is untouched. He never touches my face.
Cassaday: I have to save [them] to disk. Show me.
Miller: You promised.
Cassaday: Honey, hurry. I have to leave soon.
Miller: Jerry, there isn't really anything on my back. Main thing was to hurt the babies.
Cassaday: . . . Legs?
Miller: Some [injuries], but not a lot. . . .
Cassaday: Send [the pictures]. I love you.
Miller: Just a minute.
Cassaday: OK.
Miller: You promised.
Cassaday: I promise I will come.
Miller: I never wanted you to see these. You promised you wouldn't. Jerry, they are gross. I never wanted you to see.

The pictures finally popped up. The first showed her face unmarked; the handful that followed revealed livid purple-and-black bruises smeared across her breasts, stomach and thighs.

Cassaday: I love you.
Miller: You promised.
Cassaday: Please honey. I expected it. I'm sorry for you. I love you. . . . Where will we meet when I get there? I love you.
Miller: Done.
Cassaday: OK. Got 'em. I love you honey. Never again.
Miller: Jerry, you promised you would not open them.
Cassaday: Honey, I didn't have a choice.
Miller: Jerry, unless [these are] needed, I don't want anyone seeing them.
Cassaday: I'm sorry. I love you.
Miller: It is degrading enough.
Cassaday: I know.
Miller: I love you. Please don't show them to anyone.
Cassaday: I promise. Honey, we have to trust each other now.
Miller: Promise to burn them as soon as you know you don't need them.
Cassaday: It's on disk. If [they're] not needed, you will get the only copy.
Miller: Promise to burn the disk.
Cassaday: I promise.
Miller: I don't want them . . . ever.
Cassaday: Anything you want . . . I love you. OK.
Miller: I love you Jerry.

With the pictures taken care of, the conspirators began to plan, spending eighty minutes plotting cold-blooded murder.

Cassaday: How do we hook up tomorrow?
Miller: I need a little time in the morning to come up with a plan.
Cassaday: OK . . . What is the fastest way to the yard from [Interstate] 75?

Cassaday received directions for the quickest way to the junkyard from the nearby interstate. Miller gave him a route that would take him through dimly lit areas that would not attract police attention. She also told him how to negotiate a local intersection called "the Point," which was well known to local drivers, but wouldn't mean much to an out-of-towner.

"Did you write all that down?" Miller asked when her directions were complete.

"Yes," replied Cassaday, hitting the print icon and sending a copy of the IM transcript to his printer.

Miller: Now, you need to listen to me for a minute. I will call Bruce at 5 p.m. . . .

But just as Sharee Miller began telling Jerry Cassaday her plan to freeze Bruce in position, telephone line noise knocked them off AOL. Seconds later, they each returned to IM and continued their real-time conversation.

Miller: I hate AOL.
Cassaday: Me too. Go on.
Miller: Anyway, listen. I will call him at 5 p.m. and tell him to call me when he is leaving for dinner. Then I will tell him I will call him back to tell him when it is done. When I call him back I will tell him 30 minutes and keep him on the phone until I know he is alone. Then I will call you [and] let it ring once. And then I will call him back, just until he says you pulled up.

Cassaday: OK.
Miller: I am not really going to order dinner.

Cassaday's mind raced ahead. With nine years on the sheriff's department—some of it investigating homicides—he instinctively probed weaknesses in the plan, details that could land them in prison if something went wrong.

He instructed Miller on what to say if his name came up.

Cassaday: OK. Honey, if anyone asks, the last time you saw me was last week. They can check that.
Miller: Jerry, I am scared. OK?
Cassaday: Me too, so don't try to hide it.
Miller: Jerry if this don't work he will hurt me bad.
Cassaday: It will work. When you leave tomorrow you will never see him again.

Miller did not appear to be comforted, however, and imagined what she would do if her husband somehow escaped the trap that she and Cassaday were laying for him.

Miller: If something goes wrong, if he pulls in the driveway, I will call the police . . . not that they would help me.
Cassaday: I know. Call the state police honey. . . . Find the number. Call them first. They will head that way and then call the local assholes.

They both knew the murder would have to look like a random robbery for Sharee Miller to escape suspicion.

Miller: Now, you need to know some other things.
. . . I am taking all the work checks out of his wal-

A young Sharee Kitley grins for the camera. *(Photo courtesy Genesee County Sheriff's Department)*

This youthful photo spurred Sharee Miller to note that she was once a "nerd." *(Photo courtesy Genesee County Sheriff's Department)*

A 14-year-old Sharee Kitley tries out her make-up skills. *(Photo courtesy Genesee County Sheriff's Department)*

Karaoke was a favorite pastime. *(Photo courtesy Genesee County Sheriff's Department)*

Bruce L. Miller, seen here in his high school graduation photograph, grew up loving everything about cars. *(Photo courtesy the Miller family)*

Bruce Miller with his grown children, Julie and Jeff, at Christmas 1997. *(Photo courtesy the Miller family)*

Bruce and Sharee Miller look to the future on their Las Vegas, Nev., wedding day in April 1999. *(Photo courtesy of the Miller family)*

Sharee Miller posed for this portrait on the day she married Bruce Miller. *(Photo courtesy Genesee County Sheriff's Department)*

After their marriage, Bruce and Sharee Miller shared this home near Flint, Michigan. *(Photo courtesy Mark Morris)*

Jerry Cassaday served proudly as a Marshall (Mo.) Police Department patrol officer, shown here circa 1983. *(Photo courtesy Charlene Cassaday)*

A playful Sharee Miller sent this photo to her online lover, Jerry Cassaday. *(Photo courtesy Genesee County Sheriff's Department)*

Sharee Miller shows off the clothes she wore the night she first met Jerry Cassaday. *(Photo courtesy Genesee County Sheriff's Department)*

This photo was taken in September 1999, at Jerry Cassaday's son's wedding. *(Photo courtesy Genesee County Sheriff's Department)*

Sharee Miller sent a provocative videotape, "For Jerry's Eyes Only," to Cassaday after first meeting him in July 1999. *(Video courtesy Genesee County Sheriff's Department. Photo by Paul Janczewski.)*

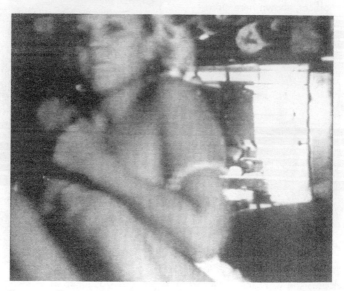

Sharee Miller switches off the camera in the concluding sequence of her videotape. *(Video courtesy Genesee County Sheriff's Department. Photo by Paul Janczewski.)*

In late October 1999, Sharee Miller sent this e-mail photo
of a home pregnancy test wand to Jerry Cassaday
to convince him she was pregnant with his baby.
(Photo courtesy Genesee County Sheriff's Department)

Sharee Miller is radiant after she gives Jerry Cassaday
the news about her purported pregnancy.
(Photo courtesy Genesee County Sheriff's Department)

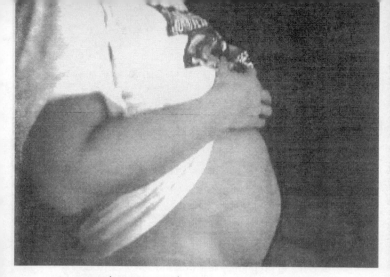

To accent her purported pregnancy, Sharee Miller sent
Jerry Cassaday e-mail photos of her growing belly.
(Photo courtesy Genesee County Sheriff's Department)

A beaming and proud Jerry Cassaday sent this e-mail photo to
Sharee Miller after she told him that she would be having his baby.
(Photo courtesy Genesee County Sheriff's Department)

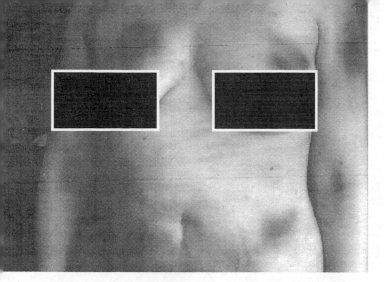

This Nov. 7, 1999 electronic photo shows bruises that Sharee Miller claimed she suffered in beatings by her jealous husband. Investigators believe she used her experience as a cosmetics saleswoman to fake the injuries. *(Photo courtesy Genesee County Sheriff's Department)*

Cassaday received this photograph that seems to show a frightened Sharee after she said her husband and his hired thugs had raped her. *(Photo courtesy Genesee County Sheriff's Department)*

In the early evening of Nov. 8, 1999, Jerry Cassaday would have had this perspective on Bruce Miller's junkyard as he approached the office.
(Photo courtesy Mark Morris)

According to Sharee Miller's instructions, Jerry Cassaday was to park his truck to the right of this door.
(Photo courtesy Mark Morris)

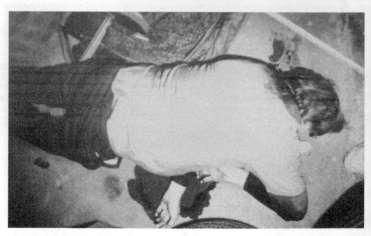

Bruce Miller's body sprawled on the floor of his office after he was blasted at close range with a shotgun.
(Photo courtesy Genesee County Sheriff's Department)

The investigation soon focused on John Hutchinson,
a former salvage yard employee.
(Photo courtesy Genesee County Sheriff's Department)

Capt. Michael Compeau of the Genesee County Sheriff's
Department supervised the detective bureau's investigation of
Bruce Miller's murder. *(Photo courtesy Mark Morris)*

Ives Potrafka was the computer-savvy detective who opened the probe into Bruce Miller's murder. *(Photo courtesy Mark Morris)*

Sgt. Kevin Shanlian took over as lead investigator when Potrafka went to work for the state. *(Photo courtesy Kevin Shanlian)*

Genesee County Sheriff Robert J. Pickell encouraged his officers to keep the probe active. *(Photo courtesy Mark Morris)*

Consumed with shame, Jerry Cassaday committed suicide in his Odessa, Missouri, apartment early in February 2000.
(Photo courtesy Genesee County Sheriff's Department)

Soon after Jerry Cassaday's death, his brother recovered this briefcase, containing suicide notes, e-mails, and other information linking Sharee Miller to the murder of her husband.
(Photo courtesy Mark Morris)

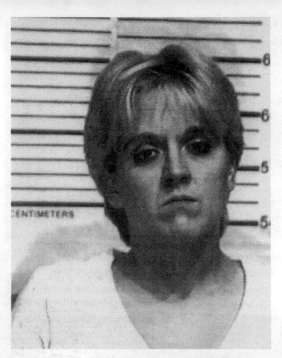

Sharee Miller was arrested in Flint, Michigan, on Feb. 23, 2000.
(Photo courtesy Genesee County Sheriff's Department)

In a search of Sharee Miller's home, deputies found this envelope, which became crucial evidence.
(Photo courtesy Genesee County Sheriff's Department)

Lawyer David Nickola defended
Sharee Miller at her
December 2000 trial.
(Photo courtesy David Nickola)

Assistant Genesee County
Prosecutor Marcie M. Mabry
was the lead prosecutor who
contended that Sharee tricked
Cassaday into murdering
Bruce Miller.
(Photo courtesy Mark Morris)

Genesee County Circuit Judge
Judith A. Fullerton presided over
the Sharee Miller murder trial.
(Photo courtesy Mark Morris)

Sharee Miller began to cry in court as guilty verdicts were read.
(Photo courtesy The Flint Journal, photographer Stuart Bauer)

Charlene Cassaday squeezes the hands of her husband, James, left, and son, Roger, right, after Sharee Miller's conviction.
(Photo courtesy The Flint Journal, photographer Stuart Bauer)

Bruce Miller's headstone in a Genesee County cemetery reflects the great loves of his life, cars and racing.
(Photo courtesy Paul Janczewski)

let tonight. He has about $2,000 in work checks. I will deposit them in the morning. He will have about $1,000 on him. He doesn't know I took the rest of the money and neither will anyone else. They will think he had more on him.

Cassaday: OK.

Miller: . . . Take his wallet the whole thing. Don't leave it.

Cassaday: . . . I won't.

Miller: Jerry, honey, I can do this. I know I can.

Cassaday: I love you.

Miller: All I have to do is look at myself and I can do it . . . without involving you.

Cassaday: No. Write this down: John P. Occonnor.

Cassaday quickly followed with two telephone numbers, both in Kansas City's 816 area code, one marked "office" and one "home."

"If anything happens to me, call him," Cassaday wrote. "Got it? Very important."

Miller fumbled around and found a torn envelope in her computer hutch. Carefully, she wrote down the exact information and dropped the envelope back into the hutch drawer.

Miller: . . . Jerry, is the gun loud?

Cassaday: Somewhat.

Miller: It is deer-hunting season here. . . . I am hearing guns all the time.

Cassaday: . . . Inside will be best, muffled. Better to look like a holdup.

Miller: Jerry, inside the building?

Cassaday: Yes. Do not go in there.

Miller: Then how will you get in without him seeing [you]? I want to know.

Cassaday: He'll come out to me. We will go inside.

Well, that won't work, Miller thought. *Bruce never leaves the counter when a customer is headed in. And what about the big window up front?* If Cassaday parked to the left of the door, Bruce Miller would see him walking toward the office with a shotgun.

Miller: Pull up to the left of the building, right to the door. [Then] get out.

Cassaday: Door opens in, right?

Miller: Pull up to the left, to the right I mean.

Cassaday: With the door on my left.

Miller: Then your door will open to the door. He will stay at the desk inside until you walk in, unless you start looking around. Then he [would] come out.

Cassaday: I want him up.

Miller: Jerry, don't look at him. Don't talk to him.

Cassaday: Don't worry.

Miller: You yourself said to me . . . that if I looked at him or talked, I couldn't do it.

Cassaday: I know, but that is different. I don't know him.

Miller: He will beg and you know it. Just do it and get the hell out of there.

Cassaday: I want him to know who I am.

Miller: Jerry, please.

Cassaday: He will know but not for long.

Miller: Just say, "Hi, I'm Jerry" and get out.

Cassaday: I will.

Miller: Please promise me.

Cassaday: I love you.

Miller: Promise me that is all, Jerry. I can't lose you.

Cassaday: I promise. You won't. Where is the light switch?

Miller: He leaves it on all night. If it is not on, someone will think something.

Cassaday: Inside?

Miller: Inside.

Cassaday: OK.

Miller: You can't see anything from the road but it is on.

Cassaday: Can you make the outside light not work?

Miller: I will try.

Cassaday: That would be best.

Miller: Wait, that is the light that is on all night, not the inside.

Cassaday: Very good . . . Where is the switch inside?

Miller: Inside light is right by the door when you walk in.

Cassaday: On the right?

Miller: As you are walking in, yes. . . . I will make sure only one inside light works.

Cassaday: OK. I need to go.

Miller: No wait. Jerry, I love you. You have to know that I love you and I am sorry.

Cassaday: I love you.

Miller: Please know how sorry I am.

Cassaday: Honey listen. When I get in town I will call your cell [phone].

Miller: I don't want to leave that on. It needs a battery for you.

Cassaday: There is a rest stop on 75 south between Birch Run and Mount Morris. We will meet there.

With preparations almost compete, Miller paused a moment. Their plans also carried a future burden, but the two would share it together, and in silence.

Miller: Jerry, are you going to be able to live with this the rest of your life? Because I can. You are so good. Are you sure? I can, you know. The rest of my life we never talk about it, never.

Cassaday: I love you.

Miller: Answer me.

Cassaday: We will never discuss it again. I love you. Yes, I can.

Miller: Answer me. I love you too.

Cassaday: Especially after those pictures.

Miller: Jerry, tell me you forgive me. Tell me one day we can have a baby and nothing will happen to it.

Cassaday: We will, honey. You and me. I love you.

Miller: Tell me you forgive me.

Cassaday: I forgive you. You have nothing to be sorry about.

Miller: Do you mean it?

Cassaday: I love you. I am doing this, ain't I?

Miller: I should have left with you.

Cassaday: No. Never leave me, never, never, never.

Miller: I should be with you now.

Cassaday: Stop, honey.

Miller: I love you so much and I wanted those babies. It hurts.

Cassaday: I know. Just tell me you will be with me soon.

Miller: Jerry, I will be with you very soon.

Cassaday: I love you.

Miller told Cassaday that she had been planning what she would say when she announced she was leaving Michigan so soon after her husband's death.

Miller: I will leave here because I am so upset. Sell everything and leave. . . . Harrah's offered me a job.

Cassaday, however, still was consumed with details. There was too much to plan and the clock was ticking.

Cassaday: Have Jenn there, or someone, anyone honey. . . . Have someone with you tomorrow night.

Miller: . . . When you are there?

Cassaday: All night.

Miller: I can try. . . .

Cassaday: I don't care who. . . . I love you.

Miller: Jerry, I love you so much. Please believe me.

Cassaday: I love you. I have to go. [I] will call you in the [morning].

Miller: Jerry, I don't want you to go!

Cassaday: I have to. Running out of time, in case I need to pull off and sleep. Need a little buffer.

Miller: Please be careful, please drive slow. Jerry . . . I love you. I miss you. . . . I will miss you. I miss you so much now.

Cassaday: I do miss you.

Miller: I am sorry. . . .

Cassaday: . . . I love you.

Miller: I wish you didn't have to see those pictures. Jerry don't leave fingerprints. It is cold here. [Wear] gloves.

Cassaday: . . . I love you.

Miller: I will worry all night and all day and all the next day.

Cassaday: See you soon. Bye sweetheart.

Miller: I love you. Bye Jerry. Promise to always love me.

Cassaday: How do I get in touch after I get home?

Miller: I will call you from [a] pay phone using card.

Cassaday: Give me lots of time, OK?

Miller: OK.

Cassaday: Then give me the number. I will go to a payphone and call you back.

Miller: Jerry, be careful please. Be careful please.

Cassaday: Love you honey. Bye.

Miller: I love you.

* * *

Cassaday was businesslike in his preparations. He had burned through his rage earlier that day when he learned of the beating and rape, and murder of his babies. Through the summer and fall, he had heard the terrible stories of Bruce Miller and his abusive relationship with Sharee.

Cassaday had argued that Miller should just leave Bruce, letting him sit in the big house all alone, dying of humiliation. But Miller feared that Bruce would come one day, find her in Kansas City and put a bullet in her head.

That would never happen. Bruce Miller, the man whom Jerry was convinced had hurt Sharee and killed his babies, would die.

He had one more thing to do before leaving.

After printing out the second half of their IM session, Cassaday dropped it with the first half in the briefcase, along with the disk of downloaded pictures of Sharee's bruised body.

On the copy of the IM transcript, Cassaday wrote that their conversation ended at 1:40 A.M. He also noted that he left at 1:50 A.M.

On a seven-hundred-mile road to murder.

Even at 2:00 A.M., Interstate 70 out of Odessa, Missouri, was filled with traffic—long-distance truckers hauling their wares and the late-night bar crowd returning home.

But no one else was on a mission like Cassaday's. Miller had needled Cassaday about dumping his Ford F-150—the payments were killing him—but now that pickup was speeding to her rescue.

Cassaday saw Odessa's yellow streetlights disappear into blackness along with the strip malls, shuttered fast-food restaurants and gas stations. Ahead, a ribbon of taillights pointed to Columbia, a university town.

Soon the streetlights disappeared, and his thoughts and the reflective white lines on the road were his only companions.

Cassaday drove with purpose and plenty of time for cool reflection—as the law called it—on the photographs he had just downloaded and the emotional turmoil of four months with Sharee Miller.

By 3:30 A.M., Cassaday turned onto I-370 east to cut off downtown St. Louis, and then drove until he found I-270, toward Chicago.

The drive around St. Louis answered one question for Cassaday: Would getting rid of the twenty-gauge shotgun now riding in the cab with him be a problem later? No, there were hundreds of places where the pieces of a disassembled shotgun could be tossed—into a lake, a river or the dark waters behind a levy.

Several hours later, Cassaday watched the eastern sky lighten as he plowed northeast on Interstate 55, through Bloomington and Normal. Such quaint midwestern names, being passed on an early-morning drive that was anything but normal.

Cassaday missed rush hour around Chicago and made good time through the industrial sinew of Joliet, Illinois, and Gary, Indiana. Still, suburban-style housing developments dotted the interstate, built mostly for young families with children and a future.

The highway paralleled the Lake Michigan shoreline, and by the early afternoon of November 8, Cassaday was in the thick of rural Michigan. There, the woods grew thick and leafy and shimmered gold and red on an autumn day.

Speeding past Kalamazoo, Battle Creek and Lansing, Cassaday neared Flint, Michigan, and his destiny—murder during a warm Indian summer.

* * *

Sharee Miller was up at about 5:30 A.M. on November 8; she was having coffee with Bruce when he returned home from his third-shift job at Delphi East. After getting the kids off to school at about 8:00 A.M., she dropped off some clothes to Bruce's mother's house to donate to charity.

By 8:30 A.M., she'd opened the salvage yard while Bruce slept. Her routine was never to take Mondays off because she'd have to spend the rest of the week cleaning up Bruce's bookkeeping. Business was light that day. She collected about $300 from customers and paid $252 in bills. Her last sale was $149 for the hood off a Trans Am. When Bruce showed up, she left.

About 2:00 P.M., Jerry Cassaday pulled into a highway rest stop near Flint, off I-75.

From a pay phone, he called Miller's cell phone, let it ring once and hung up.

Driving in from the south, Sharee spotted Cassaday's dark blue Ford immediately. They had so much to talk about, but no time just then. She handed him the cell phone and bolted. Cassaday breathed in the Michigan air and prepared to wait. The next signal wouldn't come for nearly four hours.

Late in the afternoon, Miller called Laura Ewald to suggest they go to a Mary Kay cosmetics motivational meeting that night. Ewald agreed. Angela, however, came home from school with an earache, so Miller decided not to go. Ewald told Miller she would stop over about 5:30 P.M. to see her on the way to the meeting.

At 5:43 P.M., Miller called Bruce at the junkyard and told him she would call for fish dinners from Big Brutus, a local take-out restaurant. The two spoke for less than ninety seconds.

At 6:05 P.M., Miller called the restaurant, ordered the food and hung up in less than thirty seconds.

Three minutes later, she called Bruce at B&D. Bruce

told her that he wasn't busy and would leave soon to pick up the food. After a little more than eight minutes of chitchat with her husband, Sharee hung up, satisfied that Bruce was alone.

One more call and the plan would be out of her hands. Miller punched in the number of her own cell phone. She let it ring once, then hung up.

It was the signal to Cassaday that Bruce was alone and waiting to be killed.

About 6:16 P.M., Miller called to speak with her husband one last time. Dinner was ready at Big Brutus, she said, finishing the thought by suggesting that Bruce bring home something more than dinner. Bruce got the joke and laughed.

"Not tonight, dear," he replied with a laugh.

Then he hesitated. A truck was parking outside the office, he said.

"Harold must have forgotten something," Bruce Miller said, thinking at first that one of his employees was on his way back in. "No, it's not Harold. I'll try to hurry up and get rid of this customer."

Miller said her last words to her husband.

"I love you."

Bruce Miller fired up a Marlboro Light and waited for the customer to come in as he said good-bye to his wife. Before she hung up, Sharee Miller heard the door open at B&D Auto Parts as someone walked into the shop.

Cassaday had been killing time near the salvage yard when Miller's cell phone rang once, then went silent. He pointed the truck toward B&D Auto Parts and turned off North Saginaw Street. As he closed the last five hundred yards down a dirt road toward the low-slung white building, he passed the twisted cars that represented the wreckage of too many unfortunate lives. Following the directions to the letter, he parked to the right of the door, lifted the twenty-gauge shotgun and walked in.

Cassaday immediately recognized Bruce Miller from the photographs Sharee had sent him, particularly the one where he stood next to a lady who was about her size. With the wireless phone still in his hand, Bruce Miller was sitting in a ratty metal desk chair behind the waist-high counter.

Cassaday leveled the twenty-gauge shotgun at Bruce Miller's throat, no more than a few feet away.

Bruce Miller completely mistook the sweet moment of revenge for a robbery attempt. Jerry would make it look like a robbery, but he also wanted it personal.

"Hi," Cassaday said. "I'm Jerry."

Miller's grip on the telephone loosened and Cassaday took a shallow breath and held it. He curled his index finger around the trigger and squeezed.

Bruce Miller's throat and upper chest exploded in gore.

Bruce half spun on the swivel chair as he was punched backward by the blast. He collapsed on his side, his face coming to rest on a floor strewn with cigarette butts just inches from a brimming trash can.

Cassaday flinched from the earsplitting roar but recovered quickly. He sidestepped the spreading pool of blood and reached into the dead man's shirt pocket. He took the still-warm wad of cash but didn't bother to count it. Then he took Miller's wallet.

Now Cassaday's only thought was of escape.

He pulled out of the yard, past the gate and onto North Saginaw.

Once clear of the murder scene, at 6:47 P.M., Cassaday pulled out Miller's cell phone, dialed her number and let it ring once.

He shut the telephone off as he drove away. It was the last call ever made on Miller's cell phone.

Within minutes, Cassaday was back on the expressway, heading back to Missouri.

Sharee Miller's plan was moving like clockwork, but Ewald still had not appeared, so she called her back.

"Did you stand me up?" Miller asked.

Ewald agreed to come over but said it would take a while.

Soon Miller's phone rang once, telling her that Bruce never would be home again. Not content with the pre-arranged signal, Miller confirmed it for herself.

She dialed the salvage yard. No one answered. The deed was done.

Now she must get her act together.

Complaints from three hungry children—each expecting their stepfather to be home soon with dinner—occupied Sharee Miller early that evening. Trying very hard to sound believable, she told them that Bruce was on the way home with the fish. To tide over one of her kids, she fixed a peanut butter and jelly sandwich.

Ewald pulled in just before 7:00 P.M., parking her car behind Sharee's. To pass the time, Ewald and Miller worked to download install the ICQ Internet chat program on the computer in Sharee's bedroom.

After tinkering on-line with the program from 7:19 P.M. until just past 8:05 P.M., Miller decided to give up.

"You know, I should really get off here because Bruce cusses me out all the time for tying up the phone line," Miller told Ewald.

The minutes passed anxiously and Miller wondered aloud why Bruce wasn't home yet. Miller called B&D again at 8:11 P.M., but received no answer. She began a steady stream of phone calls to Bruce's relatives.

Chuck Miller was annoyed to hear from his sister-in-law, first at 8:18 P.M. He wanted to watch the Minnesota

Vikings play the Dallas Cowboys at 9:00 P.M., and he didn't want Sharee's hysterics to get in the way of the game. Chuck always was skeptical about Bruce's marriage to Sharee, and he'd seen her laughing and joking at the junkyard several hours before.

Having had his fill of Sharee that day, Chuck tried to put her off by telling her that Bruce seemed fine when he talked to him about 5:00 P.M. about putting new rotors on a truck.

"It was nothing for Bruce to be late," he said later. "Bruce was never an on-time person."

Customers always were pulling into the yard late to look for some auto part, and Bruce would stay open to make the sale, he said.

"No big deal," Chuck told Sharee. "He's not that late."

He suggested that she drive to the yard to see if Bruce had left yet.

A son in tow, Miller hopped into Ewald's car, which was blocking her own car. Ewald stayed behind with the other kids, who had just bathed and were in pajamas.

Miller first drove to the restaurant to see if Bruce had picked up the food. Using Ewald's cell phone, Miller called her in a panic. Bruce hadn't picked up the food.

"I kept trying to calm her down," Ewald later told police. "I said that it was going to be okay."

Miller told Ewald she would drive to the junkyard to see if Bruce had broken down along the way. Miller's son noticed that Mom was panicked, and he began to cry, too. When Miller got to the junkyard, she saw that the swinging gate blocking the long driveway was closed.

She didn't get out to check if the rusty chain holding the temperamental gate was locked. Neither did she just climb the short fence and walk to the office building.

Miller then retraced the likely route Bruce would have taken from the yard to the restaurant to their home.

Miller was hysterical when she returned, telling Ewald the gate was locked.

"What do I do?" she asked Ewald. "What do I do?"

Ewald suggested they call the police to see if there had been an accident in the area.

But a call to the state police turned up nothing.

"They won't help me," Miller bawled. "What am I going to do?"

Miller began to pace the house, crying, "Something's wrong!"

She called Chuck Miller again, about 8:51 P.M.

Her second call was more alarming than her first, but Judy Miller wasn't yet worried. "I told Chuck to have Sharee call Bruce's third wife," she said.

Judy Miller was irritated with Sharee for shortchanging her on baby-sitting money. She knew that Bruce was friendly with all his ex-wives and would do anything to help them. Judy also knew that it hacked off Sharee that Bruce would do things for those other women.

But now Sharee was really crying. Judy and Chuck Miller decided to help look for Bruce.

"Now she's got me worried," Judy Miller remembered thinking.

To appease Sharee, Chuck said he would drive to the yard. Maybe a car had fallen on Bruce, he told her.

After stopping at Sharee's home to get the junkyard keys, Chuck and Judy opened the gate and approached the building. They immediately knew something was wrong. Bruce's truck was parked nearby. At the shop building, they found the office door unlocked.

After yelling out Bruce's name and getting no answer, they entered the office.

There they found Bruce lying facedown on the floor, a pool of blood surrounding his neck.

Chuck Miller approached his brother and touched his back. He felt ice cold.

"Oh, fuck, he's dead," Chuck blurted out.

As Chuck Miller called his mother on one telephone, Judy called 911 on another.

Her voice trembling with hysteria, Judy Miller told the dispatcher she needed police and an ambulance at B&D Auto Salvage and gave authorities their first account of the crime scene.

"My brother-in-law owns it and he hasn't come home in two hours and he's lying on the floor," Miller said. "And there's blood."

Bruce Miller, she said, was cold and stiff. The dispatcher immediately tried to establish whether foul play was involved: "OK, does it look like there was a robbery or anything?"

"It's hard to say," Judy Miller replied. "It looks like he was maybe sitting in the chair and that's tipped over and he's lying beside it."

The dispatcher asked if she'd like to try to revive Bruce with CPR, but Judy said that wouldn't help.

"He's not moving," she said, soon collapsing into sobs.

"Why don't you guys go in another room so you're not standing there looking at him," the dispatcher said, suggesting that they not touch anything in the room.

Under questioning by the dispatcher, Judy Miller gave authorities Sharee's version of events.

"About 6:20 P.M., he talked to his wife . . . and he was supposed to pick up food," Judy Miller said. "They had ordered takeout."

But even as police approached the junkyard, it never was clear to Judy Miller that her brother-in-law had been shot. For some time, she believed he may have just been struck in the head. Finally, after minutes of speaking on the telephone with the dispatcher Judy seemed to understand that Bruce Miller's death didn't lend itself to easy answers.

"I'm not even sure if he was hit in the head," Judy told

the dispatcher. "All I know is that there is blood by his head . . . there's blood pooling underneath him too."

After hearing from Chuck, Ruth Miller soon was on the phone to Sharee.

"There's been an accident," she told Sharee Miller. "Bruce was found on the floor. We don't know if it's a heart attack."

Ruth Miller told Sharee that they believed Bruce might have had a head injury because of the blood on the floor around him.

"She just went crazy," Ewald said later.

Miller quickly called several other people to her home, including her mother, stepfather and a few others. Miller's stepfather, Bob Adair, dropped off Miller's mother and then went to the junkyard.

Miller was trying to break free of the house and drive up to the junkyard, but the people at the house prevented her, telling her to just sit tight for a while.

"No, no, no," Miller cried when she saw police drive up to her door.

Ewald said Miller told her that Bruce had been complaining recently about back pains.

"We really thought he'd had a heart attack," Ewald said. "She was a basket case, lying on the floor, rocking and bawling."

Sweating, shivering and shocked, his thoughts filled with the murder of Bruce Miller, Cassaday raced back to Missouri to meet his self-imposed deadline of Tuesday at 6:00 P.M.

Careful not to break the speed limit, he drove and drove, through Michigan, Indiana and Illinois.

He replayed the terrifying events of the last few hours,

and still he must have wondered how a good ex-cop could kill so easily. He kept going back to Sharee, how much he loved her, how they would try to live for the rest of their lives without sharing the awful secret.

Perhaps her e-mail of September 23, 1999, rang in his head.

"Understand that I really do not want him to die," Miller wrote back then. "Yes, it would make things less complicated, but that is not what I want."

They'd come a long way since that e-mail.

The drive straight through to Missouri was exhausting—and long enough for him to replay how he had gone from boozy casino-pit boss to killer-for-love in four months.

Cassaday pulled into the driveway of his home in Odessa, Missouri, November 9, about midafternoon, traveling lighter than the day before.

Gone were the shotgun he used to kill Bruce Miller and the cell phone he used to notify Sharee. An ex-cop knew that evidence could not be saved like a morbid souvenir.

He called Mike and told him he was home.

Mike demanded to know what Cassaday had been up to.

"So what's this all about?" Mike asked.

"Mike," Cassaday replied, "you don't want to know. You *really* don't want to know."

Mike hadn't bought the story about a trip to the family's lake cabin and pressed him again for an answer.

"There's nothing so bad that it can't be undone," Mike responded.

"Yes, there are some things that can't be taken back or undone," Cassaday replied. "Leave it alone. You don't want to know what's going on."

In the next few hours and over the next few days, Jerry Cassaday ached to talk with Sharee Miller.

But he knew it wasn't the time. The police investigation and the funeral would take center stage. Phone calls from a gentleman caller halfway across the country could draw unnecessary attention to a grieving widow whose husband had just been killed.

Best to put this on ice for a while.

ELEVEN

In separate patrol cars parked on the dirt drive outside B&D, police questioned Chuck and Judy Miller for almost two hours. After detectives concluded they had nothing to do with the grisly scene in the office, police released the Millers, allowing them to drive the five miles to Bruce Miller's home on North Francis Road.

Laura Ewald, Sharee's family and Bruce's mother all were there to comfort Miller, who had spent the evening sobbing after calling everywhere for Bruce—the city police, the state police, friends, hospitals, Bruce's mother. The scene was so grim that Chuck Miller stopped before walking in and asked a friend to go get a case of beer.

Word already had filtered back from the salvage yard that Bruce was dead and Sharee Miller cried hysterically on the floor of the living room. Her stepfather and a county deputy arrived in a Chevy Suburban about 10:00 P.M. to confirm Bruce's death, but they could add few details.

"No, no, no," Sharee cried, collapsing on the floor and clutching a pair of her husband's pants to her chest.

"What did his face look like?" she asked bewildered onlookers. "I want Bruce back!"

After midnight, Sergeant Ives Potrafka of the Genesee County Sheriff's Department arrived and took Sharee alone to a back bedroom, where he gave her the official notification: her husband had been killed by a shotgun fired at close range.

Out front, friends and family heard Sharee shriek with anguish. She soon returned to her friends to sob the night away. While Ewald and her niece, Jennifer, made plans to spend the week, Miller began to rock almost uncontrollably, back and forth, as she sat on the floor of the living room.

But Miller's plan was on track, despite the glitch of not having an alibi witness with her at the moment her husband was shot. In a chat session two months before, she'd played through this moment with Cassaday.

"So if I am asked a question, I just continue to say, 'I don't know. I loved him so much. Who would do something like this,' and cry and cry?"

The murder of Bruce Miller, the forty-eight-year-old father of two grown children and a relative newlywed, unsettled the working-class suburbs north of Flint, where violent, random homicide was far rarer than in nearby Flint.

Other salvage yard owners wondered whether Bruce Miller's killer had been in their shops the day before to buy secondhand auto parts.

"We've got the same people coming through," Greg Hetzer, a nearby auto parts business owner, told a reporter from the *Flint Journal* the day after the murder.

Hetzer said Miller was an easygoing family man but may have gotten into an argument with the wrong irate customer. The salvage yard business can be tough, Hetzer observed.

Miller's neighbors also wondered if their solid, blue-collar neighborhood was still safe.

"What's this world coming to?" a neighbor told a *Journal*

reporter. "He was a nice guy. I've known Bruce for years. I'm terribly sorry for his family."

Norm Rolison, an employee of a rock-crushing business near B&D, said Miller was a likable guy, a joker with a good sense of humor.

"He was always a kidder," Rolison said, adding that the murder hit way too close to home. "You're not safe anywhere anymore."

Bruce's cousin Larry McClain remembered the good times he and Bruce shared as children, riding their bikes in the rural areas of the township.

"We used to get ourselves into a little bit of trouble once in a while," he said. "But that's common for that age."

Tom Yost, the mayor of nearby Clio and another of Bruce Miller's cousins, recalled playing with McClain and Miller when they were young, sledding at a local hill called "Grandma's farm." The murder blotted Yost's memory with the question of who had killed Bruce Miller, and why.

The day after the murder, Sharee Miller headed for a second interview with Potrafka at the sheriff's department detective bureau, a warren of cubicles on the first floor of the modern county jail in downtown Flint.

Without the hysterics of the previous night, Miller recounted her movements on the day of the murder. She also pointedly told Potrafka that her husband had at least $2,000 in his pocket when he was killed—a $1,500 cash-installment payment for the business and $500 for an insurance bill.

She also came prepared with a list of possible suspects. An ex-husband had been stalking her and wanted to regain custody of one of her children, she said. Two men also had come in the office at the salvage yard the day before and had begun hitting on her.

"They commented on my wedding ring and said I was too pretty to be working there," Miller said.

The men hit the road, however, when she picked up the phone and pretended to call the police. They left in a rusty van, Miller said, though she didn't get a license plate number.

Potrafka appreciated the new suspects, but already he had a likely candidate: John Joel Hutchinson, a former salvage yard employee whom Bruce had laid off when he bought the business.

Hutchinson, a fixture in the Genesee County auto salvage business, once had been romantically involved with Sharee Miller during a brief period a couple of years before when he was temporarily estranged from his wife. After Sharee had come to work at the salvage yard and become involved with Bruce, Hutchinson gave her a wide berth at the insistence of his wife, who had since returned home.

During Miller's teary interview with Potrafka the night before, she had mentioned that Hutchinson had owed her husband $2,000. Debt, Potrafka knew, could be a powerful motive.

Potrafka had a good feeling about Hutchinson because he already was on the sheriff's department radar screen. Hutchinson was the prime suspect in a long-standing auto fraud investigation.

The scam was simple: Use parts from several junk cars to make one serviceable vehicle. Then switch the metal plates bearing the car's vehicle identification number— or VIN—from a once-expensive junked vehicle onto the rebuilt car to get a legal title.

Thus, a buyer might think from the VIN that he was buying a 1995 Trans Am, when in fact he was buying a wrecked and rebuilt 1993 model. The scheme was more common in the automobile salvage business than consumers might have expected.

Police suspected that Hutchinson was using Bruce Miller's salvage yard license to buy cars at auction to use in a VIN-switching scheme. The previous day, fraud investigators had paid their first visit to B&D to interview Bruce Miller about Hutchinson, but Miller hadn't yet reported to work at the yard.

Murder investigators also had spoken with Hutchinson's brother that morning. Harold Hutchinson, a current employee of the salvage yard, said his brother had told him weeks before that he planned to kill Bruce Miller over the VIN-switching investigation. And John Hutchinson had boasted the morning after Miller's death that he had "disposed" of his problems at B&D, Harold told deputies.

Investigators speculated that John Hutchinson might have killed Bruce Miller to wipe out the $2,000 debt and prevent him from cooperating in the VIN-switching probe. Harold Hutchinson, however, would be a problematic witness against his brother, investigators knew. Illiterate and mildly retarded, Harold was easily led and eager to tell investigators what they wanted to hear. The case against John Hutchinson would need either a confession or strong physical or circumstantial evidence.

Potrafka quickly dispatched a squad of detectives to find John Joel Hutchinson.

The home of John Hutchinson was that of a man who loved cars his entire life. The modest one-story house, located north of Flint, was cluttered with everything automotive. Die-cast toy cars, pristine in their original boxes, dominated the decorating scheme. NASCAR logos, stickers and posters covered the walls, making the living room look more like a garage.

Resembling actor Ed Harris, Hutchinson had grown up in the tiny Flint-area town of Otisville and attended high school in Millington, not far away. After moving to Arkansas for fourteen years, the family trudged back to mid-Michigan in 1987. Hutchinson soon drifted to his roots—mangled cars, cheap auto parts and wrenching on wrecks to make a buck.

"Cars, all my life," he once drawled to a visitor in a slow, easy voice that another man might use to describe his first girlfriend. "I like working on them and building and rebuilding wrecks."

Hutchinson met Bruce Miller in the mid-1990s, and worked for him from late 1996 through 1998, until Bruce and Sharee bought B&D Auto Parts from Bruce's former business partner.

He had a chance to buy half the business earlier, for $25,000, but turned it down, saying Bruce wanted it more as a hobby than a vocation.

While Sharee did the books at the junkyard, Hutchinson and Bruce continued their friendship.

"Bruce and me were friends," he said. "We'd buy cars together and just go do little stupid stuff."

But Sharee had changed Bruce.

"He became moody," Hutchinson said. "He wasn't happy-go-lucky like he was before. Too serious."

About midmorning on November 9, a friend told Hutchinson about Bruce Miller's murder and he immediately called Sharee, who confirmed it.

What's going on? he thought.

A junkyard groupie all his life, Hutchinson knew that shady people occasionally appeared to do business.

"There's always weird people showing up, and you don't trust nobody," he said.

His surprise grew when a group of deputies, led by Sergeant Kevin Shanlian, appeared to search his home, seize his shotguns for forensic testing and question him about the murder.

"Go ahead," he said. "I've got nothing to hide."

Hutchinson also agreed to go with Shanlian to the sheriff's department for a talk.

At 1:30 P.M. on November 9, Shanlian placed Hutchinson in an interview room at the sheriff's department and told him he was the primary suspect in the murder of Bruce Miller. Still, Hutchinson agreed to give a statement without an attorney.

He started with an outline of the previous day. Hutchinson said he had gone to work early, had come home about 5:00 P.M. and basically had stayed there.

After he got home, Hutchinson said he had his stepson, Anthony Birch, run over to the home of his brother to have Harold call him.

He acknowledged owing Bruce money but said Miller was always willing to lend and had done so in July 1999. But Hutchinson said he had been avoiding Bruce and B&D since then because he did not have $2,000 to pay him back.

Shanlian questioned Hutchinson about the VIN switching. At first, Hutchinson denied knowing anything about it, but soon he grew more agitated and admitted retagging vehicles and rolling back odometers.

Hutchinson also admitted stealing car parts from Bruce Miller over the past few years and said he had broken into B&D several times to steal.

Hutchinson acknowledged having three shotguns at his home but said he had not fired any of them for two years.

He also told Shanlian that he would not have killed Bruce for such a small amount of money. Shanlian, in turn, noted in his report that Hutchinson's denials "were not very strong." Hutchinson never got upset that he was suspected of killing Bruce, one of his best friends. He never raised his voice, either.

"He would just calmly say 'I did not shoot him,'" Shanlian wrote.

Backtracking through his notes, Shanlian returned to
the telephone conversation Hutchinson had with his
brother the evening before.

Hutchinson said they talked about Harold going up
north to his father's place to retrieve a pickup truck.
With Shanlian pressing, Hutchinson at first denied talking to Harold about the VIN-switching investigation.
However, when Hutchinson realized police already had
spoken to Harold, he admitted the brothers also discussed the fraud investigation.

But he denied ever telling Harold that he killed Bruce
or knew about his death. Hutchinson also admitted that
he once had an affair with Sharee, but it was over before
Bruce began seeing her.

Hutchinson then asked to take a lie detector test. The
request surprised Shanlian, who knew a polygraph examination could prove a valuable investigative tool. He
quickly left to call a local examiner.

When Shanlian returned to say the test was scheduled,
Hutchinson thanked him, then broke down and cried
for an hour.

The twenty-four-hour anniversary of Bruce Miller's
murder approached as Shanlian drove Hutchinson to
his polygraph examination at the police station in
nearby Burton, Michigan.

As Hutchinson waited, Shanlian settled on the questions with Detective Donald A. Elford of the Burton
Police Department, an experienced operator who performed thirty to sixty examinations in an average year.
Genesee County cops respected Elford's polygraph
work, but he'd always correct detectives when they came
around asking for a "lie detector" test.

"We call it a truth verifier," Elford said.

The test, he'd explain, recorded a person's emotional
changes as they answered a series of "yes" or "no" questions. The machine registered changes in the subject's

blood pressure, pulse and respiration, measuring the "fight or flight" response.

As Elford bustled in and out of the interview room preparing Hutchinson for the examination, Shanlian watched from behind a two-way mirror in an adjacent room and became a little puzzled. When Elford would leave the room, Hutchinson actually would go to sleep for a few minutes.

As Elford settled down for the business end of the examination, he suspected that Hutchinson would be anxious and assured him he wouldn't do anything to catch him off guard.

"There are no surprise questions," Elford said. He also told Hutchinson that in the real test, he would mix up the order of the questions.

To get reliable baseline readings, and to make certain Hutchinson was comfortable and familiar with the questions, Elford ran three preliminary tests.

The actual examination was over almost as quickly as it had begun.

Elford: Do you know for sure who murdered Bruce Miller?
Hutchinson: No.
Elford: Did you murder Bruce Miller?
Hutchinson: No.
Elford: Did you have someone murder Bruce Miller?
Hutchinson: No.
Elford: Right now, can you take me to the gun used to murder Bruce Miller?
Hutchinson: No.

Hutchinson relaxed immediately, appearing relieved and happy the test was over. Shanlian, meanwhile, recorded his observations of the examination. When asked questions about Bruce Miller's murder, Hutchinson answered "no" but nodded his head "yes," Shanlian noted. And Hutchinson's "mouth was so dry you could actually hear him licking his lips," Shanlian wrote.

Hutchinson's mood changed quickly when Elford told him he had failed the test. Elford left the room quickly, but Shanlian continued to watch from behind the mirror.

Alone with the machine, Hutchinson repeated each of the questions. Answering each in turn, Hutchinson then turned to glare at the polygraph machine.

When Elford returned, Hutchinson said he must have failed because he was under a lot of pressure, feeling stressed, was having a hard time paying bills and was worried about facing the holidays without money.

Hutchinson continued to deny killing Miller after the examination, but Shanlian wrote that his denials again sounded soft and weak. Before returning home, Hutchinson accepted an offer to take the test again.

Debbie Hutchinson was dismayed at her husband's haggard appearance when he returned from more than twelve hours of interrogation late that night. To calm his hysteria, she gave him sedatives to sleep.

About 8:30 A.M. on November 12, Hutchinson returned to Burton for a second go-round with the polygraph machine, this time with a lawyer.

Shanlian watched quietly, noticing this time that Hutchinson seemed to be burping a lot. Hutchinson's lips again seemed extremely dry, and he kept nodding "yes" while answering "no."

When the test was over this time, Hutchinson looked at the polygraph machine and said, "Oh, fuck."

Indeed, Elford concluded that Hutchinson had "not told the entire truth to pertinent test questions."

Hutchinson followed the test with more denials that he had killed Bruce Miller. Others—he didn't say who—also may have had a motive to kill Miller. Indeed, Hutchinson said, he may have told somebody Bruce

Miller would regularly carry large sums of cash in his shirt pocket.

Hutchinson again came apart at the seams after he returned home.

"I'm a nervous . . . wreck," he told his wife. "I'd be better off dead than going through this."

Publicly, deputies said little about Bruce Miller's murder, releasing few details other than that robbery appeared to be a motive and money was missing.

With leads but no arrests, newly elected Genesee County sheriff Robert J. Pickell announced to reporters that his officers wanted to question a sixty-six-year-old transient known to hang out at the salvage yard. But the man was considered a possible witness, not a suspect, Pickell added.

He also noted that a suspect had been identified, located and questioned, but not charged.

Finally, Potrafka appealed to the media for help. He asked anybody who had information to please pass it along.

More than seven hundred miles to the southwest, Jerry Cassaday sat in his basement apartment and scoured the *Flint Journal*'s Web site, looking for the few public details of the investigation. But most of the articles focused on Miller's friends and background. None of the coverage highlighted, or even suggested, that Miller had a penchant for personal violence and was linked to organized crime, money laundering and counterfeiting.

It was like the community wanted to see only one side of Bruce Miller.

Sharee Miller remained inconsolable, sitting for days, crying and looking off into space. Laura Ewald remained with her for almost a week and offered to help get Bruce's affairs in order.

Digging through a bedroom drawer for insurance papers, Ewald found sex toys and several hard-core pornographic videos. Miller quickly stuffed the videos in a trash bag and asked Ewald to put them out for the next garbage pickup.

To get Sharee out of the house, Chuck and Judy Miller invited her to the funeral home to pick out the casket for her husband. She again began weeping uncontrollably.

"I don't want to be here," Sharee Miller said.

Chuck shook his head as she waited outside.

"She wouldn't even go in to look," Chuck Miller said to his wife.

Judy returned her husband's look. Both had known grief recently—each had buried their fathers in the last two years—but Sharee seemed to be spinning out of control.

"She's young," Judy Miller said.

Later, Chuck Miller called Potrafka for an update on the investigation and mentioned the upcoming funeral services. That brought a rise out of the detective.

"Whoever did this will be at the funeral," Potrafka predicted.

Chuck Miller fidgeted as the minutes counted down to the end of Bruce Miller's visitation on Friday, November 12.

Visitation had been a two-day ordeal, Miller thought, but it seemed to have had its intended effect on his sister-in-law. With hundreds of friends, family and fellow General Motors workers stopping by to pay their respects, Sharee Miller had been touched by others who loved Bruce and also were grieving. She had her bad moments during the visitation, but she seemed calmer in general and more prepared to accept Bruce's tragic passing.

Just when he was hoping it would all end quietly, Chuck Miller spotted possible trouble. John Hutchinson had slipped in with his wife, Debbie, to pay their respects.

While Sharee Miller greeted other visitors across the room, Hutchinson shook Chuck Miller's hand and slumped against a wall, his eyes full of tears.

"I can't believe they're saying I killed your brother," Hutchinson said.

Chuck Miller had heard that Hutchinson was on the suspect list but wasn't yet ready to judge him either way.

"I hope to hell you didn't have anything to do with my brother's death," Chuck Miller replied.

Hutchinson stopped by the casket for a moment, then stood beside Sharee Miller and put his arm around her shoulder.

"I'm so sorry," he told Miller, who didn't respond.

Hutchinson had turned to speak with other visitors, when all heads whipped in Sharee Miller's direction.

"Mommy, Mommy, Daddy, Daddy," she shrieked. "Get him out of here! He's the one who killed my husband!"

Miller's stepfather quietly asked Hutchinson to leave, while Chuck Miller guided him down a nearby stairway to the funeral home's basement. Hutchinson also was distraught.

"There is no way," he said. "Me and your brother were best friends."

Chuck Miller was sympathetic but firm.

"John, I'm not blaming you for this, but we've spent three days getting Sharee calmed down," Chuck said. "You will have to leave."

Hutchinson tearfully complied. Later, Sharee sidled up to comfort her brother-in-law, and perhaps make amends for the outburst.

"I'm so sorry you were the one who found him," she said.

The next day's funeral was somber and made even more austere when a musician engaged for the service failed to appear. Bruce Miller was dressed in his black Dale Earnhardt jacket, which Sharee had bought for him. A discreet turtleneck shirt hid the worst of the shotgun's damage. Dried flowers and pictures of his grown children were with him in the casket. A toy replica of Earnhardt's car sat on the casket. One of Bruce's factory friends, a union committeeman, delivered the eulogy.

His casket was carried through the cemetery on the back of a flatbed car hauler, a fitting last ride for a man whose life centered on a salvage yard.

At his grave, Bob Adair, Sharee Miller's stepfather, sent Bruce Miller to eternity with a rousing "Gentlemen, start your engines!"

Afterward, family and friends gathered for a wake. Sharee Miller finally seemed to be holding up pretty well, they concluded. She'd been a correct widow throughout, crying at the appropriate moments and showing proper sorrow.

But why, they wondered, had she avoided looking at her husband's casket throughout the service?

The funeral was not the only family ritual to celebrate Bruce Miller's life that month. A couple of weeks after the funeral, the daughter of one of Bruce's ex-wives was wed. Bruce Miller had remained friendly with both mother and daughter, despite the divorce, and had planned to give away his former stepdaughter at the ceremony.

To honor Bruce Miller at the wedding, the bride stitched a small black Dale Earnhardt patch to the train of her gown. And she inscribed the guest registry at the back of the church, "In memory of Bruce."

* * *

In truth, Sharee Miller bounced back pretty quickly. A week after the funeral, Sharee asked Chuck and Judy Miller to watch her kids for a weekend. She told them she'd rented a room at the nearby Otisville Hotel, a local roadhouse, and had planned a first-class bender.

"I'm going to get drunk," Miller said. "I've got me a room and I'm not going to drive home. I'm going to have a good time."

She also said she'd been to the cemetery recently in the middle of a rainy night, trying to find Bruce's grave with her cousin. She told them she had been drunk and crawling around on the ground.

"That's, like, a grieving thing," Sharee Miller said.

Judy Miller didn't buy it, however.

I'm grieving more than she is, Judy Miller thought as Sharee pulled out of the driveway, heading for Otisville.

Others at this time found Sharee Miller genuinely distraught and grieving. When word of her loss filtered back to Harrah's in Reno, Carol Slaughter called her Michigan friend to offer some comfort. The conversation was emotional.

"I can't even believe I'm thinking this," Miller blurted. "I mean I just don't even want to say it."

"Just tell me," Slaughter replied.

"I thought that Jerry could have been the one that did it," Miller said. "I just felt so horrible even thinking that thought."

"He's a lot of things," Slaughter said, "but he's not a murderer."

Sharee replied: "Oh, no, no, I know that for a fact. I told the police, gave them Jerry Cassaday's name. They went up to Missouri and cleared him. He was not in the picture as far as the murder went at all."

* * *

The forensics report was firm and unequivocal: The shotguns taken from John Hutchinson's home could not have been used to kill Bruce Miller. Sergeant Ives Potrafka's hope for an early resolution to the case was looking more and more remote. The crime scene itself also had come up completely clean of evidence. There was just nothing there that pointed to *anybody* as the killer.

Could anybody else have had a financial motive to kill Bruce Miller?

At Potrafka's behest, Miller lugged insurance and financial paperwork to the sheriff's department, but even a cursory review showed she had little real money to gain. A large portion of the estate would go either to Bruce Miller's mother or his grown children by a previous marriage. And because Bruce Miller died without a will, a probate court would have to sort out most of his estate.

When it came to liquidating the assets, Sharee Miller's grief turned quickly to resolve. She made a deal with Bruce Miller's grown kids. Sharee Miller got the salvage yard, while they received a $78,000 General Motors insurance policy.

But others in the family found the money hustling offensive. It reminded them of how Sharee Miller had once needled her husband about upgrading his insurance policy.

Life was blurring a bit for Sharee in the aftermath of her husband's death. Just after the murder, she resumed using marijuana, then piled on the alcohol, each day consuming up to nine glasses of rum and Coke, nine Bud Lights or two bottles of Asti Spumante.

Miller spent much of her time in the evening at a bowling alley in the Flint suburb of Clio, not far from her home. Jeff Foster, a young man about Sharee's age, ran the business's karaoke show.

One evening, Miller impressed Foster with her karaoke

singing. Later at home, Miller heard a knock at her door and found Foster standing outside.

"We partied the rest of the night," Miller would remember later. "It's okay to grieve like that."

Karaoke was just a sideline for Foster, however. During the day, he sold frozen food and ice cream for the Schwan's food service, delivering ice cream and other refrigerated items to homes and businesses. He'd first met Sharee Miller when he made sales calls at the salvage yard. After the murder, Miller asked him to start delivering groceries to her home.

Foster was ending a difficult relationship of his own and found that Miller had a good shoulder to cry on. Miller was happy to help.

"We talked for hours about our pain," Sharee Miller wrote at the time. "Then we began to laugh together."

Later, Miller would say that drinking with Foster gave her a way to forget the pain that was easier than the method her family suggested.

"My family wanted me to read the Bible, and that was hard," Miller said. "In a way, I was using [Foster] as comfort."

The Millers first heard of Foster several weeks after the murder. Foster soon became a fixture at Sharee Miller's home. For a while, Chuck Miller was there every day, doing drywall construction work that Sharee had requested. And there, without fail, sat Jeff Foster at the computer.

Chuck Miller, who never spoke with Foster, once asked Sharee what Jeff was up to.

"Doing the cybersex thing on the computer," Sharee replied.

Miller explained her frequent evenings at the bowling alley by saying she needed to get out of the house. Someone was calling at odd hours and hanging up. She said she believed her husband's killer was now after her.

She was right, in a sense.

Once glancing at Sharee Miller's caller ID, Chuck Miller noticed a steady stream of telephone numbers from the 816 area code in western Missouri.

"I get those all the time," she replied breezily, dismissing his question. "I think they're just wrong numbers."

Okay, Chuck Miller thought, but what about that call that Bruce's stepdaughter received at Sharee Miller's home not long after the murder?

A man had called asking for "Yankee babe."

Biding his time in Odessa, Missouri, Cassaday was growing impatient with the pace of his relationship with Sharee Miller. Bruce was dead and buried, and deputies were publicly leaning toward robbery as the motive for the murder, thus letting Sharee off the hook. He and Sharee should get down to planning their lives together, Jerry concluded.

Slowly and furtively, the two began to exchange e-mail messages. Finally, on November 30, only three weeks after Bruce's murder, they shared a long phone conversation in which Cassaday again expressed his boundless love.

The next morning, Miller phoned Cassaday with a wake-up call so he could get to a doctor's appointment on time. He followed up with an e-mail that stated how her voice started his day with a smile.

He told Sharee he would call her after the appointment and tell her what the doctor said. Sensing she still had the jitters about Bruce's murder, he touched on the topic indirectly, couching it with assurances of unconditional love.

"Our love can endure anything," Cassaday wrote. "It has so far, and we've been through a lot."

On December 2, he wrote to Miller that he was

disappointed that he was unable to talk to her on the telephone the night before.

"I tried to call, no answer," he wrote. "I miss you."

Cassaday dealt with his anxiety by deciding to make a bold move. Acting on impulse in early December, Cassaday drove to Flint. He retraced the murder route—this time not for homicide, but for romantic commitment. As they shared a night in a motel not far from her home, Cassaday proposed marriage and Miller accepted.

"I was so happy you said 'YES,'" Cassaday wrote after returning to Odessa the next day. "I knew in my heart as I watched you that you will be so happy, so free, so much in love everyday."

Cassaday's missive also had a darker undertone. He must have wondered why she had steered him away from her home, which he had seen before. And bubbling to the surface were his own worries about why he had killed Bruce Miller, and for whom.

Cassaday had been frightened lately. But the night before, he had feared nothing. He had watched Miller sleep, and again he imagined her as his angel. She seemed so at peace, and that had settled his nerves.

But had Cassaday already seen things that caused him to doubt Miller's commitment, or question whether she had always told him the truth?

Instead of the house of a rich widow, Sharee Miller lived in a simple middle-class home. Certainly not the picture of wealth she had painted, nor what Cassaday had envisioned.

And didn't she say Bruce had raped her on the pool deck, causing her first miscarriage?

This pool was not nestled in a tree-studded backyard, hidden in privacy.

It was an inexpensive aboveground pool, sitting almost next to the house in view of the street. How many

motorists may have seen Bruce rape Sharee? Did her
screams disturb neighbors, who were just a few dozen
feet away?

Aspects of Cassaday's visit also troubled Miller. Her response to Cassaday's assurances of love was unsettled.

"I know I haven't [written] for some time now," she
messaged on December 5. "I am depressed today about
several things."

She'd been happy he visited, even for just a night. But
she was disturbed about another money discussion they
had at the motel, and it depressed her. Cassaday had
again pressed her for money and a car.

Then Miller went silent, ignoring her telephone and
turning off her new cell phone. Cassaday was concerned,
but first he responded with jokes.

"Did you give up on me?" he asked. "Got all horny and
had to go out again?"

Days later, he was desperate.

"Where are you?" he begged in a short note.

At her Texas home, Charlene Cassaday also couldn't
get Sharee off her mind. She remembered an e-mail in
which Sharee introduced herself saying, "Let's get acquainted because I'm gonna be with Jerry forever."

Though Charlene had wondered why a woman would
get involved with a man with as many personal problems
as her son, she decided to make a nod in Miller's direction for Jerry's sake.

Charlene Cassaday framed a photo taken of Jerry at
the wedding of his oldest adopted son just a few months
before. It showed Jerry, handsome in a black tuxedo,
standing next to a mirror. Charlene mailed the photo to
Sharee. "Thank you for loving our son," she wrote on the
accompanying Christmas card.

It's a goodwill gesture, she thought.

* * *

Sharee Miller had gone silent, not responding to phone calls or e-mails. And Jerry Cassaday knew that when Sharee went quiet, it always meant bad news was coming soon. After Bruce's taunting notes back in early November, Jerry had gone into full investigator mode, frantically combing the AOL chat rooms and calling friends and hospitals. Then he had learned that Sharee had been beaten and gang-raped by Bruce and his thugs.

This time, though, his research turned up something far more disturbing, if that was possible: the woman who had agreed to marry him just days before had a new boyfriend camped in her bedroom, which explained why she was so eager to keep him away from her home during his visit in the first week of December.

That always was the threat, even when Bruce was alive. And how she would throw the trust issue back in his face.

"I would rather not have you telling me how scared you are I am going to fuck someone else," Sharee had written back in August.

Well, it looks like my worries are correct, Jerry must have thought.

She had taken up this time with Jeff Foster, her Schwan's ice cream deliveryman.

Just a few days after returning from Flint, Cassaday called his mother in Texas and begged her to let him charge an airline ticket on her credit card.

"Things are broken off with Sharee," he said. "I don't know what's wrong. Mom, I have to go to Michigan. I have to know what's going on."

"Okay, fine," Charlene Cassaday said, relenting. "We'll let you charge an airline ticket. But, Jerry, I've got to have the money back. I can't afford this."

"Mom, you will have it," her son responded.

"Who's paying for it, you or Sharee?"

"It doesn't matter," Cassaday responded. "It's one and the same."

Cassaday quickly checked flight schedules out of Kansas City International Airport and ordered a ticket for Detroit that afternoon.

Then, enraged and pitiful, Cassaday sat in the big recliner that dominated his basement apartment in Odessa, fired up AOL and rapped out a passionate ultimatum.

"This is very important," he wrote in the subject field of the e-mail program. "I wouldn't ignore it if I were you."

Cassaday told her that her reluctance to communicate was pushing him over the edge of sanity, realizing his worst fears. Cassaday had dedicated his life to her. They had opened their hearts to each other, and she had accepted his proposal of marriage. But now she ignored him and was cheating on him.

"I am taking control of my life one last time," Cassaday wrote.

He told Sharee that he was flying to Detroit and had reserved a rental car for the hour-long drive to Flint, but he pleaded with her to meet him at the gate. Where they went from there was up to her, but they needed to make a decision about their lives.

If she didn't meet him at the airport, Jerry wrote, he would choose one of three options: find a hotel, drive to her home or "get back on the plane and never look back."

Instead of hitting the Send key, Jerry configured his AOL software to send the message after he already was in the air. That would forestall the inevitable call from Sharee, begging him not to come.

He chucked some clothes in a bag and headed for Kansas City International Airport. By the time he emerged from the Jetway at Detroit Metro Airport, he would know just what Sharee Miller was willing to do for him.

Hours later—angry, but still nursing hope—Jerry arrived in Detroit.

No Sharee.

Though he earlier had threatened to return to Missouri immediately if she wasn't there, he knew that wasn't an option. He and Sharee always had worked things out before.

From a pay phone, Jerry called Miller, who sounded annoyed. The visit was "bad timing," she said, and she scolded him for not waiting a week.

But Jerry wouldn't be put off. After picking up the rental car, he detoured to a liquor store.

The knock came at about midnight while Sharee was at the computer, alone and on-line. At the front door, she found Cassaday with a case of beer under his arm—minus the few in his belly—and babbling about "getting married that night," she remembered later.

She refused to drop everything and get married, but didn't argue when Jerry suggested they go to bed and patch things up with sex. It had worked before.

After some awkward foreplay in bed, Sharee spurned Jerry's sloppy advances.

"I have never made love in that bed with anyone but Jeff," she said. "I am sorry because I thought I would be able to."

With the proof of her infidelity before him, Jerry called her a whore. Then his mind cleared. If he couldn't have Sharee, he could at least have some of her money.

For emphasis, Cassaday heaved the suitcase across the room and demanded cash, or at least some of the counterfeit that Bruce had made. Bruce's criminal wealth was now hers, and didn't Jerry deserve his share? His financial burdens had become crushing, he was out of work and more than $14,000 in debt. His truck soon would be repossessed and the woman he loved—the woman for whom he had killed—had to help, at least as much as he had helped her on November 8.

Miller resisted. Over and over, she had tried to explain it: my finances are not as simple, or as liquid, as you think. But Jerry Cassaday knew simple, too.

Simple as blackmail.

In a safe place, far, far away, sits a briefcase, Cassaday explained. Inside are your photographs, e-mails and IMs—the kind of material that cops in Genesee County could take a keen interest in.

Miller's mind raced. She desperately needed to be alone and Cassaday was just getting hotter.

"I made him leave," Miller later recalled. "He was really angry. He called me a whore. He said he was sick of me."

As Cassaday pulled the rental car out of her driveway and lurched back toward Detroit, Miller realized that he had raised the stakes.

He actually has saved *all that stuff,* she thought. *This could be real trouble.*

When Cassaday arrived back in Missouri, two days early, he again called his mother.

"I didn't feel welcome. I wasn't wanted. I left," he said.

Charlene Cassaday ached for her son, who was in genuine anguish about poor decisions he had made in his life.

"Mom, I've done things that I would never have thought I would do, and it's something—"

"Son," Charlene Cassaday interrupted, "there's never anything that can't have a way out."

Her son would not be consoled.

"Mom, I don't know, and I don't see a way out."

Charlene Cassaday thought Jerry was talking about his failed marriage to Barb.

Sharee Miller composed a conciliatory e-mail almost before the wheels of Cassaday's plane lifted off from Detroit Metro. In it, she tried to soothe him and keep him quiet.

She started off light and warm, describing a birthday card she had received from his mother. The accompanying photograph of Cassaday had touched her heart.

But in an instant, Sharee got down to the business of figuring this thing out and explaining her own behavior. She apologized to Jerry for not being able to make love to him after he appeared. Then she appeared to agonize quietly over the subject they had argued about so loudly the night before. For the first time in her life, she had been unfaithful to a man she loved, Sharee Miller wrote.

"Now I guess I can label myself as a cheater," Miller wrote. "I did not know I could do something so horrible."

As she had before, Sharee encouraged Jerry to be angry with her. Miller said she had hurt him badly, and surely, she wrote, there was no way he ever could trust her again. Still, it was her own fault, she admitted.

The admission was difficult, but she said Jerry had taught her the value of complete honesty in the relationship. She had learned not to keep secrets from Cassaday, and because of that she knew she had to admit her infidelity.

But Cassaday's demand for cash had scared her. He had offered her a bargain: give me money and I'll leave you alone. He was dead serious.

She offered him $3,000.

Not much really. But blood money doesn't always amount to a lot.

The e-mail and the promise of cash worked. Even though Jerry Cassaday had killed for Sharee, even though Sharee had cheated on him and lied to him, he couldn't resist her.

Jerry sent Sharee a few short e-mails telling her he still loved her. But he promised to quit calling.

Cassaday also e-mailed Miller his address, just to make

certain she understood his seriousness, and settled in to wait for the money.

He never would see it.

Though Miller was reluctant to spend money on Cassaday, she didn't hesitate to lavish it on herself. She was ridding her home of all things "Bruce" and replacing just about everything. In a two-week shopping spree, she bought new furniture for her bedroom, refurbished the kitchen counters, laid new carpet, replaced the living-room furniture and drapes, installed a new furnace and purchased a one-carat man's diamond ring, all at a cost of more than $23,000.

Miller kept one chair that belonged to Bruce, but only because his mother insisted she keep it. She even gave her friends seven or eight cars from the junkyard.

Chuck's take from his brother's estate amounted to a set of tools, which he would see every day as he walked through his garage.

With a depression-soaked holiday season in full swing, Jerry mounted a well-worn plea to Sharee on December 15, 1999.

"I miss you terribly and am going crazy," he wrote. "I just want to hear from you."

Three days later, Miller opened her e-mail file to find a note labeled "please read this" in the subject field.

In it, Cassaday forwarded an e-mail that she had written to him on November 5, three days before he would kill for her and just after he made a quick trip to Michigan.

"I want you back," Sharee had written. "I think I am going to go to bed and dream sweet dreams of you and I together in Kansas City."

Miller had written then that she felt safe and loved

when they were together and warmly recalled their orgasms together.

For Cassaday—secure in Miller's love and believing Sharee was pregnant with his twins—it was the sunniest time of their months together.

For Sharee, the November 5 e-mail was just another reminder that Jerry had saved all that stuff.

A few days later, Cassaday called his mom, again torn by his own anguish and Miller's silence.

"I don't know what's going on," Jerry said. "She won't communicate. She won't answer my phone calls. She has changed her e-mail address."

Christmas 1999 also was subdued in the Chuck and Judy Miller household. For three consecutive years, the family had endured heavy losses. In 1997, Chuck and Bruce's father had died. In 1998, Judy's father passed away. And with the murder of Bruce just a month before, times were glum.

Sharee Miller stopped in with the children that day. Angela was ill, but she said she missed Bruce terribly.

Sharee said nothing about Bruce.

With Jerry pining more than seven hundred miles away, Sharee's holidays were going just fine. And on New Year's Eve, 1999, she and Jeff Foster prepared to celebrate a new century together.

Sharee once again enlisted Chuck and Judy Miller to watch the kids, though they were shocked when she dropped them off.

"She came down here looking like a whore," Chuck said later.

Her hair poofed up to perfection, and her face made up just right, Sharee wore a tight black leather miniskirt, black nylon hose and high heels. She topped off the slinky outfit with a black leather coat.

"I'm just going over to the Clio bowling alley," she announced.

Judy Miller avoided a scene but later told her sister-in-law that Bruce's family thought it was way too early for her to be involved with another man, particularly since Bruce had been in his grave for less than two months. Miller's response was typical Sharee.

"I just want to go out and fuck somebody," she said. She asked Judy Miller what she thought Bruce would think of her.

"He would not approve of it," Judy replied. "But if you have to go out, be discreet, even if you're looking for a new life."

And she offered Sharee Miller new batteries for her vibrator.

Detectives at the Genesee County Sheriff's Department plugged away at Bruce Miller's murder, but new leads were scarce.

Detectives Ives Potrafka and Kevin Shanlian, among others, knew that John Hutchinson had motive. He owed Bruce about $2,000 and had come up "inconclusive" on two polygraph examinations, but motive and inadmissible polygraph tests wouldn't make the case. Forensic tests of two shotguns taken from Hutchinson's home showed they couldn't have been the murder weapons.

On January 4, 2000, a weary John Hutchinson again trudged into the sheriff's department with his lawyer for yet another taped interview, this time with Ives Potrafka.

The two months since the murder had worn on Hutchinson. Once word got around that he was the prime suspect in Miller's death, the auto-rebuilding business that Hutchinson ran out of his home had shriveled to nothing. And old friends at the auto auctions would shy away from him as he looked for junkers to buy and fix up.

"Look like I have bio-jungle disease?" he'd ask as they eased away from him.

But Potrafka always had time for him.

Hutchinson settled into the familiar interview room as Potrafka began covering old ground. "What about the day of the murder?" "How were you going to repay your $2,000 debt to Bruce Miller?" And always, "What about the VIN switching?"

Potrafka figured the VIN switching was a good motive for murder. After all, Sharee Miller had said Bruce was steamed about the investigation and likely would have cooperated against Hutchinson.

"That's one good reason," Potrafka said. "[Two] thousand dollars in his pocket is another good reason."

"You're looking at the wrong person," Hutchinson replied.

"No, I don't think so," Potrafka answered, "but I've been wrong before in my life."

"You're wrong now," Hutchinson shot back.

Potrafka probed Hutchinson's affair with Sharee Miller.

"Oh, I fucked her one time," Hutchinson responded. "We slept together a couple times when me and my wife split up. Went out to eat at a motel. Played hooky."

Hutchinson said he Sharee were involved for only "two months."

"I don't know if you want to call it an affair, seeing each other," Hutchinson continued. "And I was seeing other girls."

Potrafka then laid out his cards for Hutchinson.

"I think you have a lot more knowledge than you're giving me," Potrafka said. "I think you are either directly involved or know a lot more than you're willing to give up. . . .

"At this point, this is your chance. If you know something, then you better be telling it now. Because once you walk out the door, attorney or no attorney, and I prove this, you're gonna get the maximum of the law. So if you know something, today is the day. I'm just like anybody else in this world. The harder I work, the less I give a care. You know what I mean?"

"I know what you mean," Hutchinson said.

Potrafka continued with the heavy hand.

"You are our number one suspect. There's no doubt about it and I don't think that's a surprise to you."

"It's a real surprise to me," Hutchinson cracked as the interview wound to its conclusion.

Finally away from the sheriff's department, Hutchinson began to feel the walls closing in around him. Potrafka was sounding more and more ominous and Hutchinson had nothing new to tell him. He needed to go someplace to chill for a while, anywhere. Hutchinson was under orders to remain in the area, but he wasn't yet under arrest.

Hutchinson made plans to scoot south, out of state, for just a few days to get his head straight. Debbie Hutchinson worried, though, about whether that was such a good idea.

"I just don't . . . care," Hutchinson replied.

By mid-January 2000, the world had become a colder but far clearer place for Jerry Cassaday. He hadn't written to Sharee in a month, but when he would call occasionally, she brushed him off.

"Well, you did it again," he wrote, beginning an e-mail to her on January 12.

But Cassaday shook off his frustration with the most recent phone call and moved to the letter's real purpose—a dispassionate review of the emotional toll of their affair.

They'd had a great time, loved each other and had incredible sex, he remembered. The sound of Miller's voice captivated him when she sang to him or told him that she loved him.

He had fallen for her, pledging his love to her months before, and he always had kept his promises. They had dreamed of buying a house or a horse ranch together, and, always, of jointly raising their kids. The promise of that life together had sustained him through some very dark moments, he wrote.

And it was from love that he'd tolerated her roller-coaster mood swings and catered to her every whim. When she begged for him to come, he'd driven to Michigan and stayed hidden to avoid Bruce, consequences be damned.

Jerry had positioned his life to fit Sharee's needs and wants, and all he ever wanted was her love. But she would dribble out the truth, little by little, proving to him that she couldn't be trusted.

He scolded Sharee for lying about money, how well off she was, her cash, her bank accounts, her stocks, her trust funds, her businesses, her homes, her insurance policies, her lawsuit settlements. He'd believed all that because they offered the hope of new life, love, happiness and a fresh start.

And the wound of her infidelity with Jeff still festered. So many times Miller had cooed that no one but Jerry ever would touch her again, and now he knew that wasn't true.

Now Cassaday had nothing.

No love, no money, no babies, no life with Sharee.

Just the deep guilt and shame that go with being duped into committing cold-blooded murder.

Cassaday acknowledged that he always had been her fool for life.

"I have always believed everything you have told me and taken it at face value, regardless of how strange it may have seemed at the time, or how it looks in retro-spect," he concluded. ". . . I am just to the point that I can look at things with a clear head and clear mind and reflect back over the last year of my life."

The note of finality was profoundly intentional and certainly prophetic.

Sharee Miller caused an epidemic of head scratching at the Genesee County Sheriff's Department with a visit she made in mid-January. She appeared unannounced at the detective bureau and confronted Potrafka and his boss, Captain Michael Compeau, demanding to know more about the investigation and scolding them for their lack of progress.

Questions and demands for arrests from the grieving families were not unusual or even unexpected, but stories about this grieving widow's boisterous life in Flint's northern suburbs already were circulating in the sheriff's department. Why was she so hot for them to arrest somebody? She barely remembered her late husband!

Detectives scheduled another interview with Miller for January 26, 2000. During it, Potrafka told her that their leads had been all but exhausted. Miller knew Potrafka was suspicious of her when he asked her to take a lie detector test.

"You know I can't pass," she later told Chuck and Judy Miller. "I'm taking so many nerve pills that I wouldn't be able to pass that thing. Besides, I talked to a lawyer who told me I don't have to take it."

That annoyed the couple. They urged her to take the test if it would help the deputies.

"If you've got nothing to hide, don't worry about it," said Chuck, irritated. "Just tell 'em the goddamn truth."

Sharee also vented in a call to Carol Slaughter.

"I don't like all this medication the doctors have put me on, nerve pills," Miller said.

Miller had told Slaughter months before that she was a nurse.

I don't know of any nurse who would refer to medications as nerve pills, Slaughter thought.

Miller declined the polygraph, denying detectives a lead that could identify her firmly as a suspect. But that didn't matter much.

Within days, detectives would have more new leads than they possibly could handle.

TWELVE

For the second time in three months, Cassaday made elaborate and painstaking plans to kill a man. He finally had enough, and for him it was finished. The lies. The promises. The hope.

Cassaday had been haunted and ruined by the events of his last half year. How could he have done all this to himself, his family and his son? The answer always came back to Sharee Miller.

Miller always had given him broad suggestions to run and never look back. But Cassaday was blinded by his love, his yearning to save her and, ultimately, his mission to rescue her.

"I can not believe you have put up with the pain I have dished out," Miller wrote to him on September 9, 1999.

In that same message, Miller reminded Cassaday of his earlier threat of suicide when things between them were unsettled. Miller had blasted Cassaday for his weakness and for heaping guilt and responsibility on her shoulders. It was not her fault that Cassaday had childish feelings, she said.

"Jerry if you ever say anything like that again, I will end everything between us," she threatened. ". . . I would never stay with such a weak man who would end [his] life over a woman."

And the lies! They came like a never-ending tidal

wave. Yet she always had a way of smoothing things over, keeping the waves at bay for just a little longer.

"I am sorry you think everything I have said is a lie," Miller wrote on September 23, 1999.

Cassaday also would be sucked in by the roiling self-pity of this high-maintenance woman.

"I guess when I look at my life I see all the mistakes I have made," she wrote. ". . . I love you and right now I can't give you what you deserve . . . a much better woman than me."

The words were right there for Cassaday, but he was too love-blind to see.

Another warning soon followed under the suggestive screen name getoutwhileucan.

But he didn't listen. She kept the game alive, pulling him in, pushing him away.

"Honey, please don't worry yourself to death over me. I am not worth it," Miller wrote.

After telling Cassaday of her constant pain and her love for him, she played Bruce against him.

"I can't leave [Bruce] right now," she had written. "And if you continue to be with me it is only going to get worse for you."

It had gotten worse. He'd killed a man and fallen into a web of deceit woven by a true black widow.

He'd been Sharee's fool for life. Cassaday soon would be his own fool in death.

On February 9, 2000, Cassaday wrote his good-byes and explained, as best as he could, to the people he still loved.

In a one-page letter to his parents, he apologized for the pain he was about to inflict upon them, but he was determined to explain why.

In a wrenching confession, Cassaday told his parents everything.

Cassaday explained that after he and Sharee had become acquainted, he learned she was married. Lies and false promises soon followed, he wrote, and he believed all of them. She became pregnant with Cassaday's child, but Bruce raped her and killed the baby. Miller was defenseless against her husband's onslaught and was afraid that she would be killed if she tried to leave or have charges brought against him.

Cassaday's pain tumbled out as he wrote of the first baby being killed, and of Sharee's subsequent pregnancy with twins. After Bruce ordered his thugs to gang-rape his wife, he taunted and threatened Cassaday mercilessly. But that was nothing compared with the loss of the babies, Cassaday wrote.

Then Cassaday wrote the words that never appeared in the e-mails he sent to Miller, but they came easily now.

"I drove there and killed him," Cassaday wrote. "Sharee was involved and helped set it up."

Now Cassaday's parents could understand his depression and why drugs, alcohol and counseling never helped. For months, he had carried a horrible secret that he could not share with anyone. Laying bare his own stupidity, Cassaday said he now understood that Miller's promises meant nothing, and that all she had wanted was Bruce Miller's money.

With his last reserves of courage wasted on a faithless woman, Cassaday acknowledged he was taking the coward's way out. Ex-cops, he said, can't go to prison. He pleaded with his parents to make certain his youngest son, Kenny, was taken care of.

Cassaday said his greatest regret was that he had to leave his son and blamed Sharee Miller for driving the last wedge between himself and someone he loved.

At the end of the letter, Cassaday wrote, "I love you!!" before signing his name.

But he was not yet ready to leave.

Cassaday wrote a letter to Barb, his ex-wife, telling her

that he loved her, was sorry he had ordered her out and that everything had gone terribly after that. And he also wrote a letter to Kenneth.

Cassaday had one last letter to write, but its tone would not be so kind. It was fitting that the relationship between Cassaday and Miller, which began in an on-line chat room months before, should end on AOL.

Cassaday sent his final missive to SHAREE1013 and titled it "Something for you to think about."

The tenderness and devotion that he once had lavished on Miller were gone. The only thing left was bitter anger.

Cassaday was finished with Miller's lies, mind games and false promises, he wrote. She'd used him to get everything she had wanted, a life of her own with Bruce's money. Cassaday had desired nothing but a life with Miller and her children. She had promised it all, but none of it had come true. Since killing Bruce in November, Cassaday had waited for her, even writing checks on her promise to send money. The checks bounced and now Cassaday was afraid to leave the house because he might be arrested.

But Cassaday also was finished with fear, he wrote. He thought of the briefcase and the evidence he had assembled. It was Sharee Miller's time to be afraid.

"Now, you get to live in fear for a while, wondering and waiting when will they come," Cassaday wrote. "Well, let me assure you, it's real fucking soon."

She could have avoided all of it if she hadn't been so greedy and selfish, he wrote. Miller was responsible for every evil thing that had come into his life. He had done everything for her, and she had returned it with lies. He had only hate for her now.

He no longer was her fool for life.

"Fuck you, bitch!!!!!" he signed off.

Cassaday's good-byes were finished. There was only one thing left to do.

Cassaday pushed the briefcase back under the bed. Along with some CDs and casino trinkets, the briefcase held the IM transcript between him and Miller, written hours before Cassaday killed Bruce Miller. He hoped it would lead police to her. Cassaday also taped his suicide notes to the top, along with a letter to attorney John O'Connor.

On the windowsill of his apartment, Cassaday had carefully arranged photographs of the important people in his life and other mementos.

Pictures of his sons. A photo of Sharee. His divorce decree. His wedding ring. The picturesque lake behind the house framed it all.

He moved the recliner around so he could take it all in one last time.

His eyes moved from object to object. Cassaday must have reflected on how much joy—and sadness—each item brought him. He had killed in the name of love; now he would kill from shame.

Cassaday settled into the recliner one last time. He gazed once again at the pictures. Cassaday opened the Bible cradled in his lap and read for strength and forgiveness.

In his last moments, he looked down to the pages that contained Matthew, chapters 4:17 through 5:26.

These scriptures deal with murder, the law, reconciliation and the promise of life ever after.

"Rejoice and be glad, because great is your reward in heaven; for in the same way they persecuted the prophets who were before you," read a section he had highlighted at the end of the Beatitudes.

Leaning the stock of a .22-caliber rifle against his left knee, Cassaday must have felt time growing short. He placed the cold barrel between his lips, took a deep, last breath and pulled the trigger.

A blinding flash and it was over. Silence. And peace.

Later, the trill of a ringing telephone broke the apartment's deathly silence. No answer. Later, it rang again.

Miles away, at a Kansas City mental-health center, a psychologist hung up the phone. She had called twice to remind Cassaday that he had been cleared to go back to work at Harrah's.

Receiving no answer, the psychologist wrote a note to Harrah's, saying the same thing.

Soon a letter from Harrah's director of table games would be on its way, warning Cassaday that his job was in jeopardy.

"According to our records, you were released to work for regular duty effective 1/15/00 but have failed to contact us regarding a return date," he wrote. ". . . It is critically important that you contact me upon receipt of this letter."

Later on February 9, Earl and Lyn Lewellen's daughter walked softly into Cassaday's room. The family hadn't seen much of Cassaday lately and an envelope had arrived for him.

From behind the recliner, the girl noticed Cassaday sitting quietly in the recliner, his head lolling to the right. Thinking he was asleep, the girl left the envelope on a couch and quietly slipped out. The envelope contained $3,000 from Sharee Miller.

A note in Sharee's hand accompanied the cash: "I didn't lie. I was telling the truth."

Cassaday's parents would use the money to cremate their son. In a final irony, Bruce Miller paid for the funeral of the man who killed him.

After Lyn Lewellen found Jerry's body on the morning of February 11, Mike Cassaday pulled up and spoke with the investigating sergeant. Cassaday said he had talked to Jerry two days earlier. The two were supposed to meet that night because Jerry had talked about taking off and just "hitting the road."

He also had tried to contact Jerry after learning that he had planned to go out for a drink. That concerned Mike Cassaday because Jerry was supposed to be in counseling and attending AA.

The two also had spoken recently of Jerry's desire to move in with Mike.

Mike identified the pictures Jerry had placed on the windowsill. Pointing to the photo of Sharee, Mike told the sergeant that Miller was one reason his brother had gotten divorced.

James Cassaday was alone in his Texas home when he received the call from Earl Lewellen.

Charlene Cassaday was at an exercise class nearby.

"When Jim came to get me, I knew something was wrong," Charlene Cassaday said later. "He caught my eye and motioned to me."

When she walked up to her husband, he told her to gather her things.

But James Cassaday could not keep it inside any longer. He blurted out that their son was dead.

As time stood still, Charlene Cassaday remembered a period, not long before, when such news would not have surprised her. But that was before her son had begun treatment. *Not now,* she thought.

Jerry's hollow words echoed in her head.

"Mom, I don't know what I'm going to do," Jerry Cassaday had told her from the depths of his depression.

Charlene Cassaday had almost heard the suicide, the gun's blast, in her son's words then.

She also remembered her own words to him, words of comfort that she wished now she could have followed with a hug.

"Honey, nothing is so bad that you can't find a way out," she'd told him then.

But things had seemed to be looking up for Jerry since his move to Odessa. He was attending therapy, talking with Earl and seeing old friends from a happier time.

"We thought he was coming around," Charlene Cassaday said. "He seemed to be coming back out of it and making plans to get back to work."

But immediately, the family—and especially Charlene Cassaday—thought of a woman in Michigan.

"Our first instinct was that Sharee had something to do with this," she said.

Even as her son seemed to be coming out of his funk, he had clung to the fantasy of a life with Miller, Charlene Cassaday said.

"I've got to know what's going on with her," he told them as Miller pulled even further away from him the previous December. "She won't take my phone calls; I've got to find out what's going on."

After his disastrous trip to Michigan two months before, Cassaday had pretty much clammed up about Miller. But still, he told his family that he loved Miller and if she ever wanted him back, he would try again.

James and Charlene began preparing for a trip they never wanted to make—to lay their son to rest. Charlene Cassaday knew that her son's dreams had ended in gruesome tragedy, but she could not understand why.

About then, back in Odessa, Mike Cassaday had begun cleaning out his brother's apartment. Sweeping his hands under the bed, he found the briefcase.

And the answers.

The other detectives in the Genesee County Sheriff's Department could not believe what Sergeant Ives Potrafka had just told them.

Potrafka had just received a call from a lawyer in Missouri, John O'Connor, who said he had evidence about

Bruce Miller's unsolved murder on November 8 at the salvage yard.

"They said we have information that will solve your case," Sergeant Kevin Shanlian said.

After hearing from Potrafka, Captain Michael Compeau headed across the lobby to the office of Sheriff Robert J. Pickell. Compeau described the information, letters, e-mails and chat sessions. Potrafka would be good with this because he was something of a computer nerd himself. He already managed a Web site for the Genesee County prosecutor. The new evidence, Compeau said, could be invaluable.

"We'd like to send somebody down [to Missouri]," Compeau said.

Pickell instantly approved the travel request.

"We'd be guilty of malfeasance if we didn't," Pickell said.

As Compeau hustled out to make arrangements to send Potrafka and another detective to Kansas City, Pickell leaned back and gathered his thoughts.

"This is the smoking gun," Pickell said to himself. "This is what flips the case."

The trail of Bruce Miller's killers had gone very cold lately. Detectives initially had focused their attention on John Hutchinson. Sharee Miller had fingered him as the prime suspect, saying Hutchinson had owed her husband thousands of dollars. Police also were looking at him for his involvement in vehicle identification number switching at the junkyard.

But all hunches about Hutchinson had come up empty and, at best, he had emerged as a very weak suspect. Though his polygraph test showed he had been less than truthful, there was no solid evidence—physical or circumstantial—to tie him to the murder.

Pickell warmed quickly to the idea of Sharee Miller as a suspect. In her interviews, Miller had omitted information about her past affair with John Joel

Hutchinson—an affair to which Hutchinson readily admitted.

"She never told us she had an affair with John Hutchinson," Pickell said later. "She told us everything about how he was stealing money and flipping the VINs, but she never told us she'd had an affair with him. Her credibility was suffering."

The troops in the detective bureau had been split about Miller's involvement in the slaying.

Some detectives always had a funny feeling about Miller and believed she had a role in the murder; others were not sure, or had eliminated her entirely, based on her spectacular displays of grief and a lack of motive.

But now, the detectives had a solid lead, and it took them right back to their own backyard. Just after the murder, Potrafka had told the Miller family that the killer might just have the gall to attend Bruce Miller's funeral.

Potrafka may have been right after all.

On February 18, 2000, Genesee County detectives Ives Potrafka and Jerry Willhelm settled into the comfortable chairs at John O'Connor's Kansas City office and began the interview of Charlene and James Cassaday. By then, the detectives already had reviewed evidence from the briefcase and were convinced Miller was responsible for the deaths of two men.

"She's very good," Potrafka told the Cassadays. "I believed her. . . . I've interviewed this lady three times and until I got John's call, we're arguing back and forth, 'I'm telling you, this woman doesn't have anything to do with it.' She's very, very good. I could see why people believe her, because I bought her lies."

To smooth the way, Willhelm assured the family the police would try to avoid shining a bad light on Jerry.

"We feel the problem is Sharee," he said, adding that he believed Jerry was "a caring person." Sharee had just hit the right buttons to play on his emotions.

"It may not be that he was so gullible, it's just, she's that good," he said.

Still, Willhelm knew that to make the case against Miller, prosecutors would have to paint Jerry Cassaday as her willing triggerman. With the pump primed, the Cassadays began telling them about a side of Sharee Miller that they could not have imagined.

Charlene Cassaday vividly recalled conversations with her son at the beginning of the relationship, recounting Miller's visits to Reno, Jerry's trips to Michigan and the e-mails Sharee sent to Cassaday family members.

The Cassadays spoke of the trip their son Roger made to Reno to convince Jerry to move back to Missouri to seek counseling and of Roger's time with Miller that week.

Charlene told the detectives how Sharee Miller had helped Jerry obtain a medical leave from Harrah's. And she said that Miller had vowed to help Jerry out financially.

Charlene Cassaday also told the cops about the stories Miller told Jerry about her brain-dead husband, Jeff, how she married his brother, Bruce, how she owned nursing homes and had wealth, and how much she wanted to share her life with Jerry, but only after he kicked his drug and alcohol dependency.

"The stories that she spun were too much like a soap opera," Charlene Cassaday said.

"If this woman is who she says she is, and she's got all this money and all these houses and businesses, she can have anything she wants," Charlene Cassaday said. "But at the time she met him, he had some real psychological problems. Let's face it, he was an alcoholic; he was on prescriptions. . . . So why is she taking this on?"

Widening the list of possible witnesses, Charlene Cassaday told the detectives of other people in Reno, such as Carol Slaughter, who knew of her son's relationship with Sharee Miller.

Bit by bit, the detectives began to grasp the breadth, depth and complexity of Miller's lies. They also made lists of things to check. First on the list was the hard drive from Cassaday's computer.

From Cassaday's rubbish in Odessa, they also recovered two videotapes featuring Sharee, one with her family and one with her stripping and masturbating.

The detectives returned to Michigan with a mountain of new leads to process. Waiting to help were agents and a prosecutor from the newly formed High Tech Crime Unit of the Michigan Attorney General's Office. They were entrusted with uncovering the secrets buried deep in Jerry's computer hard drive.

The preliminary report struck gold: Jerry Cassaday had saved hundreds of e-mails to and from Sharee Miller.

Witness interviews began anew. Police learned that Sharee never could have become pregnant because of a tubal ligation—elective sterilization—she had undergone years before.

She "tolerated the procedure well," the physician wrote in a July 21, 1995, report from Hurley Medical Center.

And they determined that the ultrasound pictures Cassaday received in October 1999 were dated from the early 1990s. Detectives concluded that Sharee faked pregnancy in the e-mail pictures she sent to Cassaday merely by pushing out her stomach.

They also settled some things they already knew but hadn't mattered much before. Bruce Miller never had beaten his wife, never was involved in organized crime or counterfeiting. Police had never even been called to the Miller home for something as simple as a domestic abuse call.

Neighbors and others described Bruce as a loving family man.

Sharee never owned a nursing home and the stories of numerous stock portfolios and lucrative pending insurance settlements were fabrications. She just wasn't particularly wealthy. After Bruce's murder, she sold the junkyard for a small profit, took about $16,000 from the bank accounts and received a little stock and pension money.

With the Presidents' Day weekend looming, detectives pulled together enough evidence to move on the lone surviving suspect in the conspiracy to murder Bruce Miller.

Before leaving with Jeff Foster for a holiday trip to Reno on February 16, Sharee Miller asked sister-in-law Judy Miller to baby-sit the kids, saying that she and Jeff Foster were going out to gamble and party.

But at the last minute, without telling Judy Miller, Sharee asked another friend to watch the kids. The move again irritated Judy Miller, who had arranged to take time off from her job as a clerk at Kmart to baby-sit the children.

With lots of advance notice via e-mail, Carol Slaughter was watching for Sharee Miller and Jeff Foster as she worked the Harrah's blackjack tables during the Presidents' Day holiday week. And when Slaughter first caught sight of her, Miller was alone.

"Her hair was cut and styled, it looked so cute, and her makeup was done to perfection," Slaughter remembered later.

Miller quickly sidled up to Slaughter and reminded her to say nothing to Foster about Cassaday.

"I just really don't want to go into it with Jeff," Miller said. "Jeff knows about Bruce. He doesn't know anything about Jerry. I just want to keep it that way."

Nothing odd about that, Slaughter thought, agreeing that the new boyfriend probably didn't need to hear about an ex-boyfriend who recently had committed suicide. Or be indirectly reminded of the recent murder of his girl-friend's husband.

Slaughter and Miller had maintained a sporadic on-line correspondence, which had taken an odd turn recently. Miller had begun sending Slaughter religious material.

"Just wacko e-mails, like angels and spiritual sayings," she said.

And that didn't match the Miller she thought she knew. This was, after all, the woman who was ready and willing to engage in wild sexual play with Cassaday, on-line and in person. Slaughter also had begun to suspect that Miller had somehow played a role in Cassaday's suicide.

"He was spiraling down, and she was the element that caused him to go out of control," Slaughter said later.

Slaughter earlier had become suspicious when Miller questioned her about Cassaday's suicide.

"She told me that she had been talking to Jerry on the computer," Slaughter said. "Jerry had told her flat out that he was going to kill himself and that she would pay for it. He abruptly signed off the computer. Sharee was upset by that. She didn't think that he would kill himself, but still thought she'd better contact Barb so that some-body could go check on him.

"I believe her sole purpose for her coming out here with Jeff was to see me face-to-face to see what I knew," she said.

Later during the trip, Slaughter finally saw Miller and Jeff Foster together, dressed casually in jeans and T-shirts.

"He was really plowed," Slaughter said.

Looking at her through bloodshot eyes, Foster told her in a slurred voice how glad he was to meet her.

Slaughter sized up Foster as young, average and unim-pressive.

Elton John was playing in Reno then and Miller, who

imagined herself a high roller, decided that she deserved complimentary tickets to the show from the casino.

But the casino, which already had sized up Miller's finances, turned her down.

Whenever she appeared at Harrah's, Miller routinely would ask for a $1,500 credit limit. Just as routinely, Harrah's would turn her down, granting her a modest $400.

"Sharee wasn't the queen bee she thought she was," Slaughter said.

But the Elton John concert snub miffed Miller, and she and Foster promptly checked out of Harrah's and moved to the Peppermill for the rest of their trip.

Miller then made it a point to call on Slaughter and tell her how much nicer the Peppermill was.

"They have a Jacuzzi right next to our bed," Miller bragged.

Slaughter rolled her eyes. *Like that is some kind of big deal,* she thought.

Miller also noted that she and Foster had flown out first class and had spent a lot of time shopping. They even had to buy new luggage at Wal-Mart to lug all the clothing and boots—five or six pairs—she had purchased for herself and the kids.

Her vacation in Reno over, however, Miller and Foster boarded a flight on February 22, 2000, and prepared to return to Michigan, where they would continue to play house and spend more of Bruce Miller's money.

Miller did not know as she entered the airport that she had just concluded her last trip to Reno, or anywhere else outside the state of Michigan.

Hustling through the Reno airport, Miller and Foster paid scant notice of Nick Chiros as they cut in front of him in line for the flight to Michigan. A retired Genesee County Sheriff's sergeant now working for General Motors, Chiros was returning home to Flint from a business trip and was annoyed when the couple barged in front of him.

What's the deal? he later remembered thinking. *There's plenty of time and the flight won't leave with passengers waiting at the gate.* Watching Foster, Chiros thought him a bit comical, wearing a long coat and cowboy boots and following Miller around "like a puppy dog."

He recalled that Sharee "gave the impression she was the one wearing the boots in that family."

On the plane, Chiros watched the couple take their seats in first class and recalled later that Foster looked angry.

In Detroit, the three took a brisk walk to the connecting flight to Flint. Chiros was assigned to a seat next to Miller on that leg of the trip. But before takeoff, Foster asked if he minded changing seats with him so he could "sit next to my wife."

Chiros said fine. Putting some space between him and that couple wasn't a bad idea.

Chiros felt his heart sink as he stepped off the jet at Flint's Bishop International Airport at about 10:00 P.M. A knot of old friends from the sheriff's department appeared to be waiting for him. Imagining that something terrible had happened to his family, Chiros stepped up to Captain Mike Compeau, prepared to hear some very bad news.

But the news wasn't too bad at all. Compeau said the deputies were there to meet the couple that had cut in front of Chiros in Reno.

Still drunk and weary from travel, Miller recognized Compeau, who asked her to come to the sheriff's department. She agreed, but Foster was puzzled.

"What's going on?" he asked as Compeau left with Miller and deputies led him toward baggage claim.

While waiting for the luggage, Foster told deputies that he began dating Miller on December 10, 1999, a little more than a month after Bruce Miller's murder. He said he had quit working his Schwan's frozen food job on February 5 and now was living with Miller in the home she once shared with Bruce.

He said all they did in Reno was gamble. The only person he could recall meeting out there was a woman named Carol, a friend of Miller's who dealt cards at Harrah's. Deputies then gave Foster a ride to the sheriff's department to see what was going on with his girlfriend.

Compeau told Foster that Miller would be there for a while. He was driven back to the airport to get his car and luggage. Foster told deputies that he was going to his aunt's home.

Interview room #2 at the Genesee County Sheriff's Department is small and yellowish, about the size of a walk-in closet. Like police interview rooms everywhere, it has no distractions, only a couple of chairs and a small table bearing a tape recorder.

Once inside, Miller agreed to talk to Compeau in what would stretch into a three-hour taped interview.

It began slowly. At about 10:45 P.M., Compeau assured Sharee that "you're not under arrest right now" and should feel free to leave anytime. The opening marked the beginning of what lawyers would call a voluntary, noncustodial interview. Courts have ruled that such interviews do not require a Miranda warning.

Compeau began with a few preliminary questions about her life with Bruce, where they met and how the marriage was holding up before he was murdered.

"Our marriage was good," Miller replied. "It was beautiful."

She told Compeau that Bruce got along well with her three kids and was planning to adopt her two youngest children.

She told Compeau that between them, they had been

married seven times—three for her and four for Bruce. Miller said she and Bruce used to laugh about divorce.

"It was our joke, that we weren't never gonna get divorced again," Miller said. "Neither one of us. If we couldn't live together, we were gonna get a duplex and he would live on one side and I'd live on the other one."

Compeau quizzed Miller on her financial status since the murder, and she said that Bruce's mother and his children from a previous marriage had ended up with most of his estate in the form of about $129,000 in life insurance.

But she said Ruth Miller, Bruce's mother, had given her $10,000 "because she said that I was married to him and that I was entitled to it."

Miller said she had blown most of that on a car.

She also received about $50,000 from Bruce's personal savings plan through General Motors, and she also was in the process of selling the junkyard for just over $100,000 because she and Bruce had accumulated so much debt. Miller rambled on about other bills that were going to eat up almost all of that.

Miller then launched into a rant about how she had to put a new roof on her home and buy a new furnace. She told Compeau she was not working and was collecting about $2,400 in Social Security benefits every month.

Miller said she and Bruce were doing fine financially until he bought out his business partner at B&D.

"From then on out, it went downhill," she said.

But Compeau noticed her evasiveness on the financial picture. She told Compeau that she had cleaned out several bank accounts but had no clear picture of her financial condition.

Miller estimated that she had, maybe, $13,000 left.

Compeau inquired about VIN switching at B&D, but Miller shot back that Bruce wasn't involved.

"Because I know my husband," she said. "You guys cannot label him bad."

She said Bruce "was hot" when he learned that police had been to the junkyard asking about the VIN scam.

Preliminaries over, Compeau asked Miller if she had any affairs while she was married to Bruce.

"No, I did not," she said emphatically, adding that she had no plans to divorce him. Miller also denied that Bruce had ever hit her.

Compeau pressed her on why she went to Reno.

" 'Cause I wanted to," she said. "I gambled, I vacationed, I seen comedy shows, I drank, I smoked and I slept."

She said she went with her current boyfriend, Jeff Foster, whom she described as "my Schwan man."

She said Foster had delivered frozen food to B&D. But after Bruce died, she had a hard time going back to the business, so Foster began delivering to her home.

Miller also told Compeau that she had been to Reno before, with a friend to sell Mary Kay cosmetics.

And because "I like to gamble. And that's a problem."

She said each trip to Reno was with Bruce's knowledge and approval.

"I mean, it wasn't a big deal," Miller said. "Bruce had no problem letting me go; I had no problem with him going to races."

Compeau probed Miller to learn if there were any problems in her marriage to Bruce. But after answering patiently, Sharee began to get upset about the repeated questions.

"Everything was going [fine]," she said. "Come on, I had a week left, or two weeks left, before we'd be going to court for him to adopt my kids. I mean, you're talking about a man that's almost fifty years old adopting two babies."

With her protestations of marital bliss firmly on the

record, Compeau asked if she ever knew a man named
Jerry Cassaday.

Miller was noncommittal.

"I met several people," she said. "There was Jerry, um,
I met, talked to a lot of people."

Compeau asked her how she knew Cassaday.

"I met him out there," Miller replied. "Talked to him
on-line, along with the rest of the people out there."

Did you have a relationship with him? Compeau
asked.

"No."

Anything?

"A friendship."

Where's Jerry now? Compeau asked.

"You know the answer to that," Miller spat back.

Why don't you answer that? Compeau asked.

"I'm not answering no more," Miller said. "Not if
you're—"

Compeau interrupted, telling Miller that deputies
knew quite a bit more now than they did earlier in the
investigation, including information about Cassaday's
suicide.

He asked her when it happened.

"I don't even know," she said. "I don't know."

Miller again denied that she and Bruce were having
problems, or that he was getting physical with her. Compeau's suggestions that she had a relationship with
Cassaday and that he was trying to help her out of a
tough situation at home also met flat denials.

Compeau asked her when was the last time she had
seen Cassaday.

"I don't even know," Miller said, her memory getting
fuzzy. "Last time I was out there?"

When was that? Compeau pressed.

"I don't remember," she said firmly. "I don't know. I'd
have to look on a calendar or dates, I don't know."

Compeau told her that Cassaday died just a week or so earlier and asked if she had any contact with his family.

"I talked to his ex-wife, 'cause I have talked to her on-line several times," Miller said. "Um, but that's it."

Compeau continued to push, telling Miller that some-times things get difficult in life, situations pop up and marriages are strained by other relationships.

"You're wrong," she said.

He asked if she had been pregnant lately. Miller replied that her tubes had been tied for nearly four years. He asked if Cassaday ever believed she was preg-nant with his children.

"No."

Did she ever tell Cassaday she was pregnant during their on-line chats?

"No."

Compeau again tried the back door, hinting that deputies knew of her problems with Bruce.

Miller erupted.

"There was nothing," she bellowed. "You guys have lost your minds completely. You know what? On-line is a game, okay? Bruce did it. I did it. He looked up pornography on-line. I did it with [him]. We sit and shared it together. We talked to people on-line together. I mean, we had two separate phone lines at one time and we used to sit and talk on-line on two different [lines]. Come on, everybody does it. There is nothing wrong with him looking up pornography and me . . . talking to people on-line, or him and I both sitting there talking to people on-line. There's nothing wrong with this."

Compeau admitted that, no, there was nothing wrong with chatting on-line. What were her screen names? he asked.

"I have SHAREE1013," she said, beginning the list. "I have SEXYKITTEN4ONLYU. I have SPM1013. I've had a hundred different names."

Compeau again suggested that Miller had become involved in an extramarital relationship.

"No, I wasn't."

With Jerry Cassaday?

"No, on-line," she answered firmly. "I developed . . . I have a list of people. I have probably fifty people on my buddy list that I talk to. I've got a guy named Tom that I sit and talk to."

Miller deflected another question about a physical relationship with Cassaday.

"I sit and talk to him on-line," Miller said, growing more exasperated. "Me and Bruce both talked to people online. When you are on-line, sometimes you say stuff . . . and everybody does it. Nobody knows you. They can't see you. They don't know you."

Compeau asked if Cassaday ever came to Flint to visit.

"He showed up here because . . . when Bruce passed away . . . I just went nuts. I mean, I was very upset about this and I talked to several people on-line about it. In fact, two people showed up here."

Who else? Compeau asked.

"I'm not gonna disclose who the other person was," Miller said flatly.

But one was Cassaday?

"He was here for, like, six hours," Miller said, opening the door a little more with each question. "And I said, 'I don't want you here,' and he left. That was it."

That was after Bruce's death? Compeau asked.

". . . He thought I was gonna do something stupid to myself because I was so upset over Bruce passing away."

She said Cassaday showed up in a cab, visited for a short period, then left at her urging.

Miller clearly knew where Compeau was headed.

". . . Bruce didn't lay a finger on me, so you're wrong," she said.

Did she ever tell Cassaday that Bruce had hit her?

"No. You're wrong."

Did she ever tell Cassaday she was going to divorce Bruce and be with him?

"No."

Did she tell him those things on-line?

"No," she said, and then reconsidered. "Now, you know what? I don't know some of the stuff that was said on-line. I really don't. Because on-line is a game, so I don't know. I don't know everything that was said on-line. I don't know what Bruce said to people on-line. I don't know. I know we went into certain group things, but I don't know what he talked about and he didn't know what I talked about. I don't know."

What would Miller say if Compeau told her that Cassaday left behind things that showed they were having a physical relationship?

"I don't know."

Is it true?

"No."

It's not true that you were having a physical relationship with Jerry?

"Maybe on-line."

In person?

"No."

Compeau asked her if she ever sent Cassaday pictures.

"Yes."

What pictures?

"I don't know. We sent all kinds of pictures. . . . "

Like what?

". . . Pictures through the years when I was a kid," Miller began. "Pictures of my kids. Pictures of Bruce. Pictures of my cat. Pictures of my whole family. I mean, I send pictures of everybody. I don't know. I scan 'em; I send 'em."

What pictures did she send specifically to Cassaday? Compeau asked.

"I don't know," she began evasively. "I've sent pictures. I don't remember. I don't remember every picture I sent. I don't know."

How did she and Cassaday meet? Compeau asked.

After a bit of babbling, Miller said she met him in Reno and also talked to him on-line.

Then Compeau asked her if she had any idea who killed her husband.

"You guys made me think it was John; then I was having a bad feeling it was my second husband; then you guys make me think again it's John," Miller rambled. "I don't know."

What would she think, Compeau asked, if he told her that Cassaday saved e-mails and IMs between them?

"I would tell you that you can change them and you know that and everybody knows that," she said. "I can change any e-mail that somebody sends me . . . highlight it, delete it and type in what I want. . . . I mean, anybody can do that. So it doesn't matter who saves what."

Compeau asked her if she ever sent naked pictures of herself to Cassaday or any films of her naked.

"No," she said. "Films of me naked?"

Compeau was no longer asking Miller—he was telling her that things had gone bad with Bruce. She'd met a new man and didn't know how to get out of the situation.

Miller denied all of that.

Compeau bounced quickly through his questions, keeping Miller off balance and unsure of herself. Why would someone even want to change e-mails or IMs? he asked.

"I don't know," Miller replied. "But you can. I've done it before. So I don't know. I mean, I've done it before."

Why would she change messages?

"Just messing around," Miller said. "I mean I mess, around on-line all the time, just to figure out something new to do. I mean, everybody does it."

Compeau again told Miller that Bruce was beating her, and she didn't know how to get out of a bad situation, adding that Jerry's e-mails did not appear to have been changed.

"But they could have been," Miller insisted. "Because Bruce never hit me, so you're wrong."

Did she ever try to make Cassaday think that Bruce hit her? Compeau asked.

"No. No. From what I get out of Jerry . . . something was not right up there. So no, I quit speaking to him altogether like, um, I don't know, five, six months ago. Wouldn't speak to him no more. And then he would e-mail me once in a while. Well, okay, I'll e-mail him back and I did. So no."

Compeau brushed past the jumbled answer and asked why she stopped speaking to Cassaday.

"Because he was a fruit. . . . He was sending me all kinds of weird stuff."

Like what? Compeau asked.

"Trust me, weird stuff."

Did she think Cassaday killed Bruce?

"No. How?"

Now Compeau asked if she ever had a discussion with Cassaday how to handle this situation if it ever came up.

"No."

Did she know Cassaday was an ex-cop?

"Yeah, he told me he was," Miller said. "I don't know if it's true. But he told me he was. I guess he was a bad cop . . . and he got fired."

Did she ever discuss with Cassaday what to say to police if Bruce was killed?

"No . . . that . . . This is crazy," Miller stammered. "I want my car and I want to leave . . . because this is nuts. You guys have completely lost it."

"You're free to leave anytime you want," Compeau assured smoothly.

But Miller did not leave, and Compeau said he wanted to share a few things that police knew. Deputies had e-mails in which Miller appeared to be telling Cassaday that she loved him.

"No," Miller again insisted. "You can change those."

Did Bruce Miller and Jerry Cassaday know each other?

"They talked on-line," Miller replied. "Yes . . . I introduced them on-line. I mean, they talked on-line. I talked on-line. I mean, come on. We talked on-line."

Compeau's questions grew direct and pointed. Did you help Jerry Cassaday plan the murder of Bruce Miller?

"No . . . No."

Had she called Bruce that night, ordered food, kept him on the phone, knowing that Cassaday was going there with directions from her?

No, no, no, no, no, Miller repeated to the series of questions.

"Isn't it true that you helped plan his murder?" Compeau asked.

"No."

Deflecting more questions about her relationship with Cassaday, Miller again lashed out against Jerry.

"He had drug problems," she said. "He had drinking problems. I would sit on-line for hours and talk to this person about drug and drinking problems."

Compeau again told Miller that he had a computer message that said she and Cassaday were involved in the murder plot.

"And he could have, anybody could have, changed that," Miller said. "Anybody. You're wrong, because that did not happen."

Miller acknowledged talking to Cassaday and others on-line about Bruce's murder.

Compeau pressed again, focusing on the IM that appeared to show planning for the murder.

"That's wrong."

Why would Cassaday change something like that?

"I don't know. . . . I don't have a clue," she said. "Maybe because he was mad because I wouldn't have nothing to do with him. I don't know. I do not know. I quit talking to him altogether because he was a freak to begin with. I mean, I quit talking to him altogether. Yeah, I did."

"You just told me that you didn't [talk to him anymore]," Compeau responded.

Confused and caught in another lie, Miller fell back, acknowledging that she had spoken on-line with Cassaday after Bruce's murder.

"Yeah, after Bruce passed away, yes, he seen me on-line and I was upset that night. And yeah, I explained to him what happened; yeah, I did." Miller was scrambling. "He's a freak. He thought, 'Okay, well . . . she's gonna talk to me all the time.' So I quit talking to him again. I mean, come on. There's nothing wrong with talking to people on-line."

Compeau bore in again, and Miller announced she wanted to leave.

"Are you keeping me here?" she demanded. "You're wrong. You are wrong. Completely wrong. . . . I happened to meet a fruit and ended up talking to him on-line. . . . You know, there's nothing wrong with me sitting and playing on-line games with anybody."

Compeau then told Miller that Cassaday had left a briefcase behind, explaining the whole thing.

"I don't understand what you're talking about," she said.

Compeau offered to read a little bit of what Cassaday left behind if she agreed to stay and continue the interview.

Miller consented, too curious to leave.

"Go on," she said.

Compeau provided a few excerpts: "If anyone asks,

you last saw me last week; Jerry, I'm scared; don't try to hide it; Jerry, this won't work; he will hurt me bad; you will never see him again; call the local assholes."

"Makes no sense," Miller said, her confusion growing.

Reading from the IM, Compeau described how Miller would remove checks from Bruce's wallet that morning.

"This is bull," Miller exploded. "This is all screwed up. . . . After Bruce died, I sat on-line with Jerry and told him everything they stole from him . . . so that is bullshit. That isn't even right."

Compeau said police had confirmed those things were written before Bruce was killed.

"But I did not write that stuff," Miller contended. "Oh, this is bull. That is not even right. I did not write that stuff. I did not write that stuff. I don't know who changed that stuff, but I did not write that stuff."

No, Sharee, you did write it, Compeau said.

Miller stood up, angry.

Compeau asked her to sit down and relax.

"No, because you guys are, that is bull . . . I want my car."

The interview was over, Compeau decided. To let her leave could compromise evidence at her home and on her computer.

"You are under arrest for murder," he said.

Miller expressed no surprise as she was led upstairs to jail. Preparations for her charges already were under way: first-degree murder and conspiracy to commit the murder of her husband as an aider and abettor with Jerry Cassaday.

"She stuck to her guns," Compeau reflected. "She never wavered from her denials."

But, at last, Sharee Miller had met a man who hadn't fallen for her lies.

Miles to the north, Sergeant Ives Potrafka would spend the night searching Miller's home for evidence.

A review of her computer hard drive found no e-mails between her and Cassaday.

But the search yielded one very big prize.

Inside Miller's cluttered computer hutch, deputies recovered an envelope on which the name of Missouri lawyer John O'Connor had been scribbled in Miller's handwriting.

But the name was misspelled—Occonnor—and the home and office telephone numbers did not match O'Connor's real telephone numbers.

But those three elements identically matched the name and phone numbers that Cassaday passed along to Miller in the November 7 through November 8 IM, the chat session where they planned the murder. To deputies and prosecutors, it was the critical piece of corroborating evidence that cinched Miller's guilt.

The envelope also meant that if Miller rejected a plea bargain, she would have to explain the envelope at trial.

Sharee Miller would have to testify.

THIRTEEN

The Genesee County Jail, staffed and operated by the sheriff's department, is a nondescript five-story brick building in downtown Flint. Built in the mid-1990s to replace a crumbling and cramped lockup, the jail was filled instantly upon its completion, leaving county officials to complain that budget problems had prevented them from adding another floor.

Overcrowding is such a persistent problem that periodically some inmates simply are released to prevent the jail from violating state capacity regulations.

But release never was an option for the woman charged with conspiring to murder her husband.

Clad in ill-fitting and faded green coveralls, Sharee Paulette Miller made her home in the pods with other women on the third floor. And without a daily infusion of Mary Kay cosmetics, Miller blended with others who were accused of prostitution, drug dealing, theft, assault and murder.

Her transition was difficult. At about 6:00 P.M. on March 12, Miller's cellmate reported to guards that Sharee had wet the bed and was unable to get up. The deputy went to cell 23 in Pod 3D and found Miller lying on the top bunk crying.

"I was reading my Bible; next thing I know, I wet the bed," Miller told the deputy.

A nurse soon came in and Miller was taken to a hospital, where doctors treated her for a stress-induced seizure. The pressure was showing in other areas, too. Just after her arrest, she began taking medication to treat a nervous habit she had developed—digging at her own skin. She began seeing a jail psychologist and psychiatrist.

For a while, Miller became friendly with Mary E. Keimer, a woman almost as notorious as she.

On July 27, 1999, Keimer and her accomplice, Thomas E. Flum, poured a toxic cleaning liquid over the head of her mother, Bonnie M. Burdt, sixty-seven, and then covered Burdt's head with a plastic bag.

A pathologist found burns in Burdt's lungs and said she lived for some time, inhaling the toxic fumes, before dying of asphyxiation. Police said Keimer had spent nearly $40,000 in four months from her mother's savings account to fuel a $500-a-day drug habit.

In June 2000, Keimer and Flum were convicted of murdering Keimer's mother. The two were tried simultaneously in the same courtroom, but with separate juries. Flum's jury deliberated for several days before reaching its unanimous decision. Keimer's panel returned its verdict in thirty-five minutes. A month later, Keimer was sentenced to life in prison.

But between February and July 2000, Keimer shared some advice with Miller. Keimer was instrumental in persuading Miller to ignore a plea bargain that would have netted her a second-degree murder conviction with a sentencing guideline of between thirteen and twenty-two years, said Detective Sergeant Kevin Shanlian.

Quoting a jailhouse snitch, Shanlian said Keimer persuaded Miller to reject the deal because "you didn't confess." So with trial a dead certainty, Miller settled in, leaving the jail only for court appearances. Miller later would say, however, that she rejected the plea bargain because she was not guilty.

Miller eventually was made a trustee in the jail, which

allowed her to move about while performing routine duties, such as mopping and sweeping.

Sheriff's Lieutenant Mike Becker, who oversaw parts of the jail, noticed that Miller had gained weight while she was incarcerated. Generally, she maintained a cheery disposition.

"She was always very pleasant," Becker said.

As time progressed, Miller occasionally would try to become "much more friendly than we want to be with inmates," Becker said.

He said Miller would fuss over him and strike up conversations. Miller would gossip about other inmates and describe the jail as "terrible."

"Like she was different from them," Becker said. "She made me uncomfortable, just the vibes she was putting out. She was just too friendly."

Becker viewed this as Miller's clear attempt, once again, to manipulate a man. "Guys will fight you. Women are sneaky," he said.

Miller also attended therapy meetings and spoke to sixth graders who toured the jail as part of D.A.R.E., a youth drug-resistance program. She believed her role in such sessions was to terrify the children so they would never consider a life of crime. Still, she caused a stir when she announced to the children: "I used to be married to men, but now I have a beautiful girlfriend."

A ten-year-old girl who attended one of the sessions was particularly struck by the hazel-eyed blond inmate. The girl would remember Sharee vividly when her father served as Miller's jury foreman a few months later.

Though Miller gradually acclimated to jail, she still wanted to control the small world around her. She expressed that through a series of written requests made to jail administrators.

"I would like 'Poems from Prison Cells,' by Chaplain Ray," she wrote on April 5.

Two days later, a sergeant wrote her back.

"We do not offer a book service."

Two weeks later, Miller complained that another inmate had disturbed a movie and Bible study.

"She was rude," Miller wrote. "We could not concentrate on our movie or prayer. She kept opening the door and making all kinds of noise. Could you inform her . . . we don't need her rudeness?"

A sergeant again reminded Miller that she must face certain truths about her living arrangements.

"You don't run the jail or make the rules—deputies monitor inmates and maintain security. The end."

The next request came when she complained about the jail's disciplinary policies.

"I would like to know why the girl who was choking Ronda Hultz is walking freely around in the pod," Miller demanded. ". . . Everyone in the pod is paranoid about where this girl is at and what she is doing."

A sergeant responded to Sharee that same day.

"Do your own time," he wrote.

Miller's chirpy written requests grew no easier for her guards to take over the months. She eventually began making personnel recommendations.

"I am requesting that Ms. Dillard remain on female housing even after October 2000. She maintains a tight pod and smiles while doing it," Miller wrote, finishing the thought with a smiley face. "Oh, but she wears contraband in her hair and won't let us."

The next day, a weary administrator responded: "She isn't incarcerated. She can wear what she wants in her hair."

In April 2000, David Nickola, Sharee Miller's defense lawyer, pored over the state's evidence against his client. He already had concluded that the case had everything a lawyer could want—sex, murder and plenty of media attention.

You can't get a more zesty case than this, he thought. *It's got all the elements.*

Nickola, thirty-seven, was widely known in Genesee County as a flamboyant defense attorney, renowned for his bluster and theatrics. And once he took a case, he threw his full support behind his clients, defending them with gusto.

Nickola was not above smirking, shaking his head or looking up in disbelief when a prosecutor questioned a witness.

He knew, however, that the style that usually served him so well before a jury would have little effect at his next appearance on Miller's behalf. He and prosecutors were assembling the final evidence they'd need late in April for Miller's preliminary examination before Judge Richard L. Hughes of the Central District.

The hearing, which would not employ a jury, was to determine probable cause. Prosecutors wanted to present just enough evidence to convince Hughes that Miller should stand trial for conspiracy to murder her husband.

Hughes would decide neither innocence nor guilt, simply rule on whether there was enough evidence to order the trial. But after hearing Nickola's evidence and arguments, the judge also could simply dismiss the charges.

That would be another coup for the defense lawyer nicknamed "Rage." Nickola picked up the moniker years before when he and several other lawyers were defending a trio of men charged with gang-raping a woman. The case lacked a DNA test to prove that Nickola's client was conclusively involved and Nickola pushed the point hard, arguing the woman was lying.

Afterward, his lawyer buddies began calling him "Raging Bull" after the movie.

Square-jawed and big-boned, with slicked, jet-black

hair, Nickola mixed easily with people outside court in a carefree, laid-back sort of way. However, a switch went off when he stood before a jury.

"The jury has seen so many trials on television, so I try to keep them entertained," Nickola said. "I want this jury to understand right out of the chute that it's important to my client."

Nickola, though, was much more than bluster. He worked hard at winning. To stay up on his cases, Nickola routinely went to his spacious office on Sunday mornings in a building he owned with his father. It was a time when the telephones didn't ring and there was no one there to distract him.

At such a quiet moment—after talking with Sharee Miller and reading her interview with Captain Compeau—the broad outlines of his defense strategy began to emerge.

Jerry hadn't killed Bruce Miller, Nickola concluded. Cassaday had grown despondent and killed himself after Sharee refused to move to Missouri. But before pulling the trigger, Cassaday had faked the Internet correspondence to strike at her from beyond the grave. But jurors would want to know: who killed Bruce Miller?

John Hutchinson, Nickola decided, Bruce Miller's friend and onetime employee who owed him $2,000.

Nickola never apologized for getting accused criminals acquitted. He blamed the cops for not doing their jobs.

"If there is an acquittal and the person is guilty, the police screwed up the case," he said.

Across downtown Flint, assistant Genesee County prosecutor Marcie M. Mabry prepared for the same hearing in a far smaller office in Flint's district courts building. The disparity in office size between Nickola's and Mabry's work space could not disguise the advantage in resources she could bring against Sharee Miller.

A half dozen or so sheriff's deputies and evidence technicians had worked the case in some capacity. Mabry also could count on help from Michigan's assistant attorney general Peter L. Plummer of the state's High Tech Crime Unit.

Ives Potrafka, who led the sheriff's investigation, was preparing to retire, but he planned to begin a second career as Plummer's investigator assigned to the Miller case.

Leadership of the sheriff's investigation would move to Shanlian, a likable detective whose comprehensive grasp of the evidence worried Nickola.

When the case got into the courtroom, it would be Mabry, forty, doing the heavy lifting. And again, the contrast with Nickola and even his client couldn't be greater.

Modest and reserved, Mabry's courtroom style could charitably be described as "methodical," were it not for her remarkable ability to connect with jurors. Radiating plainspoken midwestern decency, Mabry's personal integrity regularly challenged jurors to step up and do the right thing for the community.

She came by that honestly. The daughter of a Dow Chemical analytical chemist and a social worker, Mabry grew up in Midland, Michigan, a "sheltered community with good education and good parks, a *Leave It to Beaver* kind of town," as she'd described it.

"I had the idyllic childhood," she said.

At sixteen, she worked for a McDonald's restaurant, preferring cleanup duties to the counter shift, where the false cheeriness offended her sense of honesty. Life and people are just not always cheery, she reasoned.

In 1982, she graduated from Michigan State University with a degree in food systems economics, thinking that one day she might open a restaurant. But almost immediately, Marcie Mabry, like Sharee Miller, took a dead-end job in a nursing home.

That sort of thing was troublesome for a high-achieving family. Mabry was the youngest of five children. The other siblings were on their way to successful careers as a neurosurgeon, geologist, dietician and computer architect. So one night after dinner, the family called her away from the dishes and suggested she go to law school.

Mabry gave in and enrolled in the Thomas M. Cooley Law School, working her way through as a telephone solicitor and doing workers' compensation and Social Security claims for the Michigan Bureau of History. She graduated in September 1986.

Mabry was appointed law clerk for former Genesee County Circuit Court judge Val Washington; she loved it. She remembered dancing in chambers with the judge to Motown hits before the two walked solemnly into court just seconds later.

In law school, Mabry had enjoyed advocacy class, but she didn't like the idea of having to hold someone else's briefcase for several years before getting a case of her own. She wanted trial experience and felt that the best place for that was as a prosecuting attorney.

"Being a prosecutor is the only job where you can get in court immediately," she said.

And there was another feature she liked about the job.

"I can always be right," she said. "Even if we are wrong, we can always dismiss the case and still do the right thing."

During the April 2000 preliminary examination, Mabry and Plummer gave Judge Hughes just a hint of what they would unload on a jury at trial.

Trying to establish motive for murder, Mabry had Potrafka testify that Sharee Miller received about $200,000 from her husband's estate after he was killed. Also, she called an expert computer witness who testified that Sharee Miller and Jerry Cassaday were on AOL simultaneously on November 7 and 8, 1999, during the crucial period when they allegedly plotted Bruce Miller's murder.

The records couldn't explicitly corroborate the IM found in Cassaday's briefcase.

And while Potrafka and the computer expert testified flatly that the IM could not have been fabricated, Nickola argued that it could have been faked or altered by anyone with knowledge of computers. Cassaday, furthermore, was a suicidal, alcohol-infested loser who was exacting revenge on Miller for dumping him, Nickola contended.

Nickola also tried to tempt Hughes with his John Hutchinson theory, saying Bruce Miller was killed over a $2,000 debt and Hutchinson's VIN switching at the salvage yard.

But faced with compelling evidence, Hughes had little doubt that Miller used deceit and manipulation to coerce Cassaday to kill, and he ordered the widow to stand trial in the death of her husband.

Genesee County Circuit Judge Judith A. Fullerton, a no-nonsense judge who was very tough on crime, pulled the trial assignment for yet another murder case—*State of Michigan* v. *Sharee Paulette Miller.* And it wasn't likely to linger long in her court. Soon after getting the case, Fullerton assigned it to the grease board in her secretary's office that was labeled ROCKET DOCKET. Fullerton set the trial for December 12, 2000, just ten months after Miller's arrest.

Fullerton's draw delighted Genesee County prosecutor Arthur A. Busch, who believed Fullerton was the right judge for a complex case.

"She's a quick study," Busch said. "Of all the eight circuit court judges, she is upheld most in the appeals court. And this is the kind of case you don't want to try twice."

Given the volume of e-mail and Instant Messages the prosecution would seek to admit, the case was primed for evidence questions. Nickola quickly filed suppression motions to at least keep Cassaday's suicide note to his parents and the November 7 through November 8 IM away from the jury.

During a rare Saturday evidentiary hearing, Nickola argued that those documents fell under rules banning hearsay evidence, that the authenticity of such evidence could not be proven, and that he could not cross-examine Miller's accuser, Jerry Cassaday, a dead man.

But Fullerton, whose distaste for the case was plain, ruled that almost everything was admissible. Her only concession to the defense was on the sexually provocative video *For Jerry's Eyes Only*, recovered from the rubbish at Cassaday's apartment. To maintain courtroom decorum, she ordered substantial cuts to the explicit video.

The rulings incensed Nickola, who nevertheless had to play with the ground rules he'd been handed.

"We're only getting half the story from a ghost who isn't alive," Nickola said, heading back to his office to figure a way to make the government's evidence work to his advantage.

Just days before the December trial, Nickola described the broad outlines of his strategy to a *Flint Journal* reporter.

He said Miller's e-mails to Cassaday would show that she was trying to frighten him away because he was becoming a pest. Her interest in Cassaday, Nickola would argue, was based on an Internet fantasy gone wrong.

Nickola also predicted that prosecutors would try to smear Miller by showing jurors the nude pictures she had sent to Cassaday and the masturbation video.

"She may not be a Roman Catholic, but she's not a murderer," Nickola said.

Miller also had begun to prepare for trial. For months, she had been stashing her medication, hiding pills in her jail cell. From what she knew about prison—mostly from movies and television—Miller had decided she didn't want to go.

That summer, guards had suspected that Miller was suicidal. Midevening on July 27, a deputy remarked that she looked depressed. Miller responded that she felt about as good as could be expected.

But when the deputy left, Miller's roommate told other deputies that Sharee had told her she was going to kill herself. Immediately, Sharee was then moved to a safety cell for eight days of observation.

Later, Miller would contend that her roommate had lied to get her isolated and then take her jail trustee's job, which gave her more responsibility and freedom of movement.

Miller's time in isolation did little to clear her darkening thoughts. She had settled on two plans to deal with that approaching day when a jury would return its verdict.

Under plan A, Miller would be acquitted and she would walk triumphantly out of the courtroom a free woman.

If not, she would move to plan B. She would return to her cell, take the stashed pills and follow Jerry Cassaday into suicide.

With cold-weather activities such as snowmobiling, cross-country skiing, skating and ice fishing, even industrial Flint, Michigan, can pass for a winter wonderland. However, outdoor enthusiasts were surprised on December 12, 2000, when the skies opened and dumped more than a foot of snow on central Michigan.

The blizzard, the worst for a quarter century, not only delayed the opening of Miller's trial but paralyzed Genesee County.

Public offices and private companies closed up shop and schools canceled classes because of a snow emergency that barred all unnecessary traffic from roads and

streets. The *Flint Journal* was unable to publish an edition
that day, the first time in the daily's 150-year history.

While most residents were digging out the following
day, Miller's trial opened at the Genesee County Courthouse. By then, news of the case had spread across the
country, leading some to bill it as the "first Internet murder case." Readers and viewers were captivated by the
case's sleazy elements—sex, suicide, death and deceit—
and news organizations filed in for their place in court
for firsthand coverage.

The case had drawn the most print attention from the
Flint Journal—after all, the slaying occurred in Genesee
County—and from the *Kansas City Star*—Cassaday was a
former local cop. But television news organizations also
viewed the lurid case as a gold mine of compelling news.

Besides the local outlets, the case commanded the full
attention of Court TV, the network that came into
prominence with live coverage of the O. J. Simpson murder trial years earlier.

Court TV would feed footage to NBC for a future
piece on its *Dateline* newsmagazine. A crew from *Inside
Edition* also settled in for the two-week trial.

The first order of business was jury selection.

In most Genesee County murder cases, a pool of up to
forty-five people is paraded into court for voir dire, or
the winnowing process to pick the final panel. For the
Miller trial, the pool was expanded to sixty-four panelists
because of the publicity surrounding the sensational aspects of the case. Court officials and the attorneys
wanted to make sure they had enough potential jurors
left in case many had heard about the case.

Throughout the morning, lawyers whittled away at the
panel, using peremptory challenges to get rid of those
potential jurors they simply didn't feel good about.
Nickola and Mabry had twelve challenges each.

By late that morning, Mabry used only two of her

twelve challenges, and Nickola had used all but one of his dozen.

Nickola was faced with an interesting decision.

With one challenge left, he faced a difficult choice. For the jury that would decide the fate of his client, Nickola could choose either Michael J. Thorp, an anchorman for ABC-12 TV WJRT, or a woman wearing a pink sweater and sporting a crucifix.

With a jury of housewives, my client is dead meat, Nickola thought.

The best jury for Miller, he reasoned, would be one with more men than women.

He opted to keep Thorp. Mabry did not object, and a journalist made the jury.

Thorp was shocked.

Oh, my God, he thought.

Journalists usually are stricken quickly from panels and rarely are selected for juries in high-profile cases. Often they are familiar with the case or somebody involved in it. Or they just know too much about the legal system. But that wasn't the case with Thorp. He could recall little about the Miller case, which after all had started out as a simple robbery-murder. And though he was a lifelong Flint resident, the only person he knew in the courtroom was Judge Fullerton.

Mabry was comfortable with Thorp. During a break, she learned that her boss, Prosecutor Art Busch, was not. Though Busch was close to Thorp personally, he felt the anchorman could be too forgiving. Busch was dumbfounded with Mabry's decision, which he described as a "mental error."

"Why would you do that?" he demanded, pacing a circle in his office. "That wasn't the best decision."

Mabry stood her ground, however.

"They know the real world," she said.

Busch blew off steam for a while, then began to soften.

Perhaps, Busch conceded, Thorp could help other jurors understand the complexities of the case. Which reminded him of one more point he wanted to make with Mabry before opening statements. Do not, he said, overwhelm jurors with technical computer jargon.

"We're not talking about a jury of high-tech silicon geniuses," he said. "If these jurors have a computer, it hasn't been there very long."

Before the jury and alternates—ten men and five women—were sworn, Miller entered the courtroom in handcuffs, wearing a modest maroon blouse and gray slacks. The long ten months in jail had taken their toll on Miller. She was pale and her shoulder-length blond hair was done plainly, with bangs covering her forehead.

Miller walked stiffly because of a restraining device she wore under her slacks that would prevent her from running. Before sitting down, Miller reached down to push a button on the contraption that allowed her leg to bend. Because of the restraint, she could not wear a dress or skirt to court. Showing off the device not only would be unflattering, but it also would remind jurors that she was under arrest.

Miller smiled weakly to her mother, who was sitting in the second row of wooden benches on the left side of the courtroom.

The right side of the gallery was filled with members of both the Cassaday and Bruce Miller families. Print and television reporters and court observers filled out the rest of the seats.

After the jurors were sworn, Marcie Mabry smoothed the wrinkles from her blue suit and lavender blouse and composed herself. She rose and pointed at Miller with a pen she held in her left hand.

"This is about Sharee Miller using and manipulating

her lover, Jerry Cassaday, to kill her husband, Bruce Miller," Mabry began. "She used a computer and his emotions to get him to do it."

Mabry spoke of Jerry's love for Sharee and his willingness to do anything—even commit murder—to have her.

As Fullerton watched intently, Mabry told jurors how Miller used sex and sympathy to rile Cassaday enough to kill.

"Jerry believed he had impregnated Sharee Miller," Mabry said, again pointing to Miller. "And he believed Bruce Miller had caused a miscarriage."

And Cassaday, dumped by the woman he had killed for, had become so despondent and guilt-ridden that he committed suicide, Mabry said.

But he left behind crucial evidence for police in the form of e-mails, pictures and other computer correspondence, Mabry added. That legacy left his family with an awful choice.

"So now his family is faced with the dilemma of what to do," Mabry continued. "They can keep quiet. They can just read that suicide note to themselves and go home and not expose their loved one to all this attention. But they don't. They go to the authorities."

Mabry, who was suffering from a bad cold, rolled a lozenge around her mouth during the statement.

Mabry told jurors that investigators had strip-mined Cassaday's computers over the months and discovered hundreds of e-mails Cassaday and Miller had exchanged that showed the full arc of their relationship.

"It starts out very rosy," Mabry said. "It starts out intense, a very hot relationship."

But, Mabry said, the e-mails also would expose the lies that Miller told Cassaday.

"He's a former cop; he's a saver," Mabry said of Cassaday's trove of e-mail.

She also told jurors they would see and hear the IM chat session that Cassaday and Miller participated in hours before the murder in which the two planned the slaying.

"You will understand the emotional roller coaster that Jerry was on that led him to kill for Sharee Miller," she concluded.

David Nickola attacked Jerry Cassaday in his opening statement, characterizing him as an alcoholic, suicidal liar who only wanted Sharee's money.

"There's absolutely no motive for her at all to kill her husband, a man that was willing to [become] her two youngest children's natural father pursuant to law," Nickola said.

He told jurors that Miller was a sexually active woman who became "addicted" after she discovered the indulgence of Internet pornography; she enjoyed it, alone and with Bruce.

"There are a lot of things that you can get on the Internet," Nickola said. "You can get anything you want as a matter of fact. If you have sexual, bizarre fetishes, you can get any of that there.

"The Internet is the major tool for fantasy in our society."

Wearing a pin-striped black suit and striped white shirt, Nickola told jurors some of Miller's background, how she and Bruce Miller got together and what her older husband offered her.

"Although there was a big age gap, Bruce offered Sharee something she hadn't had before: a man who really respected her and cared for her. And Sharee brought excitement to Bruce's life."

Nickola spoke of their mutual enjoyment of pornography and how the couple played around with sexual fantasies.

Nickola said that Miller also was engaged in a fantasy with Cassaday.

"And Sharee tells him some things that are absolutely ridiculous. And you'll be able to read them and realize that what they are talking about is ridiculous. She's living . . . as a housewife. . . . She creates this fantasy where she is the wife of a Mafia boss. And that she has a lot of money. And that they have this empire. That he's involved in racketeering. And that her husband beats her. So she's longing for somebody to protect her.

Nikola then drilled to the core of his analysis of Cassaday's troubled psyche: Jerry's obsession with the money that Sharee had bragged about. ". . . One thing in particular sticks in his mind . . . the money. That's what the facts are going to show what was on his mind."

To hammer home his theories, Nickola dragged out a large notebook on a stand. Flipping pages with a sneer, Nickola launched into his Cassaday postmortem.

"Jerry 'Cassanova' Loves $haree," he had written, crossing the *S* in her first name to create a dollar sign.

Later, Nickola wrote the slogan from *Jerry Maguire*—"$how me the money"—again using a dollar sign for the *S*.

Nickola also told jurors that Cassaday, with his college education, police experience and computer knowledge, knew exactly what he was doing.

"He's no pawn. He's no sucker. He's no wimp. He's his own man. He has his own intentions," Nickola said. "The money issue is what keeps him motivated.

"[But Miller is] always putting him off because she has no intention, no intention at all, of leaving her husband," Nickola said.

Nickola also read some of Cassaday's more poetic e-mails, mocking his intentions.

"If you would believe the prosecutor . . . you would think he's very much in love," Nickola said.

Then, with a sly grin, Nickola took a sip of water from

a Styrofoam cup before landing an uppercut on Cassaday's fidelity to Miller.

"But, ladies and gentlemen, we also got his hard drive," he said.

Nickola said that Cassaday, who portrayed himself as turning his life around in Missouri, beating alcohol and drug addiction and attending church, actually was deeply involved in Internet lust himself.

He said prosecutors would not show jurors the photos of other women that Cassaday downloaded, or of e-mail he exchanged with other women, or of the nude photos of Miller that he sent out, posing as her, or his own Web surfing to gay Internet sites. But Nickola would show those, he said, so the jury could see that Cassaday was not the choirboy that prosecutors presented.

Nickola read one e-mail that Cassaday wrote to another woman.

"Will we ever meet?" the message cooed.

"Jerry's got a lot of women on the side," Nickola said. "He's a real Casanova."

And Cassaday's bitter correspondence with Miller after November 8, 1999, showed that he knew the relationship was over after Bruce Miller died, Nickola said.

"When Bruce Miller died, so did the fantasy," Nickola said.

"His fantasy about the money was no longer there. He wouldn't stop drinking. He wouldn't stop lying. What happened was he became bitter, hostile and vengeful toward her."

Nickola also attacked the suicide note.

"When you see that suicide note, [you see] all the hostility in life, all the hostility he has. Everything is her fault. No responsibility whatsoever for his problems."

But Nickola saved his big guns for last, attacking the veracity of the alleged IM plotting the murder, saying it could have been manipulated.

And he told jurors they would see and hear the person who was responsible for Bruce Miller's death.

"We have a killer in this case," Nickola said. "And I'll tell you something, [it's] not my client. Wait till you hear about this.

"Your real killer is John Hutchinson."

Nickola claimed that "Hutchinson was facing some serious prison time, serious prison time" for VIN switching.

He told jurors that Hutchinson owed Bruce Miller $2,000, and that Bruce wanted his money.

"And when Bruce Miller died, the evidence against John Hutchinson [was] gone," Nickola said. "He found himself free, with no prison. Free with no jail.

"Not only does he wipe out the thousands of dollars he owes, he gains thousands of dollars. And he wipes out prison."

After suggesting that police also bungled the investigation, Nickola told the jurors that prosecutors could not prove their case beyond a reasonable doubt.

He said Sharee Miller received very little from the Bruce Miller estate, so money was not a motive.

"She didn't do it," he said.

FOURTEEN

The prosecution's evidence against Sharee Miller began at about 4:20 P.M. with Chuck Miller, who quickly dispelled Sharee's violent e-mail portrait of his brother. Bruce Miller, Chuck said, was a simple, quiet man who worked at GM. His only dream was to own a salvage yard and attend NASCAR races.

Marcie Mabry also chipped away at Sharee's notion that her husband was an Internet sex geek.

"Did you ever see your brother on a computer?" she asked Chuck Miller.

He answered without hesitation.

"I've never seen my brother use a computer," Chuck Miller said. "I wouldn't consider him a real good speller. And if he was typing something, it would be with one finger."

Under Mabry's questioning, Miller said he and Bruce never had a brother named Jeff, who was injured in a construction accident and subsequently died.

Chuck Miller also recalled the evening of November 8—the frantic telephone calls from his sister-in-law, the drive to B&D and finding his brother's body.

Mabry then played a tape of the 911 emergency call that Judy Miller made from the junkyard.

Chuck Miller dropped his head as the tape played, his memory flooding with awful sights and feelings. Sitting just a few feet away, Sharee Miller showed no emotion, appearing more like a reserved librarian than an Internet temptress.

Miller sat passively the entire day, much as she would through most of the trial. Occasionally, she would sit with her hands clasped to her chest, reflecting a pose she described to Cassaday in a September 24 e-mail.

"You are always trying to take my hands away from my chest when I am scared," Miller wrote. "But that protects me Jerry."

Now, facing an intent, focused jury, she needed all the protection she could get.

Dr. Terry Krznarich, a pathologist at Hurley Medical Center in Flint, followed Chuck Miller and told of his findings at Bruce Miller's autopsy.

Autopsy testimony usually is gruesome and some jurors squirmed as Krznarich told them in cold clinical terms that the shotgun blast hit Bruce Miller between his chin and sternum, shredding the sweatshirt he was wearing.

The pathologist saved pellets from the corpse for evidence.

Mabry shifted scenes for her next witness, from a junkyard in Genesee County to an idyllic lakeside setting in Missouri. Detective Sergeant Brian Gillespie of the Lafayette County Sheriff's Department told of being called to a home and finding Cassaday slumped in a chair with a rifle, surrounded by pictures of his ex-wife, children and Miller.

Nearby were a wedding ring, an asthma inhaler and medication bottles for Prozac.

"We had all the key indicators this was a suicide," Gillespie said.

Testimony that first day ended with Roger Cassaday, who told of his only meeting with Sharee Miller in Reno.

Roger Cassaday told jurors how he held up a sign—YANKEE BABE—at the airport so Sharee Miller would be able to find him, of their drive to Jerry Cassaday's apartment and of the stories she spun.

He said Miller told him about owning a nursing home and a salvage yard and of plans for her to buy an expensive home with Cassaday in Reno, Nevada.

Although the first day's testimony hardly was explosive, the day ended with fireworks.

Before the day had begun, Judge Judith Fullerton put reporters on notice that she would tolerate no media foolishness. The only television camera allowed in court would be operated by Court TV, which would have to share its feed with the local and national outlets.

And Fullerton instructed reporters that jurors were not to be photographed.

At the end of the day, her law clerk saw a hallway crewman from *Inside Edition* pointing a camera at jurors as they filed from the courtroom. Fullerton exploded, ordering the crew into the courtroom for a stern face-off.

Fullerton opened by wondering out loud if she should convene a contempt hearing.

A producer for the newsmagazine program pleaded with Fullerton, explaining the camera was not operating and only *appeared* to be videotaping jurors. He offered to show Fullerton the tape, saying the entire incident was an unfortunate misunderstanding.

Unmoved, but needing evidence, Fullerton checked with her clerk, who said the taping appeared intentional. Fullerton instantly settled on swift and immediate punishment.

"You are out," she said, banning *Inside Edition*'s cameras from the courthouse.

Out-of-town reporters were stunned, but the locals just smiled. This was how Fullerton always operated, they explained: she would not allow her court to become a circus.

* * *

With little flash, Mabry built the case against Miller brick by brick. On December 14, 2000, she questioned Dr. Celestine Joseph, an obstetrician and gynecologist, who confirmed that she had performed Miller's tubal ligation at Hurley Medical Center in 1995.

Next up were Carol Slaughter and Gloria Taylor, two Harrah's casino employees who worked with Cassaday.

Slaughter told Mabry about how she saw Bruce Miller's obituary on the *Flint Journal* Web site and noticed something odd. The obituary said that Bruce and Sharee were married in April 1999, but Slaughter had never heard that Sharee and Bruce were married, only that Bruce had shown a romantic interest in Sharee after Jeff had died.

"I was very surprised that it said she was Bruce's wife," Slaughter said.

"She said her mother-in-law wanted it written that way and she was upset. Then she said they had run off and gotten married the Monday before Bruce was killed."

Taylor also spoke of her contact with Sharee Miller on one of her visits to Reno, when Cassaday would show her off to his fellow employees.

"They had stayed on the casino floor so he could introduce her to the graveyard shift, all the foremen and the dealers," Taylor said. "They were happy. They looked like they were having a wonderful time. He was showing off the woman he adored."

Though Sharee Miller had changed into a brown pantsuit, jurors and others could see little change in her demeanor. She was attentive and observant, but she still showed little emotion.

After testifying, both Slaughter and Taylor said they were surprised when they saw Miller in court. Unlike the flashy debutante image Miller had presented in Reno, she now appeared mousy, wearing ill-fitting glasses that the Reno Miller never would have worn.

"It was like night and day," Slaughter said.

Taylor agreed.

"The person I saw sitting in that courtroom was not the same person I saw in Reno," she said.

Mike Cassaday, Jerry's brother, took the stand next, choking up as he talked of finding his brother's suicide notes and the briefcase under the bed. As Mabry read the suicide note, jurors watched attentively. Miller's face was blank, but for a moment she drew her hands to her chest, again betraying internal stress.

Nickola, however, responded to the letter with a smirk.

Charlene Cassaday followed her son to the witness stand, describing her son's troubled past and mysterious fling with Miller. Mabry closed her examination of Charlene Cassaday with a compelling question: "Does your family believe Sharee Miller is responsible for the death of your son?"

The mother's reply surprised no one.

"We have no doubt," she said.

After showing jurors the *My Family 1999* video, prosecutors called Don Colcolough, AOL's senior manager for network security and investigations in Dulles, Virginia.

Michigan assistant attorney general Peter Plummer, a computer crimes expert who had not taken an active role in the trial until now, coaxed the stiff computer specialist through dry testimony that threatened to put jurors into a glazed-over stupor.

Though Colcolough's testimony could hardly be called compelling, it was necessary for prosecutors to show how Cassaday and Miller used the Internet.

Colcolough said that Miller and Cassaday were among AOL's 100 million users spread out in 26 million accounts, and they were also 2 of the 70 million subscribers using the company's Instant Messenger service.

Using company records, Colcolough told jurors that Cassaday and Miller—or someone using the screen names JLC1006 and SHAREE1013—were on-line simultaneously from roughly midevening November 7 through the early-morning hours of November 8.

Plummer asked if he could falsify an IM, print it out and make it look believable, and Colcolough said it could be done, but it would be difficult.

"Depending on the capability of the user, it could be easy or hard," he said.

"For somebody who is our usual member, who's not very technical, it would be hard. For somebody who is savvy with a computer, you could do it fairly easy."

He explained that manipulation of the information would require better than average computer skills and a basket of other abilities—knowledge about AOL software, printing, word processing and applications, and the capability to change fonts, colors and spacing.

"It could be done," he said. "I could do it."

But after examining the IM in which Cassaday and Miller allegedly plotted the murder, Colcolough said he was certain of one thing.

"This printout is consistent with those produced by America Online products," Colcolough said. "It appears to be consistent with an Instant Message. It appears to be authentic."

But Colcolough's admission that an Instant Message could be faked was a victory for Nickola, who pulled another concession out of the expert the next morning, December 15, when court resumed.

Colcolough said that if Cassaday knew Miller's password, he could have sent e-mail to himself under her screen name to make it look as if Miller had sent it.

An e-mail forger also could change dates and times on the e-mail to suit his purpose.

Other witnesses that day included a motel front-desk supervisor who presented records showing that a "Sharee Cassaday" had checked in on October 4, 1999, and checked out the next morning. Those were days in which Cassaday could have been in Michigan, though it never was firmly established.

Next, the night auditor for a motel in nearby Birch Run showed a reservation made for Jerry Cassaday on November 3, 1999, that was canceled ten hours later that same day.

Mabry followed with witnesses, many of them Sharee Miller's closest friends, whose testimony suggested that she was a practiced and accomplished liar.

Laura Ewald, in obvious discomfort because she was forced to testify against her friend, took the stand for an account of the trip she and Miller took to Reno in July. She said Miller never left with Cassaday, and she saw them spend time alone only while Miller was playing blackjack.

Ewald also fought tears as she described what she and Miller were doing the night Bruce Miller was killed. Ewald also gave jurors a sad picture of her friend's crying jag after learning that Bruce Miller had been killed.

The next witness, Jennifer Dege, testified how she and Miller used the Internet to meet strangers.

Mabry called to the stand a mathematician, who calculated that the odds of Miller making the same mistake on the envelope found in her computer desk—the misspelling of Missouri attorney John P. O'Connor's name and transposing the digits in his home and office telephone numbers—independently of Cassaday were 1 in 6.4 billion.

After a firearms expert testified about tool marks on shotguns, Mabry called Ives Potrafka, now an agent for the Michigan Attorney General's High Tech Crime Unit, but formerly the lead investigator for the Genesee County Sheriff's Department's probe of Bruce Miller's death.

The relative dullness of the preceding 2½ days of testimony had lulled observers and jurors to expect just another investigator with another notebook full of careful corroborating evidence. They couldn't have been more wrong.

The trial was about to erupt with tension and graphic images; it would morph into a mini–passion play.

On the trial's third day, Miller looked a bit more attractive than usual, opting for a peach-colored blouse and cream slacks. And though her demeanor hadn't changed, Potrafka was one witness who could hurt her the most, or help her, depending on how her lawyer handled him.

Nickola, who painted the police as bumbling boobs in his opening statement, had his main foil on the stand and listened intently for opportunities.

Potrafka started slowly, describing to Plummer the three formal statements he had taken from Miller before he left the sheriff's department.

He said that almost immediately Miller had pointed him to potential suspects—John Hutchinson, several people who were in the junkyard that day, an ex-husband and another customer who was not happy with the price Bruce Miller had paid for a car.

Potrafka also told Plummer that he had checked Miller's computer after her arrest but had found nothing related to the death of Bruce Miller. The material could have been overwritten by subsequent computer material, Potrafka speculated.

However, he said investigators uncovered a wealth of information from Cassaday's hard drive in February and March 2000. Using forensic software and key-word searches, Potrafka said investigators found more than five thousand hits and recovered about five hundred significant e-mails and other correspondence between Miller and Cassaday relating to their relationship or Bruce Miller's death.

Jurors eventually would be given three-inch-thick binders containing those e-mails.

The most dramatic moment yet in the trial opened when prosecutors introduced the long Instant Message chat session Cassaday and Miller had on November 7 through 8 when they allegedly plotted the murder.

Instead of having Potrafka read the IM that was found in Cassaday's briefcase, prosecutors sought to bring the words to life.

Two Genesee County Sheriff's Department deputies were called to read the e-mails—aloud—for jurors.

Deputy Diane Watson would read Miller's words, and Sergeant David Dwyre posed as Cassaday.

Nickola objected strenuously, but Fullerton allowed the deputies to play the parts as long as they read the text in a flat, unemotional tone.

Still, the readings were dramatic, the conspirators' words chilling. The courtroom hushed and everyone fixed on the deputies who became Miller and Cassaday. As the words and phrases tumbled from their mouths, they embodied Cassaday and Miller, plotting murder in a blur of chopped sentences, instructions and declarations of their love.

"What is the fastest way into the yard from seventy-five?"
"I will call Bruce at five P.M."
"And keep him on the phone."
"Jerry, if this don't work, he will hurt me bad."
"You will never see him again."
"Take his wallet, the whole thing."
"I can do this."
"I love you."
"Is the gun loud?"
"Inside will be best."
"Don't look at him, don't talk to him."
"Just do it and get the hell out of there."
"I want him to know who I am."

"Are you going to be able to live with this for the rest of your life?"
"We will never discuss it again."
"Tell me you forgive me."
"Don't leave fingerprints."

When the IM was finished, the court remained still for a few seconds as everyone absorbed what they had heard. Even reporters who had read the IM dozens of times before the trial were struck by the power and the purpose of the exchange.

The case against Miller had now picked up momentum, and Mabry sensed that now was no time to slow down.

The prosecutor moved to introduce the masturbation video, *For Jerry's Eyes Only.*

Though Nickola had argued before trial to keep the video away from jurors, he again moved to get it off the table. He told Fullerton he would stipulate to jurors that a video of Miller "undressing and masturbating" exists.

But Fullerton was loath to dicker over settled rulings. She already had ordered that the most explicit portions of the video be excised.

"Maybe I shouldn't take into account the defendant's privacy rights, but given the decorum of this court, I didn't feel [jurors] needed to see all of it," Fullerton said.

Before playing the tape, Fullerton told jurors the ten-minute video was edited because it was "graphic, explicit [and] pornographic."

Miller's mother quietly left the courtroom.

Fullerton allowed jurors to see what was happening on the tape until Miller began disrobing. At that point, the picture reverted to a blue screen, though jurors could hear the music.

Miller lowered her head and put her hands over her forehead, covering her face and hazel eyes from the jurors as the video opened to the sweet, sexy sounds of a country ballad.

As "Angel" played during the tape's second segment, Miller put her hand over her mouth, took her glasses off and turned her face down as she rubbed her eyes. Miller sat and endured the humiliation of a video she had made for her Internet lover.

It was the only time during the prosecution's case she showed outward signs of distress, emotion or shame.

To buttress the authenticity of the IM, Potrafka clicked off a list of more than twenty similarities between the plan as described in the Internet correspondence and what police found while investigating the homicide.

Those included the discovery of bruised photos of Sharee Miller in Cassaday's briefcase; the accuracy of directions to and from the salvage yard; references to "the Point," a Flint description of an odd intersection near the junkyard that an outsider wouldn't likely know; the missing money from Bruce Miller's pocket; the signs that the killing was part of a robbery; the order of Sharee's calls to law enforcement, state police first, "local assholes" last; the timing of Sharee's calls to the junkyard; and, of course, the hard, indisputable fact that O'Connor's misspelled name and twisted telephone numbers appeared identically in the IM and on the back of an envelope found in Miller's computer hutch.

Potrafka then read the BDJUNK e-mails that taunted Cassaday about Sharee Miller's abortions.

Nickola's cross-examination focused heavily on errors Potrafka made early in his investigation, including the detective's assumption through the preliminary examination that Instant Messages could not be altered or faked. Nickola also hammered Potrafka on mistakes he made in calculating Miller's financial situation after her husband's death.

The IM also wasn't a perfect predictor of the homicide, Nickola observed. Potrafka acknowledged a number of inconsistencies between the murder and the Instant Message, including the point at which Miller allegedly says she will tell her husband she's ordered dinner, but assured Cassaday she would not.

Indeed, Miller had called the restaurant and ordered fish.

But investigators believed that was merely a last-minute refinement the conspirators made at the Interstate 75 rest stop as Miller passed her cell phone to Cassaday.

As jurors filed out during an afternoon break, they were puzzled about what they had seen—or, rather, hadn't seen—on the sex video.

Because the nudity and masturbation sequences were edited out, all they saw was Miller walking in front of the camera and getting on the water bed before the screen turned to blue.

Michael Thorp, the anchorman, briefly discussed his bewilderment with other jurors during the break. Then he asked Fullerton's law clerk if he could ask a question.

"I can't answer you," the clerk replied.

"Well, I'm going to ask you anyway," Thorp pressed. "Are we supposed to take the judge's word for it that this is pornography?"

The question caught the clerk off guard.

"I'll ask the judge," he said.

Thorp's question prompted a crisis meeting in chambers between Fullerton and the lawyers. Mabry, who always had pushed to have the entire video played unedited, said she was "concerned that evidence has no value now."

Nickola strenuously objected to Thorp's question, but Fullerton tabled the discussion for now. There would be plenty of time to sort through the questions before the prosecution finished its case.

When jurors returned, the two deputies began reading page by page through hundreds of e-mails exchanged between Cassaday and Miller between July and November 1999. But the recitation began too late on Friday afternoon. They would not conclude until the following Tuesday when the trial resumed.

One evening early in the trial, Thorp returned home and discovered that even he couldn't leave the case at the courthouse. Though his colleagues at the TV station knew better than to ask Thorp for his thoughts on the case, his ten-year-old daughter had no such reservations.

Brimming with news, she tried to tell her father about a trip she made to the Genesee County Jail as part of the D.A.R.E. program, which teaches kids the dangers of drugs.

When the little girl said Sharee Miller was the woman who had spoken to her class, Thorp lunged to silence his daughter.

"Stop!" he almost screamed.

Thorp didn't want to scare his daughter, but he also didn't want to hear anything about Miller or the trial outside the courtroom, as Fullerton had ordered.

Months later, Thorp called the Genesee County Sheriff's Department, demanding answers.

"Why are you introducing my daughter to a [suspected] murderer without my permission?" he asked.

He also was concerned because Miller was not charged with a drug offense, which is the whole purpose of D.A.R.E. Department officials explained that Miller was used to balance the racial component of the inmates who talked to students.

Most of the inmates in the jail were black, and Miller, a white woman, was used to show kids that white people also could go to jail.

* * *

When the trial resumed on December 19, Miller again entered the courtroom handcuffed and hobbled by her leg brace; she wore a maroon sweater and blouse.

The deputies completed their e-mail recitation.

Mabry introduced telephone records showing calls made between Miller's house and her cell phone to various other numbers, which police believed showed her setting up an alibi and signaling to Jerry that Bruce was alone.

Fullerton still was concerned about the jurors' take on the masturbation video, so she allowed Mabry to call Detective Sergeant Kevin Shanlian to the stand to explain the video. Miller, Shanlian said, was masturbating and writhing naked on a water bed.

With that, the prosecution rested.

After failing to receive a directed verdict—a customary tactic in which defense lawyers ask a judge to dismiss the charges because prosecutors have not proven their case—Nickola pushed ahead.

Nickola would call seven witnesses in his ardent defense of Miller.

His first was Paul Albee, a private forensic computer expert, who said that anyone with a good working knowledge of computers could fabricate e-mails and IMs.

"On a scale of one to ten, how difficult is it to save an IM to disk and then make changes?" Nickola asked.

"I'd say two to save it to disk and three to make the changes," Albee said. "If you're familiar with word processing, you can do it."

As part of his demonstration, Nickola showed jurors a faked IM, with Potrafka's name inserted in several spots.

Under cross-examination by Plummer, however, Albee admitted that he could find nothing about the November 7 through November 8 IM to suggest it had been saved, altered or faked.

Nickola fought to rehabilitate his expert's testimony.

"How could you tell that document was authentic?" he asked Albee, showing him the IM.

"I would have to ask Mr. Cassaday," Albee responded.

"I have no further questions," Nickola said, walking briskly back to the defense table.

He next called Peter Doerr, the lawyer who was working with Sharee Miller on Bruce's adoption of her two youngest children.

Doerr said he had never met Bruce Miller and was working on the adoption plan because Sharee Miller hired him.

Another lawyer, probate specialist Ira Bare, followed to describe his work on the estate of Bruce Miller, who died without a will.

Bare said at the time of Bruce Miller's death, the Millers were carrying about $46,000 in credit card debt. And in all, their debts amounted to $150,000, he said.

Bare said because of mortgages and debts, the estate's financial picture was a mess.

"I've never had an attorney's fee as high for an estate this small," he said.

He called his fee of $12,000 or $13,000 "obscene for the size of this estate."

Bare said that when all was said and done, Sharee Miller received about $70,000 of her husband's money— not the $200,000 as prosecutors had claimed months before—after selling the junkyard and paying off debts following her husband's death.

The next three witnesses Nickola called all played a major role in his theory of who really killed Bruce Miller.

They included Anthony Patrick Birch, who was a nervous teen and the stepson of John Hutchinson, Harold Hutchinson, a junkyard employee who was the brother of John Hutchinson, and John Hutchinson himself, the man who murdered Bruce Miller, Nickola told jurors.

Birch was first, and he said his stepfather was acting

strangely the night of the murder. He said John Hutchinson was away from their home about the time of the slaying, and his stepfather later ordered him to find Harold Hutchinson and tell him to call his brother.

Anticipation rose in the courtroom as Nickola then prepared to square off with John Hutchinson.

Despite the frigid weather outdoors, Nickola's accused murderer took the stand wearing a short-sleeved polo shirt with broad vertical stripes of white and gray. Clean shaven and lucid, he nevertheless appeared shifty and uncomfortable, which was to be expected given that Nickola had accused him of a crime he vehemently had denied from day one.

Nickola asked about a statement Hutchinson had given to officers in which he nodded his head affirmatively when asked if he killed Bruce Miller.

By now, Hutchinson hated Nickola and his portrayal of him as a killer, but he was cool on the stand and would give no more than he had to.

He told Nickola he did not nod his head, no matter what a police report said.

"It's been a year ago and my memory ain't that perfect," he said. ". . . I did not nod my head yes."

He explained that he worked at the junkyard until Sharee and Bruce Miller bought out Bruce's original business partner and Hutchinson acknowledged owing Bruce Miller $2,000 at the time of his death.

"Bruce expected to be paid in cash and in full," he said of the debt.

John Hutchinson also acknowledged stealing auto parts from B&D, but denied telling his brother he would kill Bruce Miller over the VIN-switching investigation. He said that he and Bruce Miller were friends who got along fine, and that he was able to borrow cash from his friend by simply asking.

"He was tight-fisted, but he'd loan it to me 'cause we got along good," he said.

He told Nickola that he subsequently had been charged with a felony in the VIN-switching case but had pleaded it down to a misdemeanor.

Nickola then asked him the question everyone wanted to hear.

"Did you kill Bruce Miller?"

"No, I positively did not," John Hutchinson replied without hesitation.

He said Bruce Miller liked to "flash cash," his term for carrying a hefty wad of bills in plain sight to those who dealt with the junkyard owner. Hutchinson also acknowledged recently bouncing a $750 check.

Throughout, John Hutchinson appeared unflappable, and he actually yawned after one of Nickola's questions.

Nickola then asked his setup question, one that Hutchinson's brother would answer later in an altogether different manner.

"Do you remember telling Harold Hutchinson before Bruce Miller was murdered that if you got in trouble for that car out at B & D that Bruce Miller would be in trouble, too?"

"No," John Hutchinson spat out.

Nickola asked another pointed question.

"Did you call your brother approximately a week before Bruce Miller's death [and say] that you were going to kill Bruce Miller over this loan?"

"No," he answered.

He said he thought he talked to Harold Hutchinson on the night of the murder, but he denied any role in "disposing" of the man over the VIN switching.

Mabry's cross-examination of John Hutchinson was brief. Prosecutors did not want him on the stand too long, since he was not *their* suspect, and they believed placing too much emphasis on him would distract jurors from the real defendant, Sharee Miller.

Hutchinson told Mabry that he had a plan to repay Bruce Miller the $2,000 through a friend. He said a man who had just purchased a home from him would pay Bruce Miller the money he owed. Hutchinson said he had paid Bruce Miller off in that manner in the past. Bruce Miller, however, did not know of the plan at the time of his death because Hutchinson said he hadn't yet told him about it.

He also denied any favorable treatment from prosecutors in the VIN-switching case to help prosecutors in this murder trial.

To many in the court, John Hutchinson did not look, sound or act much like a killer, which would have dealt a fatal blow to Nickola's case.

But the only opinions that mattered at this stage were jurors', and their poker-faced expressions were impossible to read.

Next on Nickola's list was Harold Hutchinson, a man who almost failed to appear for trial. As with most witnesses, Hutchinson had received an expense check to assure he made it to court. After Hutchinson had cashed the check and never contacted Nickola, the court sent state police to bring him in. They found him living in a car near Alpena in northern Michigan.

Gaunt, bearded and unkempt, Harold Hutchinson appeared confused and borderline retarded. His testimony, though, was crucial to Nickola's case.

Hutchinson said he had worked for Bruce Miller for more than four years and that he liked him.

"Bruce was a great friend of mine and a good guy," Harold Hutchinson said. "I never had any problems with him."

He told Nickola that on the night Bruce Miller was

killed, Birch came to him and told him to call John Hutchinson.

"He told me it was urgent for me to get a hold of him," Harold Hutchinson said.

Nickola asked if his brother had told him he had disposed of Bruce over the VIN-switching investigation.

"Yes," he said.

The admission was a solid victory for Nickola, and one that Mabry had to assault on cross-examination. She first asked Harold Hutchinson about the call to John Hutchinson the evening of the murder, trying to get the gist of the conversation.

But Harold Hutchinson couldn't follow her question.

"When I talked to him on the phone, from then on back?" he asked.

Mabry rephrased the question, hoping it was simpler.

"Do you understand my question?" she asked.

"I understand your question," Harold Hutchinson said. "But you can't go at the back tail end of the cat and figure on having all the meat, 'cause you ain't gonna get it. You're missing three-quarters from the first. That's what I'm trying to explain."

The courtroom erupted in bemused laughter, and even Mabry chuckled, wondering aloud how a cat got into the discussion.

But she coaxed an answer of sorts from Hutchinson about what he meant when he told police that his brother had "disposed" of Bruce Miller.

Harold Hutchinson said that after he told his brother he needed more money than he was making at the junkyard, John Hutchinson told him to go there the following day and collect his tools. After that, John Hutchinson would get him a better job and his issues with Miller would be "disposed of."

Mabry then asked Harold Hutchinson if he ever told

police that his brother had admitted murdering Bruce Miller.

"No, he did not," Harold Hutchinson said.

But Harold did admit that he had taken Prozac the day he had spoken to officers, and he had been drinking to forget his own problems.

"When my nerves get shot, everything kind of goes blank on me," Harold Hutchinson said.

Fullerton recessed court after Hutchinson stepped down. Nickola had but one witness left, and he knew she'd need a good night's sleep to turn this case around. Sharee Miller was handcuffed after jurors left the courtroom. As deputies led her from the court, she turned to her mother, who was sitting in the audience.

"I love you," Sharee said.

FIFTEEN

For days, people close to the case knew Sharee P. Miller would testify.

She had to. She had too many questions to answer about conflicting statements she had made to her family, friends and Cassaday, about infidelity to her husband, about her e-mails and how that torn envelope with the misspelled lawyer's name and mixed-up telephone numbers had turned up in her computer hutch.

But the question everyone wanted answered was the most obvious: Did she plot to kill Bruce Miller? If not, how could she explain away the vile descriptions of him in her e-mails to Jerry Cassaday?

Through Nickola's opening statement, his questioning of the prosecution's witnesses and into his own case, he had hammered home the theory that Sharee Miller had more to gain by living with Bruce than by having him killed.

Nickola dismissed Cassaday as a flake who had pressured Sharee Miller for money to escape his own financial burdens. And before his death, Nickola argued, Cassaday fabricated an Instant Message to frame himself and Sharee Miller for a murder they did not commit. John Hutchinson, not Cassaday, was the real killer, Nickola contended.

The jurors had heard all that. But now, they would hear it from Miller herself.

Anticipation swept Fullerton's courtroom the morning of December 20, 2000, as Nickola called Miller to the stand. Wearing wire-frame glasses, a maroon top and slacks, Miller blew a kiss to her mother as she stood and walked gingerly to the witness-box.

Most attorneys drill their clients on how to look, act and answer, rehearsing and revising the script to make the defense case credible to jurors. When the dress rehearsal was over, however, only the accused could carry the day.

Nickola at first took a quiet, easy approach to this client, tossing out soft questions aimed at warming her up on the stand and letting the jury see her as a mother, a wife, a grieving widow.

Sharee Miller began by telling jurors she graduated from Kearsley High School in 1988. It sounded convincing, but jurors could not be expected to know that she graduated a year later from the school's adult education program.

From there, Nickola took Miller through her life, her abusive childhood, her failed marriages and her children.

Quickly, he moved to her relationship with Bruce Miller. She said she met him in 1998 and was working at B&D before Bruce Miller bought it from a business partner.

Miller said that both she and Bruce were living with other people at the time, but after Bruce's father died, they became romantically involved. When their significant others learned of the affair, those relationships disintegrated, leaving the lovers a smooth path to intimacy. "He made me laugh," she said of Bruce Miller.

"We had a lot in common. We could talk about anything," Miller said.

At first, Sharee Miller said, she and her kids began spending nights at the Bruce Miller home on West Francis Road in Mount Morris Township.

In December, she and Bruce went to Las Vegas. Before

leaving, Bruce gave her a diamond two-carat band that he had received for a car at the junkyard. Miller said she'd worn it on her left hand as a sign to others to stay away.

She said Bruce Miller proposed to her in February 1999, and in April they flew back to Las Vegas to get married.

Miller told Nickola that the security and softness that Bruce Miller offered meant a lot to her and the kids. Her voice quivering, Miller glanced at the jury.

"I don't even know if there's a word to describe the feeling that I had that somebody was finally, actually taking care of us instead of hurting us," she said. "I don't know how to explain that. I didn't even know how to act, to finally have somebody active in my children's lives, wanting to be a dad."

Nickola gently led her into the July 1999 trip to Reno with her friend Laura Ewald and her first meeting with Cassaday.

During the police interview before her arrest, Sharee Miller initially had denied having an affair with Cassaday. But now, with too much evidence showing a substantial relationship, Miller had no recourse but to acknowledge it. She was trapped in her earlier lies and had to speak frankly about her involvement with Cassaday.

Miller said she had gone out for a short vacation with her friend Laura Ewald to unwind, see the sights, gamble, go to shows and see if she could sell cosmetics.

"I was at my high point," Miller said. "I hadn't been selling Mary Kay very long, but I had a lot of customers."

After getting dressed up, the two went to the casino. Miller said she had worn a long dress, had her hair fixed and was wearing the $14 costume-jewelry rings. She also wore her two-carat wedding band.

Miller said Cassaday tried hitting on her that night at the blackjack table, and he was more impressed with her fake diamond rings than with her wedding band.

"Did you ever meet with him when he was off work?" Nickola asked.

"No, not that time," she said.

That night, she admitted, she began lying to Cassaday about owning a nursing home and being married to a guy named Jeff, who had been injured and was brain-dead from falling off a roof. She spun tales that Cassaday believed.

"I told him a lot of stories that day," Sharee said. "It was fun."

When she returned to her home near Flint, Miller said, she and Cassaday began communicating via the Internet. Since she and Bruce were heavily involved in pornographic Web sites on the Internet, Cassaday also joined in the sex-chat fun. Miller said her husband knew of Jerry then, but not of her relationship with him. Miller said she and Cassaday used that as part of their own fantasy.

That e-mail relationship grew more intense and both longed for it to get physical, she said. By then, she said, she was addicted to the Internet and its ocean of pornography.

And Miller rushed to the sexual stimulation. During the trial, prosecutors introduced dozens of screen names Sharee Miller had used. Some were of garden variety, like SHAREE1013.

But Justhot2cu, HORNEY7249, IWANTTOBELAID, Lovemeslowly, Sexykitten4onlyu, Iluvsexsomuch, I69luv6969, Hotcootch and Love694140 had given jurors another glimpse of her psyche.

"You could be anybody you wanted to be," she said of the faceless Internet sex chats with Jerry Cassaday and others. "Bruce and I both made up stories about who I was."

But she said there was something about Cassaday's e-mails that was particularly intriguing.

"His e-mails were so intense; it was like a fairy tale," she said. "I was addicted to it. I wanted to see if this was the same person who was writing to me."

Miller said she did not have sex with Cassaday until her August visit to Reno, physically consummating an Internet fantasy.

To get away from her husband in August, and smooth over any qualms he may have had, she told Bruce that she was visiting a sick friend, Carol.

She also said she told Jerry about Bruce during the August trip.

"He had a lot of money," she remembered telling Cassaday. "He was a Mafia person" and also involved in counterfeiting.

But as time wore on, she said, Cassaday became a pest, and she tried to persuade him to leave her alone.

Miller said after the August trip, "our relationship started dying down.

". . . At that point, I wanted Jerry to leave me alone," she said.

When she tried to break up with him later, Cassaday used the sexually explicit video she had sent him as blackmail, threatening to send a copy to Bruce or his family. She said Cassaday also threatened to send it to her ex-husband, with whom she was involved in a custody battle over her oldest son. Miller said she believed the adult video would smear her and allow her ex-husband to regain custody of her oldest boy.

She said Cassaday had become suicidal, drinking heavily and getting into trouble with the law in Reno. She said Cassaday had shown up in Michigan unexpectedly in early October to celebrate his birthday, but that trip was a flop.

Cassaday had called her from a motel, but she couldn't spend much time with him. "I was there twenty or thirty minutes," Miller said.

"Bruce was on sick leave a lot of that time," she explained. "He wasn't working a lot and he was home that night, so I couldn't stay at the hotel with him."

She said Cassaday caught a taxi later and went out, getting supremely drunk. Miller said she went to the motel the following day and found Cassaday passed out on the bed, his room a shambles and a glass door cracked. After Cassaday told her he had lost his wallet and money in a bar, she said they spent much of the day trying to get faxes of his identification from Nevada so he could board an airplane to return home.

Miller said Cassaday had become consumed by the fantasy they had constructed on the Internet, despite the outrageous stories she had fed him. His life was spiraling downward, reaching its low points with the drunk-driving arrest and the arrest at the casino.

She said she agreed to go to Reno and help him prepare for a move back to Missouri so he could be near family and get his life back on track. To boost his spirits, she told Cassaday in October she was pregnant.

"He felt good," she said. "It made him want to get better. It made him want to quit drinking, quit pills, quit smoking marijuana."

But Miller said her main objective was to ease away from Cassaday. To push him out of her life, Miller said, she sent him three taunting e-mails, posing as Bruce Miller.

"I didn't know how to make him leave me alone," she said.

She said she wrote the last two just after Cassaday's November visit to Genesee County.

"I was really upset," she said. "I didn't want him coming at that time. Obviously, I wasn't pregnant. I was scared."

She said that during that visit, Cassaday had stayed at a Birch Run motel and she met him at a Flint Township pizza place, taking along her three children.

There the kids played while Miller and Cassaday conversed like old friends, she said.

As soon as Cassaday left, she began posing as her evil husband in e-mails purportedly coming from Bruce under the screen name BDJUNK.

The e-mails, written in screaming capital letters, were meant to frighten Cassaday away for good.

"I thought if Jerry thought that Bruce was this big man that was going to hurt him if he didn't leave us alone that Jerry would just leave me alone," she said.

"He said that he had been involved in all this FBI work before. He knew how people like Bruce were. And I just thought he would stop contacting me if I sent him those e-mails. I didn't know how else to make him leave me alone."

Nickola then turned the testimony to the day her husband was killed.

Miller said police were at the junkyard earlier that day investigating the VIN switching.

"I assumed the business was in trouble," she said. "I told Bruce everything the [police officer] had told me. Bruce was really mad. He said if the business was in trouble, John was going to pay for that."

Later that night, she became upset when Bruce did not return home from work. Later, she learned he was dead.

"I was sitting on the floor crying and I saw a police Suburban pull up and my stepdad got out of it," she said.

Miller's voice began quivering as she told jurors the events of that sad night.

Sniffling and shaking, she appeared on the verge of losing all composure, but not quite.

"They came in and [my stepfather] began shaking his head," Miller said. "He didn't have to say anything. I knew something was wrong."

But she said even her husband's murder did not deter Cassaday. She also said he still believed her to be pregnant.

As the relationship iced over, Miller said Cassaday became relentless in trying to patch things up. He even showed up at her door about midnight in early December, upset, and asked her to marry him.

After refusing his offer, she said they had a big fight. She said Cassaday had become vile, calling her a whore, saying that he was sick of her, threatening to show her mother the explicit video.

Nickola followed by asking her about how the envelope with the misspelled lawyer's name got into her computer desk.

Cassaday, she said, called in early February, concerned that he might be arrested for something. He'd already told her that he'd floated bad checks all over Kansas City.

"He gave me an attorney's name and said if he was arrested I should call that number," she said.

Nickola then proffered the question for which the gallery had waited for days.

"Did you kill your husband?"

"I did not," Miller answered without hesitation.

Nickola pressed on with rapid-fire sentences.

"Did you help someone kill your husband?"

"No, I did not," she said.

"Do you believe Jerry Cassaday killed your husband?"

"No."

"Did you love your husband?"

"Yes, I did."

With that, Miller's direct examination was over.

Now Miller would face Mabry, who would be neither as kind nor as forgiving as her own attorney.

Marcie Mabry wasted little time in moving to expose Sharee Miller as a liar and murderer. Yes, Miller admitted, she had lied to her husband, his family and her friends.

And Miller acknowledged composing every e-mail in

the binders that jurors would receive for deliberations. She admitted writing everything the prosecution had attributed to her—everything, except her portion of the November 7 through November 8 Instant Message.

Mabry was systematic, cool and quick in presenting various e-mails to highlight how Miller used deception, sex and sympathy to rile Cassaday to the point of murder.

"When you wrote that you're hoping Bruce doesn't wake up from a nap, you're telling Jerry you want him to die?" Mabry asked of one missive.

"Correct," Miller answered unflinchingly.

"Jerry wanted you to leave Bruce?" Mabry asked.

"Yes."

"But you keep coming back to this death theme," Mabry said.

Miller didn't respond. She refused Mabry's bait because it wasn't phrased as a question. Throughout her cross-examination, Miller would offer no more than she had to.

Mabry then asked Miller about the e-mail in which she expressed fear of being shot in Kansas City if she left Bruce.

"Do you remember writing that e-mail?" she asked.

"Yes, I do," Miller responded.

"You're saying, 'I can't leave until he's dead.' Do you deny that e-mail?" Mabry inquired.

"I do not deny that e-mail," Miller answered coolly.

Mabry began a series of questions on Miller's fairy-tale e-mail of October 23, 1999, where she told Cassaday the story of a woman who tried to end her marriage.

Jurors had heard the fairy-tale e-mail earlier, read to them by the deputies. The e-mail described a marriage that resembled Miller's union with Bruce, but with a heavy dose of intimidation and fear that Sharee Miller already had said wasn't real.

In the e-mail, Miller had written that a woman named

Stacy was married to a much older man for money and security, but she had become involved with another man and wanted to leave her husband.

To get out of the marriage, Miller wrote, Stacy believed that "death seems to be her answer."

Stacy needed a tool to help her leave, Miller had written.

Miller had left the moral of the story up to Cassaday, but she also said that reading between the lines was very important.

The fairy tale ended with Miller asking Cassaday if he could "come up with a beautiful ending to this nightmare."

Mabry asked Miller what she was trying to convey to Cassaday in the e-mail.

"I believe the beginning states it's a fairy tale," Miller answered. "Jerry and I had a lot of fantasy play on-line. I did write the e-mail."

Mabry pressed, trying to get Miller to answer the question, not evade it.

"Let me repeat the question," Mabry said. "What are you trying to convey to Jerry through that letter? In your own words."

But Miller danced around the answer.

"Exactly what the letter says," Miller said. "It was a story."

Mabry then asked Miller what the "reading between the lines" meant.

Miller fumbled. "I wrote a story. As far as the tool to leave. I just wrote a story. I don't know how to answer that."

After again reading a portion of the e-mail, Mabry tried one last time. Miller was no more forthcoming.

"It sounds to me like one of the other fairy tales that Jerry and I shared," she said.

Having shone a spotlight on the suggestive language

in the e-mail and Miller's evasive answers, Mabry moved on. She confronted Miller with two other October 1999 e-mails when she wrote of her desire to see her husband dead.

In one, Miller wished he would not wake up from a nap, that his heart would stop beating so hers could beat again.

"I want to live again, and living is what I will do when he dies."

Then, on October 27, 1999, Miller told Cassaday she was "to the point of going to Detroit, picking up a bum on the streets and paying him a small fortune to do what I want."

Mabry switched gears, showing Miller pictures of a bruised body. Mabry asked how the bruises got there. Investigators believed she had used makeup to make her body appear bruised.

Miller admitted she sent many pictures to Cassaday, including shots of her naked.

But Miller said she never sent Cassaday any pictures of her body bruised that way, even though she admitted the picture looked like her body.

Miller also said she sent Cassaday fake pregnancy pictures by jutting her stomach out, and she used a friend's pregnancy test wand to dupe Cassaday into believing she was pregnant.

Miller also acknowledged sending Cassaday a picture of Bruce standing next to a woman and telling him that the woman was about her size.

Mabry asked why Cassaday needed to know dimensions. Miller, again, was vague.

"He asked, maybe," she said. "I don't know."

Mabry tried to sneak in a question to rattle Miller.

"So he would know who he was killing when he came up here?" Mabry queried.

But Miller was on guard.

"Jerry Cassaday did not kill Bruce Miller," Miller shot back.

Mabry asked about the masturbation video. Miller repeated that Cassaday had used it to blackmail her, threatening to send it to Bruce and, after his death, to her husband's family.

"At that point, I wanted Jerry to leave me alone," she said.

Mabry asked Miller how she could say she wanted Cassaday out of her life, but then took action that kept dragging him back in.

"Every time I tried to break up with Jerry, he said something," Miller replied. "I don't know, that made me want to stay with him . . . made me want to keep talking to him."

Mabry paused briefly, preparing her next blow to Miller's credibility. Earlier, Miller had admitted to meeting Cassaday during her first July visit. However, she had insisted they had not become intimate until the August trip.

Mabry asked her why she had not slept with Cassaday in July.

"I was with my girlfriend out West," she said.

Mabry approached Miller and asked her to identify a photograph—the picture of her in the outfit she had worn when she met Cassaday. Police had found the photo in his apartment after he had committed suicide.

Nickola sprang to his feet and asked to inspect the picture. With Fullerton's permission, Nickola asked Miller to identify a hair extension hanging on a wall in the photograph. The question had broken a string of prosecution questions barreling toward Miller's credibility like a speeding freight train.

When questioning returned to Mabry, she asked Miller to read what was written on the back of the picture.

The question was spoken in an even, low-key manner

that hid the explosiveness of its meaning. Miller read the back of the picture.

"'July 17, 1999. The first time we made love. Sharee.'"

Mabry had handed the jury yet another reason to doubt anything that Miller said. She had admitted lying to her friends and family. Now she had lied to the jury.

Mabry continued her cross-examination, but Miller's answers seemed hollow.

Miller said she had faked pregnancy to cheer up Cassaday, who had threatened suicide.

"Did you think it was helping his mental health to tell him about babies dying? . . . You didn't care, did you?" Mabry said.

"I cared about Jerry Cassaday," Miller answered.

Mabry asked her if she told Cassaday she had been gang-raped.

"I don't remember that," Miller said.

After reading the letter left for attorney John P. O'Connor, in which Cassaday had written of a gang rape, Miller budged.

"I may have said that," she said.

And then Mabry asked Miller questions about her February 2000 statement to police, just before she was arrested. Specifically, Mabry wanted to know why she had denied knowing Cassaday.

Miller seemed to scramble.

"I had been questioned for hours," she said. "I was in my menstrual cycle. I was bleeding all over myself. I needed to go to the bathroom. I was scared."

Miller said Compeau had read an IM to her.

"I had never heard of that Instant Message," she said.

Miller also said she did not save any of the e-mails exchanged between her and Cassaday, or anybody, for that matter.

When asked about calls made to her cell phone from her own home, Miller said she had made them "by accident." She also said the cell phone had gone missing the day her husband died. And she told Mabry that she had no idea with whom she was on-line late on November 7 and early on November 8.

After a few more questions, Mabry's cross-examination concluded.

Nickola declined to follow up, and Miller sagged visibly as she left the witness-box and walked to her seat at the defense table.

In all, Miller admitted to dozens of lies, not only to Cassaday but to friends and relatives. Now she wanted a jury to believe she was not involved in a conspiracy to kill her husband.

After a short break, the parties reassembled inside Judge Fullerton's court to hear closing arguments from David Nickola and Marcie Mabry.

It had been a long day—for the attorneys, for Sharee Miller and for the families of Bruce Miller and Jerry Cassaday.

Jurors appeared to be holding up well, despite the long hours they had put in. And the case was only hours away from when they would begin deliberations.

Mabry began first.

"What you have is a cold, calculated, premeditated murder by Sharee Miller, someone who is an experienced actress, someone who admittedly craves attention," she said.

Systematically, Mabry painted a sordid picture of Miller's infidelity to her husband, of her emotionally charged e-mails to Cassaday and their physical relationship. Mabry said Miller used lies about her pregnancies and miscarriages, Bruce Miller's dark side, underworld ties and gruesome domestic abuse to provoke Cassaday to rage.

That effort, Mabry told jurors, culminated when Sharee Miller posed as Bruce Miller in a series of cruel,

violent e-mails that played on all of Cassaday's weaknesses to incite him to kill.

"This goes beyond fantasy," Mabry said.

Though Miller denied sending the bruised pictures,
Mabry said they could only have originated from
Sharee's computer.

"You can bet she did [send the pictures]," Mabry said.
"She did it as a final flame to get him to come out here,
to get him mad enough. 'He's killed two sets of your babies. He's beaten me until those twins died.'"

Mabry paced in front of the jury and attacked
Miller's fairy-tale e-mail. She held up the damaging
Instant Message that she contended Cassaday saved
only hours before he would come to Michigan to kill
Bruce Miller.

And she held up Cassaday's suicide note, asking jurors
why this man killed himself.

"Do you think he just killed himself just because his relationship with her wasn't going good?" Mabry asked.
"Or because he'd lost two sets of kids?"

Mabry answered the question.

"The relationship with her wasn't working and he'd
killed a man for nothing. For nothing! He'd been used.

"And by turning her in, he'd exposed his family and
loved ones to unfavorable attention. To humiliation and
embarrassment."

Mabry accused Miller of turning Cassaday into a pawn
for her.

"She works and molds him into a killer for her,"
Mabry said.

Mabry punctuated her arguments by occasionally
pointing at Miller, who sat passively next to Nickola.

Nickola did not let the comments pass, however,
smirking at some points, glancing up at others, letting
jurors know that he did not buy Mabry's arguments.

Mabry did not seem to notice. She warned jurors to

beware lest they fall into Sharee Miller's trap and get fooled like Cassaday.

There are too many similarities between the Instant Message and the actual murder, Mabry said. And too many e-mails Miller acknowledged writing that paved Cassaday's road to rage, hate, revenge and murder.

There were too many inconsistencies and lies in Miller's story to be believed, Mabry concluded.

Nickola's closings were loud, intense and theatrical. Moving about the court, Nickola launched into one of his patented attacks, blaming Cassaday and a bungled police investigation for the charges against an innocent widow. Meanwhile, a criminal like John Hutchinson got off with a slap on the wrists, Nickola said.

He said the prosecution's case was little more than a smear of Miller's morals, portraying her as a slut who sent out naked pictures and dirty videos and cheated on her husband.

Mabry earlier had asked a witness about an unconfirmed report that Miller had been tossed out of an Otisville roadhouse for dancing obscenely.

Nickola attacked this characterization with passion and sarcasm.

"What about the Otisville Hotel, all the dirty dancing you're doing out there?" he mockingly asked, swiveling his hips as if he were dancing. "And you're thrown out?"

He said prosecutors were portraying Miller "as if she's some sort of drunk whore out at the Otisville Hotel.

"Well, I'll tell you something, if being at the Otisville Hotel and having a few drinks and having some fun equates to being a murderer, eighty-five percent of the people in Otisville are murderers.

"There's no proof in this case about that."

In another attack on the prosecution's picture of Miller, Nickola mocked their evidence that Miller had begun seeing Jeff Foster within weeks of her husband's murder.

"Oh, she's seeing another guy?" Nickola asked, standing prudishly, hands on hips, as if he were a moralistic matron scolding a wayward child. "She's seeing this Jeff [Foster]! How soon? How soon?

"This case has a common theme, a common theme," he continued. "That theme is, 'Let's smear her because we don't believe in the sexual values she has.'"

Nickola then hammered out John Hutchinson's alleged role as the real killer.

"Did you hear anything about John Hutchinson in [the prosecutor's] case?" he asked jurors.

He followed with an attack on the IM, reminding jurors that Ives Potrafka once had believed that IMs couldn't be faked. That led Potrafka, once the lead investigator in the case, to drop Hutchinson as a suspect.

"Certainly, the Instant Message can be manipulated," he said.

And Nickola attacked Jerry Cassaday, saying he was the one who was deceiving Sharee Miller by sending out her pictures to others as he surfed the Net looking for sex. Waving pictures and e-mails that he had discovered on Cassaday's hard drive, Nickola commented: "I'm not going to sit here and read smut to you like they did just to bury somebody."

But he encouraged jurors to examine those documents in their deliberations to get a picture of Cassaday that prosecutors hadn't shared with them.

He also blasted Cassaday's romantic, dreamy writing style.

"Who talks like that?" Nickola asked in disbelief. "There was a lot of romantic stuff in there both ways. Read that stuff and read it for what it is."

He said if Cassaday was the real killer, why didn't he leave more information on the killing, such as where he ditched the gun, Bruce Miller's wallet and the gas receipts?

He again argued that Sharee Miller had no motive to kill and had more to lose by having her husband dead because he had not yet added her to his insurance papers and was preparing to adopt two of her children.

"Somebody's life is on the line," he warned jurors. "You might not like her. You might not follow along with what she does in life. She may not be your friend. But she's a human being. She's a daughter, and a sister, and a mother."

And Nickola opened a final attack on Cassaday's dependence on drugs and alcohol and his instability. He said the cash-strapped Cassaday saw Sharee Miller as a solution to his own financial problems.

"Are you going to rely on Jerry Cassaday to make the most important decision in your life?" he asked. "Hell no!"

Finally, he asked the jury to acquit her for two reasons: too much reasonable doubt and she didn't do it.

In her rebuttal, Mabry attacked the "John Hutchinson as murderer" theory, telling jurors to beware of the tangled accusation Harold Hutchinson had made against his brother.

"He wants you to have as your star witness Harold Hutchinson, who can't remember whether to put on a fuel filter or a fuel pump," Mabry said. "He can't hear things quite right."

Mabry told jurors the November 7 through November 8 IM between Miller and Cassaday was too complex, too complete, to have been fabricated.

"There are too many details and too many things that match up," she said.

She said the documentation of telephone calls made by Miller to her cell phone and AOL records showing that she and Cassaday were on-line simultaneously on November 7 and 8, 1999, were further confirmation of her guilt.

"And that is what [Nickola] avoided with the phone

calls," Mabry said. "He didn't want to get into that. Because it shows that the Instant Message is credible and corroborated by other independent evidence. I didn't hear him say the phone company lied."

Once again, Mabry asked jurors to use their common sense and find Miller guilty of premeditated murder and of conspiring to kill her husband.

On the morning of December 21, 2000, twelve jurors—eight men and four women—awoke, dressed and headed to the courthouse to decide the fate of Sharee P. Miller.

As jurors debated, the families of Bruce Miller, Sharee Miller and Jerry Cassaday lingered listlessly in the fifth-floor hallway outside the courtroom, chatting in their own small groups. The atmosphere was loose as the pressure of the trial abated for at least a while.

Newspaper reporters and the Court TV crew passed the time playing cards in a tight makeshift pressroom that was cluttered with cables, boxes and expensive television equipment. A TV producer shared a box of chocolates she'd received as a holiday bonus. Occasionally, a witness ambled over to chat or join the game. And from time to time, a group would trek into the cold December air to smoke.

Chuck and Judy Miller and Roger Cassaday were particularly receptive to impromptu interviews, taking the opportunity to keep reporters focused on the weaknesses in David Nickola's case. With just a few days until Christmas, the early line in the pressroom predicted quick guilty verdicts on both the murder and conspiracy counts.

Nobody in the jury room, however, would have taken those odds.

TV anchor Michael J. Thorp was selected jury foreman almost before the door closed. He later attributed it to his question of Fullerton's law clerk about the masturbation video, asking if jurors were to accept the judge's description of it as being pornographic.

The jurors spent about an hour warming up to the case before taking a straw poll to see where they stood. Seven of the twelve immediately said they believed Miller was guilty, while five were initially undecided.

None said they would vote to acquit her.

They discussed the John Hutchinson theory, the e-mails and the Cassaday-Miller relationship. The jurors' easygoing attitudes evaporated quickly as the discussions progressed.

"There were no fun and games," Thorp said of the testy atmosphere. "This was murder and mayhem. Three families are hurting."

Thorp said the deliberation always snapped back to Hutchinson, whom many jurors considered an entirely reasonable suspect, Thorp recalled later.

"Mostly, they didn't believe the police or any authority," he said.

Hutchinson's attraction was easy to understand, Thorp said. By focusing on him, one could skip over the prosecution's baroque contention that Miller seduced Cassaday and played on his rage to kill her husband.

"Hutchinson also was attractive [as a suspect] because his was a simpler theory of the case," Thorp said.

Almost seven hours into the deliberation, jurors said they wanted to hear Harold Hutchinson's garbled testimony played back to them. Despite the contradictions in Harold Hutchinson's testimony, some were ready to believe him.

"The people who wanted to believe said his brother [John] killed [Bruce]," Thorp said.

Toward the end of the first day, the jurors had not changed their minds. The undecided five still were undecided and the seven ready to convict were just as firm.

By early evening, jurors had had enough of each other and the case.

"We got nowhere that first day," Thorp said.

Fullerton finally sent in a note asking if the jury wanted dinner brought in so deliberations could continue. The jurors' response was quick and adamant. "Get us out of here," they answered. It was nearly 6:45 P.M. and they wanted to go home after more than seven hours of arguing.

But before deputies led jurors to the parking lot, Thorp had an idea and urged the panel to think about it. He suggested the jury begin the next day by simply reading the e-mail volume as if it were a novel.

On December 22, 2000, jurors returned to the cramped room at 8:30 A.M. Each spent about an hour reviewing the e-mails privately. An evening's rest and some quiet time with the e-mails made everyone a little more agreeable.

"The naysayers began to soften a bit," Thorp said. "We were still hung, but everybody was on the same page."

Thorp said the women on the jury had been quick to decide that Miller was guilty, confirming Nickola's initial fear of having too many women on the panel.

"The women didn't buy any of [Miller's story]," he said. "They strongly thought she was quite the manipulator."

Others also had made up their minds quickly the previous day.

"The first thing out of her mouth was a lie, so why should we believe her?" Thorp said. "After she testified, I was pretty sure where I was going."

In the courthouse hallway a few feet away, the scene hadn't changed appreciably from the day before. Family members had staked out their respective territories. Bruce Miller's family held down benches at the far end of the hall, while Jerry Cassaday's parents and a couple of brothers sat next to the courtroom doors. Sharee Miller's mother and Laura Ewald split the distance between the courtroom doors and Fullerton's chambers at the other extreme of the hallway.

Standing near Fullerton's chambers, Nickola held court for reporters, chatting amiably about his chances at a second trial if the jury hung. He wasn't convinced he could do a better job, since he already had shown his strategy to the prosecution.

The bull session came to an abrupt end with word from a clerk that the jury had a question.

In a note, jurors asked for a date on the pictures of Sharee Miller's bruised torso. Nickola asked Fullerton to tell the jury there was no evidence on that question. Fullerton, however, opted to tell jurors simply that the date question could not be answered. The jury then asked to see the pictures for themselves.

Prosecutors had their own worries. Had they spent enough time debunking Nickola's John Hutchinson theory? That thought rang louder with the jury's next request, which made Nickola smile. The jury asked to hear Harold Hutchinson's convoluted testimony again. Fullerton quickly herded jurors back into the courtroom while the tape was played. Fullerton, however, left reporters, family and other observers waiting in the hall.

The testimony and a more thorough understanding of the e-mails had begun to loosen some of the undecided votes, Thorp said.

"We began seeing evidence of her guilt on every page," he said.

One question rang in the minds of many jurors: why would Miller write e-mails saying she wanted her husband dead?

Some jurors felt the fairy-tale e-mail was crucial and thought of Miller's influence on Cassaday.

"Why is she trying to 'zoo' this guy up, to get him upset and mad?" Thorp said. "She keeps on personalizing it. 'He beat me and killed my baby.'"

They also wondered why Miller would send doctored photographs to Cassaday.

"Why would anybody fake a picture like that?" Thorp asked. "This is more than fantasy. She's saying we can live our lives together. They (the e-mails) were horrible, hurtful and asking for a response."

Some believed that the IM could have been doctored, and in the final analysis, a couple of jurors simply disregarded it. But the majority believed it was authentic.

"When you start adding together the Instant Message and the phone records, it means some of it *had* to be true," Thorp said.

Miller's elaborate scheme astounded the jurors.

"We kept going back to asking, 'Why would she send these pictures and e-mails saying her husband was a mafioso, when he is a [General Motors] shop rat?'" Thorp asked. "Why would she claim this guy was in the Mafia, beating her up and that she was pregnant?"

By early afternoon, though the jury remained deadlocked, it had made steady progress toward a verdict. The vote was eleven to one to convict Miller of *something*. Jurors did not want to consider the individual counts before first deciding that she was responsible for her husband's death.

But one lone juror, an African-American man, had stopped speaking to the others.

Thorp said the man never was very involved in the discussions. Though he was not unfriendly, he had kept to himself and remained quiet even during their lunches and breaks.

"We kept going to him," Thorp said. "He never gave us a reason [for his silence]. We said, 'Tell us your doubt. Convince us. Tell us your reservations.' He would not take part in the discussion."

Thorp tried another tactic, asking all the jurors to go back to the beginning and pick the things they believed proved Miller's guilt. To most, the fairy-tale e-mail and the Instant Message were the most convincing pieces of evidence.

But still the holdout kept a silent vigil.

The women jurors were the firmest and they pressed the man.

"Where's your problem?" they asked. "Why can't you see this? Say something."

Eventually, the other African-American jurors intervened. One explained that he had never considered the IM in his analysis, but he was ready to convict based on the strength of the other evidence.

Still, the holdout would not speak.

Driven by frustration, emotion and stress, with tears beginning to flow, the jury finally could go no further. Just before 3:00 P.M., Thorp sent out a note, announcing that the jury was deadlocked.

Thorp acknowledged that jurors were upset. They hadn't accomplished the job Fullerton had set before them: simply come to a unanimous verdict.

Wasting little time, Fullerton called jurors into her courtroom for a seven-minute closed-door session in which she issued a standard instruction given to deadlocked juries: go back in and keep working, and try harder this time.

Reporters and family members were not allowed in for the instruction, and some were fuming. Such sessions usually were open proceedings, but Fullerton said she wanted no distractions.

Returning to the hallway afterward, Nickola paced outside Fullerton's door, speculating that jurors may have been hung on the conspiracy count. The prosecution's ruminations were less public. Mabry and Plummer gathered the families of Bruce Miller and Jerry Cassaday in an adjacent courtroom and asked them to be patient, promising to keep them informed.

A rumor spread through the hallway that prosecutors were considering a last-minute plea bargain to end the case and relieve jurors of their obligations.

Reporters quickly put that fire out, citing several reasons.

First, Miller had never wavered in her protestations of innocence. She already had rejected a second-degree murder plea, which was as low as prosecutors would go. Few believed Fullerton would impose a light sentence on Miller, even if prosecutors and Nickola agreed to it. And additionally, the Bruce Miller and Jerry Cassaday families would be incensed if they perceived Sharee Miller was getting any type of favorable deal.

The ball, once again, was in the jurors' hands. And as they filed back into the jury room, frustration was written large on their faces. Instead of heading home, they were going back to deliberate. And since eleven were convinced of Miller's guilt, the task boiled down to communicating with the holdout.

Thorp realized the situation was delicate. In cases of hung juries, several things could happen. The holdout could reexamine his vote and change it. Or, that juror could work slowly to convince at least some of the others that they were rushing to judgment.

But if pressed too hard, a holdout could dig in his heels and never budge.

If that happened, a hung jury appeared inevitable. And no one knew which road this would take.

The word came suddenly at about 6:00 P.M.—the jury had reached a verdict. And with that, all the loose familiarity that had developed in the hallway over the last two days vanished.

Fearing the worst, Nickola huddled with Sharee's family, telling them that, no matter what, the fight was not over. At 6:08 P.M., three days before Christmas, deputies led Miller back into the courtroom to hear the jury's decision.

Although she appeared apprehensive, Miller had replaced her plain hairstyle with a more sophisticated look, pulled up and off her shoulders. Miller told deputies that she had fixed her hair so she would look good walking out of the courtroom for the cameras. Still, she sat next to Nickola and shivered with apprehension.

Behind the rail, members of Cassaday's family held hands on the court benches. Bruce Miller's relatives sat behind them, while the family of Sharee Miller sat on the other side of the court.

"What is your decision?" Fullerton asked.

Thorp stood and announced that the jury had found Sharee P. Miller guilty of second-degree murder and guilty of conspiracy to commit first-degree murder in the death of Bruce Miller.

Tears flowed from the families of Bruce Miller, Jerry Cassaday and Sharee Miller, though for altogether different reasons. The Cassaday and Bruce Miller families held hands, hugged and shared tears. Sharee Miller's mother crumpled into the arms of her husband, Sharee's stepfather. Hearing the verdict, Marcie Mabry looked up to the ceiling. David Nickola sat stone-faced.

Through it all, Sharee Miller fought her own tears.

As is customary in criminal cases, Nickola asked that the jury be polled individually to ensure the decision was unanimous. One by one, jurors responded with a "Yes" to Fullerton's query if they agreed with the verdict. All except for juror number 6, a man with long, curly black hair, who answered, "Absolutely!"

Sharee Miller's tears flowed as the last juror was polled, the full impact of the panel's decision finally descending over her life. Fullerton accepted the verdict and scheduled sentencing for January 29, 2001.

The judge ordered everyone seated until jurors could be escorted to the cold parking lot below.

"We wish you a pleasant holiday season," Fullerton said as jurors filed out. Sharee Miller's family quickly followed, ducking television cameras that now filled the hallway.

The Cassadays and Bruce Miller's family lingered in the courtroom, hugging each other and exchanging warm handshakes. Over the preceding two weeks, in the breaks and during the long wait for the verdict, a remarkable thing had happened in the hallways of the Genesee County Courthouse.

The families of Bruce Miller and Jerry Cassaday had reconciled, despite the bitter violence that a member of one family had done to the other. Over hours of conversation and cigarette breaks in the frigid Michigan air, the families had come to the joint conclusion that one person was responsible for both men's deaths—Sharee Paulette Miller.

"She's the cause of both of their deaths," Chuck Miller said. "Everything she has ever said has been a lie."

"We feel relieved and vindicated," said Roger Cassaday.

He credited his younger brother with saving enough information to point police in the right direction.

Mabry, still suffering from her cold, simply was glad the whole damn thing was over. Relaxing with reporters, she still framed her answers carefully, crediting the jury for taking its job seriously, thoroughly sifting through the evidence and reaching an "appropriate" verdict. Soon the Cassaday and Miller family members surrounded her. Their appreciation brought Mabry to the brink of tears.

Addressing a line of TV cameras outside the courtroom, Nickola promised a vigorous appeal, citing his inability to question potential jurors about prior media exposure to the trial and Fullerton's decision to admit the Instant Message and suicide note.

Sharee, he said, was upset with the verdict.

"She's got three children, who won't have their mother home for Christmas," he said.

Deputies led the weeping defendant down a side hallway and out of the courthouse. As Sharee Miller walked, the plan B option began to cut through the shock and the fog of the verdict. She focused on the stash of pills she had meticulously hidden over the months.

But before Miller could make it back to the pod, deputies placed her in an isolation cell for a seven-day suicide watch. She would say later that her family had requested it. They weren't certain what she would do if she were convicted.

Michael Thorp later described the turning point after Fullerton sent jurors back to deliberate after declaring the deadlock. Jurors again started at the beginning and laid out their reasons for voting guilty or not guilty.

An amazing thing then happened. The holdout spoke. "Okay, okay," he said. "Let's talk. Let's vote again."

With that, the vote was taken, and all twelve believed Miller was guilty. Then they had to discuss, "Guilty of what?"

Thorp said the vote was twelve to zero to convict Miller of conspiracy to murder Bruce Miller. But again, there was dissension on the first-degree murder charge. The holdout, again, did not believe Miller's conduct fit the charge, primarily because she had not pulled the shotgun's trigger.

Other jurors were too tired to argue the fine point, and the eleven agreed they would be comfortable convicting Miller of second-degree murder. "At that point, we were just happy to have a compromise," Thorp said.

Thorp said jurors behaved professionally and humanely with each other during the tense hours. He said they realized that someone's life was in their hands and wanted to make certain they reached the correct verdict.

"I wish she had been innocent," Thorp said. "It was a lot harder than any of us thought. It didn't get personal, but it was emotional."

He said jurors were anxious about how the holdout would respond when they were individually polled. While it does not happen often, occasionally a juror who was on the fence but who finally consented to a guilty verdict can waver during the poll and toss the entire case into a mistrial by changing his verdict.

"We were all holding our breath, wondering whether he would say yes," Thorp said later.

They all let out a sigh of relief when he agreed with the other eleven jurors.

The verdict also pleased Arthur A. Busch, Genesee County's prosecutor, who was particularly happy that the one juror whom he considered a wild card—Thorp—turned out to be the right person to lead the other eleven panel members through a sensitive case that required thought and reason.

Mabry had been right after all. The gamble had paid off.

"Juries have a gut-level reaction to things like this," Busch said later. "They just didn't like [Miller] and what she said. They were deeply offended by her conduct . . . and were in no mood to split fine hairs about it."

On January 29, 2001, Sharee P. Miller returned to Fullerton's court for sentencing.

With a *Flint Journal* reporter and several area television stations attending, Court TV again was on hand to record the case's conclusion, as were three jurors who had voted to convict Miller.

After dickering with Nickola over details to the presentence report, Mabry began her argument for a long sentence with a harsh description of Miller.

Mabry called Sharee a "cold, calculating killer" who played a deadly game of Internet deceit with the lives of real people.

"She killed Bruce Miller but used another man's life

to do it. It was all just a game," Mabry said. "Jerry Cassaday was a gullible man who was in love."

Mabry told Fullerton that Sharee Miller continued to
lie even after her conviction, offering as proof the
number of corrections she had to make to Miller's presentence report.

"She has a hard time telling the truth," Mabry said.

Plummer sat quietly and listened. He already was planning how to use the unique case to explain Internet and
computer evidentiary issues to future law school students.

Nickola said he was confident he would win on appeal, getting a reversal of the conviction or a new trial.

"This case was long on sex and short on evidence," he
said.

Miller, dressed again in her jail greens, and bulked up
to 148 pounds by starchy jail food, sat quietly. Sharee
Miller's mother sobbed during much of the hearing. She
now cared for two of her daughter's children. The eldest
boy had returned to live with his father just after Bruce
Miller's murder.

Sentencing hearings in Michigan allow for testimony
from a crime victim, so Judy Miller read a prepared letter. She accused Sharee Miller of betraying the family by
having an affair only a few short months after marrying
Bruce.

"She was playing a game with people's emotions all
in the name of fun," Judy Miller said.

No members of the Cassaday family attended the
hearing. They would not have been allowed to testify,
since Jerry Cassaday had been classified as a "coconspir-
ator" rather than a victim.

During Judy Miller's statement, Sharee sat next to
Nickola in the same jury box from which the jurors had
announced her conviction a month before. She did not
look at Judy Miller during the brief statement.

"I couldn't even look at her," Judy Miller said to her

husband after returning to her seat. "But I was so close
to her, I could feel her breathing on me."

Miller clung to her innocence, again denying that she
was involved in her husband's death.

"I did not kill my husband, and I did not have anyone
kill him," she said.

Sharee Miller later would elaborate, but only slightly,
when probation officials asked her to give a written version of the offense. Miller was succinct, using only four
of the twenty-four lines available to her.

"I did not participate in this offense in any way," Miller
wrote. "I am innocent and planning my appeal."

Nickola again argued for leniency, but he sensed that
Fullerton was about to hammer Miller. Without a jury,
Nickola's tone was restrained, even respectful. He said
Sharee's family had chosen to stick by her for the long
run.

Fullerton agreed with the jury that Miller was guilty and
deserved the harshest punishment she could mete out.

"This is ridiculous," Fullerton scoffed as she glanced
over the Michigan sentencing guidelines.

According to the tables, Sharee Miller's guideline
range was 162 to 270 months—13 years 6 months to 22
years 6 months—but probation officials had recommended the judge go over the range. Fullerton was
happy to accommodate.

She exceeded the recommended sentence by a wide
margin, explaining that Miller's plotting, planning and
purpose in the slaying had earned her a hard sentence.

In her written version, Judge Judith A. Fullerton offered this rationale:

"The extent of the defendant's involvement in the
planning and perpetration of the murder of her husband as well as the nature of the crimes, murder by
gunshot, albeit as an aider and abettor, warrants a sentence well beyond the guidelines."

Fullerton sentenced Miller to life in prison for conspiracy to commit first-degree murder.

Under Michigan court rules, a person sentenced to life becomes eligible for parole after twenty years. But to thwart that possibility, Fullerton sentenced Sharee to fifty-four to eighty-one years for her conviction on second-degree murder.

Sharee Miller would not become eligible for parole until 2055, when she was eighty-three years old.

Barring a successful appeal, Sharee would have a long time to think about her mistakes. The family of Bruce Miller found solace in the sentence.

"I'm happy with it," Judy Miller said.

Chuck Miller again blamed Sharee Miller for the deaths of two men.

"Everything she's ever told us is a lie," he said.

Somehow, living as the wife of a quiet man with simple dreams hadn't been exciting enough for Sharee Miller. Instead, she had condemned Bruce Miller to a swift and violent death.

As the hearing concluded, Miller stood and was led through a back door, her claims of innocence ringing hollowly through Fullerton's courtroom. A month before, jurors had heard another description of Sharee Miller. It came in an e-mail she'd written to Cassaday on November 1, 1999. Given the deception that ruled her life, no one could be certain if the reflection was an honest one.

"I am not shit in this world," she'd written.

Still, Sharee Miller had a life before her. She could communicate with her children, her family and friends, though it would be from the confines of a Michigan women's prison. Someday, perhaps, she would come to terms with her conviction.

But Jerry Cassaday could find solace only in death.

"I want to be cremated," Cassaday had written in his

suicide note to his parents. "I don't deserve anything better. Please take my ashes to my favorite hunting tree. . . . It's the only place I really had true peace in my heart."

SIXTEEN

Sharee Paulette Miller finally has made it into an up-scale neighborhood, an irony that strikes with an echoing clang.

The Scott Correctional Facility for Women is a high-security prison with the usual triple rows of chain-link fencing topped with shimmering razor wire. Absurdly, the thirty-five-acre prison is plopped in a bustling neighborhood of million-dollar homes northeast of Detroit. During her evening walks in the grassy yards behind the fences, Miller can see enormous houses under construction, not unlike those in the high-end neighborhood that she and Jerry Cassaday had toured in Reno.

After almost two years of declining interviews to a host of journalists, Miller agreed to sit down with the authors of this book. Neither she nor her family was compensated for the interview. The only thing she asked was that a copy of the book be mailed to her at the prison after it was published. We agreed.

Under the prison's ground rules, we were allowed to bring only pens and notepads, which a string of guards counted as we entered.

She met us in the prison's large visiting room about 3:00 P.M. on a Friday in early May 2002. She remained seated, looking a bit uneasy, as yet a third guard dutifully counted our pens and pads.

Her blond hair had grown below her shoulders since

her sentencing hearing more than a year before and she'd curled it for our visit. She was subtly made up and wearing her trademark luminous brown lipstick. She had lost all of the weight she had put on in the Genesee County Jail. Miller wore stonewashed jeans and a navy blue T-shirt that she later told us belonged to a friend.

Miller still wore a thin gold wedding ring on her left hand.

She rose as we approached and we shook hands formally. The guard led us to a small room that lawyers usually use to interview clients. Once Miller sat behind the metal desk, any apprehension she had about the interview seemed to melt away.

Miller explained that she decided to meet with us to give the public a fuller picture of who she is. She agreed that nobody is *really* at their best when they're on trial for murder, which was all that Court TV viewers ever saw of her.

A *Dateline NBC* profile that ran in the early spring of 2002 was closer to the mark. Miller's interview was taped in 2000 while she was awaiting trial in the Genesee County Jail.

And an *Inside Edition* piece that ran shortly after her trial said little about Miller outside of the case.

"I wanted you to know who I was," she said. "You don't know me as a person. I'm not a perfect person, but I'm not a horrible person."

Indeed, it was easy to imagine how Miller could intoxicate men in karaoke bars, junkyards and casinos. And it was just as easy to see how her charm derailed Jerry Cassaday's natural police skepticism. Animated, frank and outspoken, she smiled regularly and laughed easily.

She was a good listener and unafraid to make eye contact. Her answers to questions were spontaneous, glib and spoken with bracing certainty.

"That is not going to stick," she said firmly when asked about her sentence of fifty-four to eighty-one years. "I haven't accepted that."

Miller appeared completely confident that she would someday walk out of Scott to return home, certainly in time to play with her grandchildren while they still were young. Despite the jury's verdict and the weight of evidence in her own written words, she maintained she had nothing to do with Bruce Miller's death.

"Only two people know whether Jerry did it—Bruce Miller and Jerry Cassaday," she said. "I'm the only one who knows whether I was involved."

Miller also believes that Jerry Cassaday planned for her to have a successful appeal. Here's her theory:

Cassaday, the smart ex-cop, consciously offered up the kind of evidence at his death that would punish her and assure her conviction. But he knew the evidence, particularly his suicide note to his parents, never would stand up on appeal, Miller said. Had he provided other corroborating evidence—such as gas receipts, the murder weapon or even Bruce Miller's wallet—the case against her would have been bulletproof, she said.

"He gave them enough information to put me away, but not forever," she said. "I think Jerry wanted me to pay for not being with him. That's how I know Jerry didn't do it."

Miller agreed that her affair with Cassaday was the most disastrous relationship of her adult life. It was rooted, she said, in a mutual love of fantasy, which went back to childhood for her.

"Jerry Cassaday loved fantasies just as well or better than I did," she said. "He played with me as well as I played with him. When I began finding my picture all over the Internet with Jerry pretending to be me, I got a taste of that."

At trial, Miller denied sending Cassaday the photos of

her torso bruised from a brutal beating by her husband. Prosecutors contended that those were the pictures that finally pushed Cassaday to murder. Miller maintained her denials but said she now has an idea where the pictures originated, though she declined to discuss it.

She did say that Cassaday's fantasies revolved around forced sex and pregnancy.

"His fantasy was for Sharee to always be pregnant," she said.

So why fuel the fantasies of a disturbed man?

"Yes, it got out of hand," she answered. "I've messed with a lot of men in my life. Jerry was the wrong one. Instead of just dropping him, I kept coming back around."

She said his suicide has left her with a hard reminder of the mess she has made for herself.

"To have somebody write you a letter about killing himself because you don't love him . . . I carry a lot of guilt around from that," she said. "But Jerry pinned that on me. In reality, we kill ourselves for our own selfish reasons. How am I supposed to feel? I didn't believe he would do it. Now I have to deal with it."

For now, Sharee Miller must make Scott her home.

She lives in a small two-person cell that she described as her "apartment." Her day usually consists of working a few hours in the prison store, where she makes about $11 a month handling paperwork and bagging and delivering prisoner purchases. She works out each day in the prison gym. Once a week, she sees a therapist, and she spends hours at a stretch writing in a journal that she someday hopes to publish as a book to help other women. Her book, she said, "won't be entertainment.

"I know when I come home five, thirteen years from now, and publish my book, it will be so much better than your book," she said. "My book is going to help people."

Part of Miller's prison routine is dealing with mail. Because of the media exposure, Miller said shedding her sexpot image has been difficult. She still gets mail from people, including other prisoners, asking her for sex mail. But she doesn't respond.

"Sex played a big part of why I'm in here, but I will not write of it," she said.

Though Miller had a plan at the Genesee County Jail to kill herself if she was convicted, she said she now has reconsidered suicide.

"I've thought about it, but it doesn't mean I'd ever do it," Miller said. "I have too much I'm fighting for now. I want to be out of here to see my grandbabies. Am I going to [commit suicide]? No, but being here depresses you."

Miller said she misses her children, privacy and vine-ripened tomatoes. Prison, however, has not been a completely bleak experience. She said she has acclimated well to confinement and she betrayed no bitterness about being without the two "crutches" of her life: men and alcohol.

"Being here has been beneficial to me," she said. "I've learned why I've done some of the stupid things I've done. You can use prison to get better. I want to go home a better person."

But her adjustment hasn't been without issues. On July 13, 2001, a guard noticed that inmate Victoria L. Payne had covered her cell door for nearly fifteen minutes. Payne, forty-two, is serving a sentence of thirty to seventy-five years for soliciting the murder of an elderly couple and their daughter, who helped uncover the plot.

The guard knocked on the door and Payne called out that everything was all right, that she was just getting dressed. Several minutes later, Payne walked out. The guard searched the room and found Sharee Miller hiding inside a locker.

Sharee had no permission to be there and was

charged with unauthorized occupation of a cell. She pleaded guilty.

Miller acknowledged the transgression during our interview. She stressed, however, that she wasn't charged with a sexual infraction and was fully dressed when the guard found her. She declined to speak further about the incident.

Still, Miller asked us to contact an old friend from the Genesee County Jail. Catherine M. Lindsley, thirty-four, served a three-month assault sentence with Miller in the fall of 2000. As the two shared a cell, they told each other stories, played cards, watched television and grew sexually intimate, Lindsley said.

"We started just as friends, and it slowly developed into something more," said Lindsley, who described herself as a lesbian.

She added that they consider themselves to be "lovers who are separated.

"I'm not embarrassed by it," said Lindsley, who visits Miller regularly in prison.

Lindsley also is convinced Miller had nothing to do with her husband's death.

"There's no way possible someone that kind and considerate could do something that stupid," Lindsley said. "Sharee is a decent person with a big heart."

Almost invariably, it is women who speak well of Sharee Miller. That, she acknowledged, is due to the sheer brutality of her predatory relationships with men. With time now to look back at the wreckage, Miller said she has recognized a pattern. Her exclusive relationships with men, Sharee Miller said, would last only about four months before she would begin sleeping with someone else.

"I have done a lot of destruction, emotionally, to a lot of people," Miller said. "I understand I've ruined a lot of people's lives. I've destroyed marriages and lots of relationships."

Miller pointed to her relationship with Jeff Foster as the dubious exception. Miller said Foster was the only man in her adult life to whom she remained faithful.

"We were only together from December through February," Miller said. "I didn't have time to cheat on him."

Miller said Bruce Miller was a "wonderful man" who did not deserve her infidelity. She was unapologetic, however, about the most lurid manifestation of her affair with Jerry Cassaday, the video *For Jerry's Eyes Only*, which she made scarcely three months after marrying Bruce Miller.

"This was made for the private use of one person," she said. "Everybody has masturbated. Not many people have videotaped it. I'm embarrassed, but I'm not ashamed of it. I did it; I made it. We've all done things in the past we'd rather not have done. But it was tastefully done."

As a matter of course, a life of infidelity required the construction and constant maintenance of countless lies, she said.

"It didn't get me anywhere, but a lot of hurt and a lot of pain," Miller said. "I've lied to myself more than to other people. I have really screwed-up morals, that's for sure."

The exposure of that character flaw at her trial ripped her credibility, Miller acknowledged.

"I have done nothing but lie my whole life, secret after secret after secret," she said. "I have no more secrets. I don't hide stuff anymore."

The origin of these threads—lies, infidelity and fantasy—was the sexual abuse she suffered as a child, Miller said. She wondered if Nickola's trial strategy of portraying her as an adventurous, sexual free spirit, rather than as a child abuse survivor, alienated jurors.

"If I were in their shoes, I wouldn't like me, either," she said. "I wasn't a slut. I was a woman with a lot of problems."

Time with a prison therapist has given her a new per-

spective. Outside prison, her life with men never slowed
long enough for her to see what she was doing to herself,
even during periods of intense trauma.

"Buddy getting hurt didn't stop me," she said. "Bruce
getting killed didn't stop me. This stopped me."

After arriving at Scott, Miller said, she went to a prison
health fair—the "Love Yourself Convention"—where she
learned that she had been hiding from the abuse she
suffered as a child. Miller discovered that she has a dark
room in her psyche where bad things lie.

"I always was trying to shut those doors," she said.

Even her reaction to that abuse was twisted, she said.
Her relationship with her abuser was the most loving relationship of her young life, Miller said. But when she
turned fourteen, her abuser deserted her for another
girl her own age.

"Through the years, you grow up thinking it's love,"
Miller said. "I turned fourteen and saw him giving it to
someone else. I saw that and everything I had built
around this man collapsed around me."

It was jealousy, then, that drove her to tell her mother
about the abuse. That experience forever warped her relationship with men, she said.

"So being with a man, I'm just going to hurt you because you are going to hurt me," Miller said. "Love for
me is betrayal."

Every day, Sharee Miller plots her appeals and hopes
for a new trial. The Michigan Court of Appeals is not expected to hear the first round of her appeals before late
2002 or early 2003.

As Nickola did at trial, Miller railed at Fullerton for allowing the jury to see the damaging November 7 to
November 8 Instant Message and Cassaday's suicide
note.

"They would not have a case without the IM and the
suicide note," she said. "If I was going to get convicted,

they should have done it within the system. I will get another trial."

Should her state appeals fail, she hopes for a more sympathetic hearing from a federal judge, who could take a closer look at whether Cassaday's suicide note deserved the "dying declaration" exception from the hearsay rule, which says that a person has a right to face her accuser.

Dying declarations are statements made when the speaker believes that his death is imminent. It originated from the religious notion that a person would not wish to meet his Maker with a lie on his lips. Courts often have accepted dying declarations from gravely injured crime victims who told investigators who hurt them. But few courts have tested the question of whether a suicide note that describes the circumstances of someone else's death qualifies as a dying declaration.

"[Cassaday's suicide note] was not a dying declaration," Miller said. "If this sticks, I'll be in all the law books."

Judge Judith A. Fullerton, she said, overstepped her authority.

"She's nobody big enough to change the law," Miller said.

Miller said she was too easily caught off guard at her first trial, particularly at the moment when she stated that she and Cassaday hadn't made love until August 1999. Moments later, she recalled ruefully, Mabry shredded her credibility by showing her a photograph with contradictory evidence scrawled on the back in Miller's own handwriting: "July 17, 1999. The first time we made love. Sharee."

"When I was sitting on the witness stand, I was honestly confused," Sharee said.

Miller also said her first trial was marred by tension between her and her defense lawyer—though it never was

apparent to trial observers. She said Nickola ignored
some of her defense suggestions—a common complaint
among defendants—and was too demanding of how she
should act and appear.

"David told me how to wear my hair, how to wear my
clothes," she said.

Miller still gets irritated when she sees newspaper articles quoting Nickola, whom she described as a lawyer
who likes to see his name in print and stand knee deep
in a high-profile case.

She would assault the Instant Message of November 7
and 8 at a new trial by going on the stand and showing
the jury how she taught Cassaday to change and fabricate them, cutting, dragging and pasting text between
screens.

"I have never been to a computer class in my entire
life and I figured it out," Miller said. "It was easy, really
easy. Put me on the damn stand. Let me show you what
we did!"

She said she's confident that a new trial would go her
way.

"Next time around will be so much different," Miller
said. "I'm not saying [Nickola] didn't do his job. But if
I'm paying the bill, it'll be done my way."

But even if she is released someday, Miller said, she
never again will own a computer.

Our time with Miller simply flew by. Standing only
once to select pretzels and a Diet Coke from a vending
machine, she sat comfortably in her chair for six hours.
Some of that was due to prison rules that restricted her
movement with visitors. Some of that came from her desire to tell us her story.

At about 9:00 P.M., we put our pens down and waited
for a guard to tell us our time was up. We had covered
a mountain of emotional debris, but the mood was
light. Despite her brimming self-confidence, Miller

had remained polite and completely nonconfrontational throughout the session. She poked fun at us, the writers who had hung on her every word, and she accurately deduced differences in our personalities simply from the clothing we'd worn to the interview.

"You guys look real funny together," she said. "Just complete opposites."

The guard finally came and counted our pens and notepads for the fourth and final time. She walked with us to the visiting-room security station. We said our good-byes and promised to stay in touch. After the final handshakes, she stepped back, found a chair and settled in to wait for a guard.

She also waits for a second trial, one where she hopes she won't have to contend with Jerry Cassaday's messy suicide note or with that damning Instant Message. And she hopes that a new trial will let her walk away from a life of lies, infidelity, deception and murder.

Sharee Miller knows that no jury ever could find her innocent.

Not guilty would suit her fine.

EPILOGUE

Reporters sifting through the initial rush of information in the Sharee Miller case described it as the "first murder planned on the Internet." But not long after her conviction in December 2000, news stories emerged suggesting that Saudi dissident Osama bin Laden and his operatives for years had used e-mail and the Internet to plan terrorist strikes.

The tag "first Internet murder" certainly lost its distinction. But the role of electronic communication in the case cannot be overstated. In the two weeks prior to Bruce Miller's murder, his wife and Jerry Cassaday exchanged about 175 e-mails. That doesn't count the hours they spent each day on the telephone or chatting through AOL Instant Messages, the transcripts of which are not automatically saved to a computer's hard disk.

Through inexpensive and immediate communications, Sharee Miller put Jerry Cassaday on the emotional road that ultimately led him to kill Bruce Miller. Using a relentless barrage of e-mails, IMs and phone calls, some sexually charged, she constantly tore at his weaknesses—his love for her and his desire to have more children, his money troubles and, above all, his substance-impaired judgment—until she overwhelmed his resistance to murder. That simply could not have happened over the short space of four months using conventional "snail mail."

"She hit the right buttons that would play him," Sergeant Jerry Willhelm said.

But there also is something very old about the story of Bruce, Sharee and Jerry. Love triangles have been with us always. Infidelity has been with us forever. So have lies.

And the wreckage Sharee Miller has left behind is immense.

Sharee Miller's family has been profoundly torn by the ordeal. Her oldest son returned to live with his natural father shortly after Bruce's murder, while Miller's mother is raising the two youngest. Throughout the trial, Miller's mother and stepfather politely declined to speak with reporters, saying they were trying to protect the children.

Twice a month, on Sundays, Miller's mother brings her two youngest children to visit. Sharee is amazed with how they have grown, and friends say the trips can be hard on the kids.

The motive to kill Bruce Miller was one of the stickiest issues with which prosecutors wrestled in the case, even though they were not required to prove motive at trial. Money is an old standby. At the preliminary examination in April 2000, Sergeant Ives Potrafka estimated that Miller collected up to $200,000 from her husband's estate. But by the trial the following December, it was clear that Bruce Miller's estate was in shambles because he died without a will. Nobody can agree how much Sharee Miller collected after her husband's death. Observers estimated the amount from a low of about $25,000 to a high of about $125,000.

David Nickola was quick to exploit this weakness, and he continued to massage the point more than a year after the trial.

Had Miller really been intent on killing her husband,

Nickola argued, she would have laid better groundwork by making certain her husband had a will and waiting until the adoption of her two youngest children had become final.

"She could have set herself up very nicely," Nickola said. "She could have set up a will and waited for thirty days [on the adoption]. She could have had about four hundred thousand dollars coming to her. That's important to know if you think there is some sort of master plan."

Chuck Miller, Bruce's brother, developed his own theory in hindsight. He believes his sister-in-law became intent on murder in October 1999, about the time she went to Reno for the fourth time in four months.

About then, Bruce stopped grumbling to family members about Sharee's spending and frequent trips to Nevada, Chuck Miller said. He became quiet and missed a few days at work so he could be home in the evenings with Sharee. He quit talking about her, Chuck Miller said, which was a sure sign that, once again, he was thinking of getting another divorce.

Under Chuck Miller's theory, Sharee sensed that Bruce was preparing to divorce her and then planned to kill him and scrounge whatever assets she could in the confusion that would follow. She could not wait for him to adopt the children because Bruce Miller probably would have refused then. To have pushed the adoption issue would only have forced a divorce, Chuck Miller speculated.

"He was catching on that Sharee was having an affair and pissing away his money," Chuck Miller said.

However murky the motive, proof of Sharee Miller's creative writing went far beyond the e-mail evidence that jurors saw at trial. Buried deep in the sheriff's department investigative file is a scrap of paper written in Miller's distinctive hand. The story it tells bears a striking resemblance to the tale she told Cassaday on November 7, the day before Bruce Miller's murder:

"I went to the Upper Peninsula hospital. I had a D&C. Was suppose to stay in hospital, but as soon as I was out of recovery he got me dressed and we walked out of the hospital 5 hours later. He then, 4 hours later, proceeded to rape me, bleeding and all. He didn't care. Nov. 6 hospital. Left Nov. 7th, early morning hours."

Deputies believed the note contained talking points for the awful phone call she made in November 1999, when she told Cassaday that she had been gang-raped.

It's difficult to feel sorry for Jerry Cassaday. He was, after all, a murderer. It's easy, though, to understand his pain.

Many have fallen in love hard, only to find out later that they've been deceived. Cassaday heard the lies, but he didn't want to believe they really were lies. He desired Sharee Miller so much that he was willing to turn a deaf ear and close an eye to keep her in his life.

He made a lot of mistakes—he fell hard for a woman he hardly knew, he killed for her and he killed himself because of her.

"He was just so gullible and so vulnerable and he believed everything she said," said his mother, Charlene Cassaday.

But his biggest mistake may have been blocking out that voice in his head that said, "Hold on. This isn't right." Perhaps it was easier with drugs and alcohol.

Jerry's conscience led him to revenge, destruction and, ultimately, justice. Despite his despair, he left enough information behind to allow investigators to close the case.

"If they hadn't found this stuff, in all likelihood Sharee Miller would be walking the streets today as a free woman with a pocketful of money," said Sheriff Robert J. Pickell of Genesee County.

* * *

For the Cassaday and Miller families, Sharee's conviction brought peace of a sort. It punished Bruce Miller's surviving killer and at least documented what drove Jerry Cassaday to commit an unspeakable crime.

Chuck and Judy Miller buried Bruce at Flint Memorial Park Cemetery, just off one of the windy side roads, about seventy feet from a wishing well. A flat headstone, emblazoned with a NASCAR slogan and a race car, marks the grave, which sits on a gentle slope.

As of their interview with us in January 2002, Chuck and Judy have not returned to the cemetery since the funeral. But they've worked to sustain Bruce's memory in other ways. Troubled that Sharee's harsh and false depiction of Bruce would linger, the Millers still feel they must defend him. They will talk at any length and to almost anyone about Bruce Miller, finding their own peace in discussing the turmoil and sorrow that Sharee Miller brought into their lives.

Chuck Miller said his sister-in-law probably would never understand or accept what she had done.

"I believe she has the capacity to delude herself," Miller said. "She's told so many lies; she always believes what she's saying."

That's not a problem for Ruth Miller, Bruce's mother. Just after Sharee's conviction, Ruth Miller cut her image out of the wedding pictures they purchased in Las Vegas.

Jerry Cassaday's family has been far more circumspect. Immediately after the trial, family members announced they no longer wanted to discuss the case and declined opportunities to tell Jerry's story to a national television audience. Charlene and James Cassaday returned to their Texas retirement, seldom speaking of their son's tragic death, even to some of their closest friends. Jerry's brothers scattered back to their homes across the country.

It was time, they said, to get on with their lives quietly and out of the spotlight.

Immediately after Jerry's memorial service, the family scattered his ashes near his favorite hunting tree, just as he had requested.

Both the Miller and Cassaday families remain convinced that Sharee Miller is responsible. If not for her, they said, two men would be alive still.

John Hutchinson still counts himself as one of Sharee Miller's victims. By immediately identifying him as a suspect in the murder, Miller showed no compunction about possibly snuffing out his life with a long prison sentence.

Hutchinson was the prime suspect for months, though deputies never were really close to filing charges against him. Still, the agony of that uncertainty took its toll. He was hospitalized for nervous exhaustion during the investigation.

Hutchinson said that his small auto-rebuilding business never recovered from the investigation. He worked for a time as an electrician for a Flint-area machine tool company. He soon quit, however, and hasn't worked for anyone else since. He is considering moving away from Michigan entirely.

"The best thing I can do is move on with my life and move on to somewhere else," Hutchinson said recently, "but I don't have the drive to do it."

He, too, speaks willingly about his experiences, still hoping to lift the shroud of suspicion that followed him those months. He remains particularly bitter that David Nickola tried to convince jurors that he, and not Jerry Cassaday, pulled the trigger on November 8, 1999.

"I hate him as much as I hate [Sharee]," Hutchinson said recently. "He used me for his pigeon."

He found resolution, if not peace, after Sharee Miller's sentencing, which he attended. After all the television cameras and reporters had cleared out, he stood quietly on the fifth floor of the Genesee County Courthouse. Turning to leave, Hutchinson came face-to-face with one of the investigators.

"Sorry we put you through what we did, but we were just doing our jobs," the investigator said.

They shook hands, and the deputy headed for the elevator.

David Nickola remains one of Flint's most colorful, controversial and quotable criminal defense lawyers. He continues to represent Sharee Miller and vows to march her case through the federal court system, should her state appeals be unsuccessful.

He still argues that prosecutors charged Miller after police prematurely dropped their Hutchinson investigation. Miller was convicted, he contends, after Judge Fullerton allowed Mabry to argue a smutty case with uncorroborated evidence.

"She was condemned from the very beginning because of the evidence they put in her face," Nickola said. "It's okay for men to have an affair and say they're sorry, but it doesn't work that way for females."

Prosecutor Marcie Mabry doesn't see it that way and is confident the case will hold up on appeal. Working now in a larger office in Flint, Mabry is bemused by the attention the case has received. She doesn't quite understand why she's appeared on national television numerous times to explain the case, while other murders she's prosecuted have passed almost unnoticed.

For Mabry, the trial was a tedious document grind, marred by a persistent cold that distracted her from connecting more directly with the jury.

"It was overwhelming," she said. "I couldn't spend a lot of time connecting with jurors."

While watching the trial, one couldn't miss the contrast between Mabry and Sharee Miller. The panting star of *For Jerry's Eyes Only* stood little chance against Mabry's image of prim midwestern correctness.

Another interesting comparison emerged about a year after sentencing. Mabry announced to friends that she was pregnant with twins.

Unlike the twins Miller had promised Cassaday, Mabry's babies were real.

In unscientific Internet polls taken in connection with broadcasts on Court TV and with NBC's *Dateline,* up to a quarter of the audience believed that Sharee Miller was not guilty of killing her husband. Michael Thorp was there and still believes he got it right.

Thorp, who continues to anchor a morning TV show in Flint, recently described Sharee Miller as a "murderess."

"She was pretty evil with what she did to [Bruce Miller]," he said. "Everything she said was a lie. There is nothing truthful about her."

And he cuts little slack for Cassaday, whom he described as being "sick and troubled." Had Cassaday lived, Thorp said, he would have had no trouble convicting him of premeditated, first-degree murder.

"In the jury's view, Jerry was a poor son of a bitch," Thorp said. "He was a troubled person, easily swayed and a great mark for a manipulative woman. She saw him coming a mile away and it was easy for her."

Still, Thorp admired Nickola's "ferocious" defense but said it came up short when the lawyer promised too much and didn't deliver.

"In the opening statements, Nickola said Bruce played sex games and enjoyed sexual things on the computer,"

Thorp said, "but he never did. He did *say* Bruce was involved but never *showed* that Bruce was involved in pornography.

"Ultimately, that didn't matter, but it set up an expectation that wasn't fulfilled. He said they were in it together and he wasn't."

Thorp said he is haunted by the case and is trying to forget it. Still, one lesson from the evidence has remained vivid.

"If it's on a computer, it's never gone," he said.

To assess the effect Sharee Miller can have on men, one need only look at the life of her last boyfriend since her arrest. For a long while, Jeff Foster was teased around Flint about being the "Schwan man."

Though his relationship with Miller was brief, she changed his life, Foster said in a brief interview in April 2001.

"I can never forget what we had between us," he said. "It was fast and hard and we both fell into it very hard."

During that period, he said, "We raised hell. We went out and played with people's minds."

Foster ran the karaoke show at a local bar for a while and followed Court TV's coverage of the case closely. During the broadcast, he appeared anonymously on a Court TV Internet message board to announce that the Jeff mentioned in testimony was "alive and kicking." After another reader asked if he was Jeff, Foster responded, "I hate being called the Schwan man!"

As of January 2002, Foster was one of Miller's most cryptic defenders, claiming to have some remarkable insights into the case but declining to share these details.

"I have a personal opinion [on this case], but I'm keeping it to myself now," he said.

Foster said his support for Miller stemmed in part

from an eighteen-page letter Sharee sent him while in jail awaiting trial.

"She was very scared," Foster said. "But her letter explained everything."

Sharee Miller, however, has dismissed Foster's insights.

"His deep, intimate secret is that I wrote him, saying, 'Don't leave me while I'm in jail,'" Miller said.

Foster said Sharee's family also dislikes him.

"They think I should be in prison now," he said without explanation.

Police were the real villains in the case, Foster said, setting up Miller with the manufactured transcript of the November 7 through November 8 IM session.

Asked in January 2002 if his feeling about Miller had changed, Foster remained mysterious.

"It's been a nightmare," he said. "You can put that on the record, I guess."

Laura Ewald stands at the other end of Sharee Miller's defenders. She continues to speak on Miller's behalf, even though it has earned her the disbelieving smirks of smug TV commentators who interviewed her after her testimony.

Years before Sharee Miller even met Bruce Miller, she had earned Ewald's respect and love for the care she gave Ewald's brother after his car accident. Ewald later saw the spark in Miller that made her just fun to be around.

"She's one of those people with a sparkle in her eye and she loved life," Ewald said. "You could see it."

Given the ruinous outcome of Miller's own trial testimony, Ewald emerged as Miller's best witness, even though she testified for the prosecution. Her recollections were clear and roughly consistent with both the prosecution and defense theories of the case. She drew

the smirks, however, when she testified that Sharee
Miller, her best friend, had never even hinted that she
was having an affair with Jerry Cassaday.

That, however, was completely consistent with their
friendship, Ewald said recently.

"She knew I was set in my ways and believed that when
you're in your marriage, you're in your marriage," Ewald
said. "That's why she never mentioned it to me."

Ewald, a regular visitor to the Scott Correctional Facility, said Miller has moved past that.

"She said the only thing she had to do with [the mur-
der] was to have an affair with Jerry," Ewald said. "She
said that was the dumbest thing she's ever done in her
life."

As a witness in the case, Ewald was not allowed to sit in
the courtroom during Miller's trial. Still, having watched
three days of videotaped coverage on Court TV, she had
not changed her position on Miller's guilt.

"I still believe she is innocent," Ewald said. "I know she
had affairs. As far as wanting to have Bruce murdered, I
couldn't believe what I was hearing in that courtroom."

Ewald has earned the right to that opinion, no matter
how the evidence is stacked against her friend. She was
there on July 17, 1999, when Sharee Miller met Jerry Cassaday in Reno. And she was there four months later, when
Bruce Miller was murdered. And she stayed with Miller for
a week thereafter, watching her emotional response up
close and assessing it through years of experience.

Some would describe her as naive or trusting, but she
is entirely believable. None of her recorded police interviews betray the slightest hint of deception. And,
indeed, prosecutors found her credible enough to in-
clude her on their own witness list.

Ewald continues to live near Flint and keeps a room
prepared for Miller, should her appeals be successful.
But Ewald isn't just waiting around. After working in an

automotive shop for almost eighteen years, Ewald has returned to school. She's studying social work, largely because of Sharee Miller.

"I've always seen Sharee help other people," Ewald said. "I thought I would do something to help others myself."

Some good, it seems, can spring from tragedy.

And what of Bruce Miller, the almost forgotten character in this tragic triangle? There's no question he loved Sharee, adored her kids and was willing to chance a May–December romance in his search for happiness.

But murder reduced this uncomplicated man—who lived his life wrenching on junks and going to races—to a piece of evidence on a bare autopsy slab.

On a cold January day, we visited his grave and felt an eerie peace. Everyone agrees Bruce did not deserve this end. Too often crime victims are ignored. Or their lives vilified and exposed. Standing in the mist, we felt his tragedy deeply.

After saying a prayer and driving off in silence that day, we learned something about Bruce that we had not considered before. He was a simple man, with faults to be sure, but he no longer could defend himself. We hope that this book reclaims his good reputation.

Rest in peace, Bruce Miller.

POSTSCRIPT

Seldom have two criminals left a paper trail like this. The heart of this story is the enormous e-mail and America Online Instant Message correspondence between Jerry Cassaday and Sharee Miller from July 1999 to February 2000. Cassaday and Miller wrote each other virtually every day—and often several times each day—during their brief and tragic relationship. The court and investigative record contains more than 750 pages of such correspondence.

Most of that was mined from the hard drives of Jerry Cassaday's computers after his death. Other on-line friends provided a smaller set of e-mails later. Forensic sweeps of Sharee Miller's computers yielded no e-mails significant to the investigation. She has noted that she did not save e-mails because she felt they would clog up her computers' hard drives.

E-mail being an informal mode of communication, particularly between lovers, the authors took the liberty of cleaning up spelling, punctuation and grammar to keep distractions to a minimum. We used ellipses to alert readers to deletions from the original texts when they became repetitious or irrelevant.

Translating Instant Messages into a form readable for a book was a different matter entirely. Scanning the printout of a fast-moving IM is like reading the transcript of an argument between two combative radio talk-show hosts. People talk past each other in IM, with arguments and points becoming jumbled. While one person answers a question, the other is composing and presenting a new one. Correspondents often interrupt each other, disconnecting the simple elements of a single sentence.

Often the best way to understand an IM is to have two people read it aloud, as if it were a spoken conversation. That was why the deputies' recitation of the fateful November IM was so effective at trial.

In rendering the IMs for this book, we connected the dots by linking the elements of sentences with the appropriate answers. This produced a text that looked somewhat different from IM, but it kept the conversation moving without fits and starts. We also cleaned up the casual approach that Miller and Cassaday took to spelling and punctuation.

Here is how the original November 7 to November 8 IM appeared at the spot where Miller gave Cassaday directions:

SHAREE1013: take it all the way to Mount Morris road, by the bank
Jlc1006: ok
SHAREE1013: where we met
Jlc1006: ok
SHAREE1013: take it down to 75 making a right on Mt,. morris
Jlc1006: ok
Jlc1006: left on 75
SHAREE1013: that way you you don't have a town to go threw
Jlc1006: ok
SHAREE1013: lefrt on Mt morris road
SHAREE1013: no
SHAREE1013: right on mt morris road
SHAREE1013: left on 75

Jlc1006: then left on 75
Jlc1006: ok
Jlc1006: im with you

Here's how that turned out in our "translation":

Miller: Take it all the way to Mt. Morris Road, by the bank where we met.
Cassaday: OK.
Miller: Take it down to [Interstate] 75, making a [right] on Mt. Morris Road. That way you don't have a town to go through. [Then] left on [Interstate] 75.
Cassaday: Then left on 75. OK. I'm with you.

The e-mail record alone never would have given this story its rich texture. This book was written after numerous interviews with direct participants in the case. From the Genesee County Prosecuting Attorney's Office, we'd like to thank Prosecutor Arthur A. Busch and Assistant Prosecutor Marcie M. Mabry. Assistant Michigan Attorney General Peter Plummer and Special Agent Ives Potrafka, both with the state's High Tech Crime Unit, also contributed.

Though this case had an alluring Internet connection, these officials kept their focus on the human tragedy, helping jurors see that this wasn't really an electronic crime. It simply was murder.

The Genesee County Sheriff's Department opened their complete evidence file to us and provided us with mountains of records and plenty of guidance. Sheriff Robert Pickell gave us his valuable perspective, while Captain Michael Compeau, Lieutenant Mike Becker, Sergeant Kevin Shanlian, Sergeant Jerry Willhelm and Deputy Diane Watson guided us through the case step-by-step, patiently answering our questions and helping us through the evidence. Detective Don Elford of the Burton, Michigan, Police Department gave us expert insights on modern polygraph techniques.

And thanks to Nick Chiros, a former Genesee County deputy, for sharing his recollections of Miller's return flight from Reno.

Police officers often are accused of fixing on a theory of a crime and working it to the exclusion of all others. Investigators in the Miller case, however, showed real flexibility and swiftly changed directions when unexpected and compelling new evidence appeared. Though Cassaday, an ex-cop, handed them the initial evidence, the investigators cinched up the case with dedication and professionalism.

We also would like to thank Genesee County Circuit judge Judith A. Fullerton and her staff for the numerous and welcome courtesies shown to us before, during and after trial.

We interviewed many of the people closest to Jerry Cassaday and Sharee and Bruce Miller during this period. Of particular help were Chuck and Judy Miller, who generously invited us into their home for long and detailed renditions of their stories. Bruce Miller's pointless death has left a huge hole in their family and we never will forget their loss.

Jerry's family—his parents, Charlene and James Cassaday, and brothers Roger, Mike and Steve Cassaday—always were available to chat during the long days at Sharee Miller's trial in December 2000. Charlene Cassaday later consented to extensive interviews to flesh out her recollections. The family's willingness to expose Jerry's crime and then submit to interviews is a testament to their courage and desire to do the right thing. All of us owe them our thanks.

John and Debbie Hutchinson generously gave us several hours to describe the nightmare of being wrongly

suspected in a murder. And jury foreman Michael J.
Thorp provided insights into how deliberations progressed during those cold, cold days in Flint.

In Kansas City, Missouri, the Cassaday family de-
pended on the advice of criminal defense lawyer and
former prosecutor John P. O'Connor in reaching its decision to bring this difficult case to light. His help to us
was no less important.

Carol Slaughter and Gloria Taylor, Jerry Cassaday's
friends at Harrah's casino in Reno, never failed to answer their phones or our questions.

Laura Ewald consented to a detailed interview, describing for us her friendship with Sharee Miller and her
recollections of the night of November 8. She remains
one of Miller's staunchest defenders and we appreciate
and respect her perspective. Everyone needs a friend
like Laura Ewald.

As noted in chapter 15, Sharee Paulette Miller
granted us a vivid six-hour interview in May 2002 in
which she maintained she had nothing to do with her
husband's death and confidently predicted her eventual
vindication. We continue to follow her appeals closely.

Her immediate family has maintained their silence.
However, Miller's defense lawyer, David Nickola, was
generous with his time, thoughts and records. He is a
passionate and devoted advocate and has served his
client well.

Jeff Foster, Sharee Miller's last boyfriend, did not
grant us an extensive interview. After brief on-the-record
discussions with the authors in spring 2001 and January
2002, he suggested that we pay him for an extended interview. We declined.

In addition, we reviewed transcripts of recorded interviews given to investigators by the participants in this
case.

To mitigate unintended harm to innocents, we

changed the names of minor children who were drawn
into this nightmare, Jerry Cassaday's youngest son and
Sharee Miller's three kids from previous relationships.
To state it plainly, their real names aren't Kenny, Tommy,
Angela and Buddy.

Descriptions of events depicted in the two videotapes
in question, *For Jerry's Eyes Only* and *My Family 1999*, are
our own and were based on copies of the tapes provided
by the Genesee County Sheriff's Department.

For quotes we relied on the collective recollection of
participants in conversations, recorded in discussions
with investigators, court testimony or taken from interviews with us.

Seldom have true crime writers been able to quote so
many of the exact words that conspirators have used to
plan and commit murder. Quotes of discussions between
Jerry Cassaday and Sharee Miller were taken either directly from their electronic correspondence or from
letters they also wrote to family, friends and coworkers.
Others were taken from Sharee Miller's pretrial discussions with investigators, her extensive testimony at trial
and her interview with us.

Other sources of information included the Genesee
County Clerk's Office, the National Archives, the clerk's
office of the U.S. District Court for the Western District
of Missouri, the Michigan Department of Corrections,
the National Oceanic and Atmospheric Administration,
the Missouri Gaming Commission and the Reno Police
Department.

We relied on Web resources too numerous to mention
for information on battered spouse syndrome.

We also would like to thank the newspapers for which
we work. Our editors at the *Kansas City Star* and the *Flint
Journal* recognized this as an intriguing story right from
the start and generously provided us with the resources
to cover it properly. For this book, our newspapers

helped us rearrange our work schedules to find time to write it and allowed us to draw on the papers' archives and photos.

At the *Kansas City Star,* Mark Morris thanks editor Mark Zieman, managing editor Steve Shirk, assistant managing editor Randy Smith, deputy metropolitan editor Bill Dalton and assistant metropolitan editor Mike Casey.

At the *Flint Journal,* Paul Janczewski would like to thank editor Paul Keep, his assistant Karen Curtis, managing editor Brook Rausch, metro editor John Foren and assistant metro editor Julie Morrison.

Though each of the authors covered Miller's trial, we would like to thank Court TV producer Grace Wong for bringing her good fellowship and expertise to the postmortem bull sessions we conducted each day. Her enthusiasm for the case confirmed our suspicions that *Michigan* v. *Miller* deserved a fuller telling in print.

Even while this project was in its infancy, Rick Balkin, our literary agent, was a constant source of inspiration, expertise, support and determination.

Thanks to those who loved and comforted us as we pursued this tale. Without them, this book simply would not have been possible.

Mark Morris's wife and children—Carolyn Cupp and Sarah and Will Morris—tolerated more than three months of separation during six trips to Flint during the research and writing of this book. Much of that time came during the Christmas seasons of 2000 and 2001. That sacrifice was way above and beyond the call. Thanks.

Paul Janczewski relied on the input, inspiration and encouragement of several people close to him: his son Ryan Janczewski, girlfriend Karen Curtis and her daughters, Quinn and Mallory Curtis.

He'd also like to thank his Ohio family, David and Shannon Janczewski, and Kenny and Margie Janczewski. He would be totally remiss if he did not thank his mother, the late Dorothy R. Janczewski, who gave him humor, his biting wit, his feistiness and the ability to not take himself too seriously. *I really miss you, my dear old friend.*

Friends and coworkers Brendan Savage and Ken Palmer always were there when the authors needed to get away from the computer to share a story and a beer at the White Horse Tavern.

Finally, this book is the story of how colleagues became friends. The authors met while covering the Miller case for their respective newspapers. And based upon similar takes on the story, they decided to pull a book out of it. That meant spending buckets of time together, not only in interviews and in front of computers, but also at hockey games, bowling alleys and a particularly memorable Cleveland Browns football game.

We occasionally disagreed, but our friendship never faltered. We are, as Sharee observed, "exact opposites" with two different ways to tackle one major project. But we were able to compromise and hopefully write a book with a single voice.

The electronic means we used to produce this book mirrored those Miller and Cassaday used to cultivate their relationship, and from the same geographic perspective. Two people—one in Missouri, one in Michigan—talking on the phone, trading *lots* of e-mail.

There's a lesson here. At least we could work through our problems.

May 2002, Flint, Michigan

MORE MUST-READ TRUE CRIME FROM PINNACLE

Under the Knife By Karen Roebuck	0-7860-1197-1	**$6.50**US/**$8.50**CAN
Lobster Boy By Fred Rosen	0-7860-1569-1	**$6.50**US/**$8.50**CAN
Body Dump By Fred Rosen	0-7860-1133-5	**$6.50**US/**$8.50**CAN
Savage By Robert Scott	0-7860-1409-1	**$6.50**US/**$8.50**CAN
Innocent Victims By Brian J. Karem	0-7860-1273-0	**$6.50**US/**$8.50**CAN
The Boy Next Door By Gretchen Brinck	0-7860-1459-8	**$6.50**US/**$8.50**CAN

Available Wherever Books Are Sold!

Visit our website at **www.kensingtonbooks.com**.